*Women and Ordination in the
Christian Churches*

Women and Ordination in the Christian Churches

International Perspectives

Edited by

Ian Jones, Kirsty Thorpe
and Janet Wootton

t&t clark

Published by T&T Clark

A Continuum imprint

The Tower Building, 11 York Road, London SE1 7NX
80 Maiden Lane, Suite 704, New York, NY 10038

www.continuumbooks.com

British Library Cataloguing-in-Publication Data
A catalogue record for this book is available from the British Library

ISBN 10: HB: 0-567-03154-3
ISBN 13: HB: 978-0-567-03154-9

Typeset by Free Range Book Design & Production
Printed on acid-free paper in Great Britain by Biddles Ltd,
Kings Lynn, Norfolk

Contents

Acknowledgements

The editors would like to thank a number of people without whom this book would never have come to fruition. The original idea for the conference out of which this collection has emerged was generated by conversations with Professor Elaine Graham at the University of Manchester, UK. Generous support was given to the original conference by the Trustees of the Lincoln Theological Institute for the Study of Religion and Society and by the research support fund of the School of Arts, Histories and Cultures, both in the University of Manchester. A further debt is owed to participants in the conference 'Women and Ordination in the Christian Churches: International Perspectives' which took place on 14–16 July 2006 in Manchester. Grateful thanks go in particular to the conference steering group who, in addition to the editors of this book, included the Rt Revd John Packer, the Revd Dr Judith Maltby and Dr Peter Scott. Peter's support as Director of the Lincoln Theological Institute has been particularly important. Further thanks go to Professor George Brooke, Dr Anna Rowlands and, for their translation work, Stephen Brown and Alison Jones. Grateful thanks are due to T&T Clark/Continuum International for publishing this collection, and particularly to Tom Kraft, Associate Publisher, for his support and good humour in advising us on the preparation of the manuscript. Finally and most importantly of all, we acknowledge the faithful discipleship of women and men, ordained and lay, with whom the contributors have reflected and researched in order to produce this book.

Contributors

Dr Bolaji Olukemi Bateye teaches in the Department of Religious Studies, Obafemi Awolowo University, Ile-Ife, Nigeria. She is also a resource person at the OAU Centre for Gender and Social Policy Studies.

Revd Professor Dr Angela Berlis holds the Chair in Old Catholic Church Structures at the University of Utrecht. She is a priest in the Old Catholic Church and author of a historical theological book on the beginnings of German Old Catholicism in the nineteenth century: *Frauen im Prozess der Kirchwerdung* [Women in the Process of Becoming Church] (Frankfurt 1998). She has published in the fields of church history, gender studies and ecumenical theology.

Revd Dr Ellen Blue is the Mouzon Biggs Jr Associate Professor of the History of Christianity and United Methodist Studies at Phillips Theological Seminary in Tulsa, Oklahoma. She is an ordained clergywoman in the United Methodist Church. She is co-author, with Charles Wood, of *Attentive to God: Thinking Theologically in Ministry*, published by Abingdon Press in 2008. She is at work on *Rampart Street Reformers*, the history of St Mark's Community Center in New Orleans, run by Methodist women throughout the twentieth century.

Dr Helen Cameron is Director of the Oxford Centre for Ecclesiology and Practical Theology based at Ripon College Cuddesdon, where she directs a programme of research, consultancy and learning. She also contributes to the Masters degree in Consultancy for Ministry and Mission at York St John University. She co-edited the UK's first book on Congregational Studies, *Studying Local Churches* (London 2005). She is a member of the Salvation Army.

Catherine Gyarmathy-Amherd is convenor of the working group on women's contacts, Europe East-West of Schweizerischer Katholischer Frauenbund [League of Catholic Women in Switzerland] and board member of the European Project for Interreligious Learning. Between 1998 and 2006, she was co-president of the Ecumenical Forum of European Christian Women, and has worked for many years on a voluntary basis in the areas of politics, ecumenism and human rights. She divides her time between Switzerland and Hungary.

Captain Gillian Jackson has led three congregations in South Wales. It was during this time that she undertook studies at Cardiff University, gaining a MTh in Christian Doctrine. Her current role includes leadership teaching and training at William Booth College, London.

Dr Ian Jones is Director of St Peter's Saltley Trust, an educational charity based in the English West Midlands. He is a former Research Associate at the Lincoln Theological Institute for the Study of Religion and Society, University of Manchester, and is author of several publications on the history and sociology of English Christianity, including: *Women and Ordination in the Church of England: Ten Years On* (London: Church House Publishing, 2004).

Katerina Karkala-Zorba is a theologian and linguist, a member of the central committee of the Conference of European Churches, a member of the Special Commission on Women's Issues of the Synod of the Church of Greece and former co-president of the Ecumenical Forum of European Christian Women.

Dr Adair T. Lummis is an associate for research, Episcopal Church Center as well as Faculty research associate, Hartford Seminary, USA and is co-author of several books and author of articles and chapters based on research comparing clergywomen and clergymen in a number of US denominations.

Dr Gwendoline Malogne-Fer is a sociologist at the Groupe sociétés, religions, laïcités (GSRL) and postdoctoral fellow of the Institut Émilie du Châtelet/Région Île de France. She is currently doing research on migrants' Protestant churches in New Zealand and in Île de France. 2007 saw the publication of her book *Les Femmes dans l'église protestante mâ'ohi: Religion, genre et pouvoir en Polynésie française* [Women in the Mâ'ohi Protestant Church: Religion, Gender and Power in French Polynesia] (Paris: Karthala).

Dr Esther Mombo is academic Dean of St Paul's United Theological College, Limuru, Kenya, teaching church history and theology from women's perspectives. She was a consultant at the 1998 Lambeth Conference and belongs to the Circle of Concerned African Women Theologians. Her writings cover women's issues, evangelism, HIV/AIDS, Christian–Muslim relations and poverty in Africa. She is on the Inter-Anglican Doctrinal and Theological Commission and contributed to the *Windsor Report*.

Bishop Christina Odenberg studied theology at Uppsala University and was ordained priest in the Evangelical Lutheran Church of Sweden in 1967. In 1979 she became the first woman to be elected to the Synod of the Church of Sweden, serving on the central board and its executive committee from

1983 to 1997. During this time she was rector of a parish outside Stockholm and in 1988 was Chaplain to the King of Sweden. In 1997 she was consecrated Bishop of Lund (the first woman to be elected bishop in the Church of Sweden), serving there until her retirement in 2007.

Revd Dr Ann Peart is currently Principal of Unitarian College, Manchester. Her first professional life was as a teacher, and after a time as wife and mother she trained for the ministry in the 1980s. Within the Unitarian movement she chairs the national commission responsible for policy concerning ministry and is a member of the executive committee of the General Assembly. Her research is in the area of women and Unitarianism and she maintains a commitment to feminism both within and outside the churches.

Dr Julia Pitman is Programs Manager at the Australian Centre for Christianity and Culture, Charles Sturt University. Her PhD on the experience of ordained and lay women in Australian Congregationalism was conferred by the University of Adelaide in 2005. She has published articles arising from her PhD and also on aspects of the history of the Uniting Church in Australia and its antecedent churches. She is a member of the Uniting Church in Australia, and has served on its executive and on that of the National Council of Churches in Australia.

Revd Dr Kirsty Thorpe is a United Reformed Church minister interested in church history, feminism and communications. She co-authored *Daughters of Dissent* (United Reformed Church, 2004), a history of women in the URC, with Dr Elaine Kaye and the Revd Janet Lees. Her PhD researched early twentieth-century women's ordained ministry in the Congregational Union of England and Wales.

Deaconess Dr Rachele (Evie) Vernon holds the Philip Potter Chair in Ecumenical Studies at the United Theological College of the West Indies. She is an Anglican deaconess and a poet.

Revd Rosie Ward is Leadership Development Adviser with the Church Pastoral Aid Society, UK. She is ordained in the Anglican Church and is author of the book *Growing Women Leaders: Nurturing Women's Leadership in the Church* (Abingdon: BRF, 2008).

The Revd Dr Janet Wootton is Director of Studies for the Congregational Federation, UK. She was minister of Congregational Churches from 1979–2003, building up a substantial arts and community project at her last church, Union Chapel, Islington. She is a hymn-writer, and author of books and articles in the fields of worship, mission and feminist theology. Her book, *This is our Story: Women's Ministry in the Free Churches*, including a chapter by Kirsty Thorpe, was published by Epworth in July 2007.

Revd Professor Frances Young was Edward Cadbury Professor of Theology in the University of Birmingham, 1986–2005, but is now retired. She is an ordained minister of the Methodist Church. She is the author of many books in the fields of patristic theology and biblical hermeneutics, including an essay entitled, 'Presbyteral Ministry in the Catholic Tradition, or Why Shouldn't Women be Priests?', published by the Methodist Sacramental Fellowship in 1994.

Abbreviations

AACC	All African Conference of Churches
ADC	Agbala Daniel Church
CPAS	Church Pastoral Aid Society
DOC	Disciples of Christ
EEPF	Evangelical Church of French Polynesia
EPM	Mâ'ohi Protestant Church
FRLs	female religious leaders
IBC	International Bishops' Conference
HMCO	Harris Manchester College, Oxford
KJV	King James Version (of Bible)
NGC	New Generation Church
PCC	parochial church council
PCFC	Pacific Conference of Churches
UCC	United Church of Christ
UMC	United Methodist Church
UNAID	UN organization set up to deal with HIV/AIDS
WCC	World Council of Churches

Introduction

Ian Jones, Kirsty Thorpe and Janet Wootton

The last 30 years

As the final quarter of the last century began, an international conference on women's ordination would have had a very different story to tell and a quite contrasting look from the 2006 gathering in Manchester which provided the impetus for this book. In 1975 a World Council of Churches survey found that just over a third of its member churches then ordained women. These were mostly Lutheran, Presbyterian, Methodist, Baptist, united churches and some evangelical or Pentecostal groups, above all in North America and Europe. Although there were ordained women in some churches in Asia, the Pacific, the Caribbean, Latin America and Africa, they had fewer chances at that time to gain theological education, and find an acceptable way into ordained leadership.

Meanwhile, in the 1970s the Anglican Communion worldwide presented a very diverse picture, with women's ordination already a reality in some places, a theoretical but not an actual reality in others, and a topic which was not yet openly discussed within official church circles in further places. Neither the Roman Catholic nor the Old Catholic churches were ordaining women as priests, despite a growing debate about the matter among some Roman Catholics in North America. Meanwhile, Orthodox churches consistently opposed the possibility of women priests, although some people were advocating the reactivation of an ordained diaconal order for women.[1]

It was at this point that the WCC, in the person of American Lutheran minister Revd Constance Parvey (as director of the Community of Women and Men in the Church study) invited a varied group of Roman Catholic, Old Catholic, Anglican, Orthodox and Protestant Christians to a consultation on women's ordination. She found the ecumenical partners at the gathering, represented by participants from 14 countries and 26 churches, fell into three categories. One group was made up of churches which opposed the ordination of women, and for whom the subject arose only in ecumenical settings or in relation to women's role in society. A second group was made up of churches which had been ordaining women for some time, for whom the issues were now to do with ministerial placement, leadership styles,

renewal and church unity. The third group, around whom much of the consultation revolved, consisted of churches which had not yet reached a firm
conclusion on women's ordination.[2]

At the end of the resulting conference a book was produced, *Ordination of
Women in Ecumenical Perspective*, with a list of questions for future work.
Reading them now, it is evident how much the debate has moved on since 1980.
With one or two exceptions, the significance of opening diaconal ministry to
women as a half-way house towards priesthood has largely fallen out of the
debate in the ensuing decades. Questions of women's inclusion in the more
prominent leadership roles of church life are notably absent from the list of
topics that were seen as important in 1980, yet these have emerged over recent
years as highly significant issues in the developing debate about women's
ordination. The list of topics for further discussion is also silent about the over-
representation of women among the ranks of nonstipendiary clergy, a concern
which has often come to the fore over the last 25 years, as the proportion of
unpaid women clergy has increased in those churches that allow them to be
ordained.[3]

What is most striking about the book is the narrow nature of the bibliography.
At the time this was clearly viewed as an encouragingly inclusive reading list,
having contributions from Anglican and Roman Catholic and Orthodox
perspectives, rather than being confined to writers within North American and
European Protestantism. From an early twenty-first-century perspective,
however, the bibliography seems incredibly limited, with hardly any contributions from women in Africa, Asia, the Pacific, the Caribbean and Latin America.
That internationalizing of the debate on women's ordination has been one of
the most energetic developments of recent years.

The debate about women's ordination has undoubtedly undergone other
changes in the period since that ecumenical consultation almost 30 years ago.
Through the Ecumenical Decade of Churches in Solidarity with Women,
1988–98, the World Council of Churches sought to build up regional and
ecumenical networks of women who could share their stories about their
position both in the Church and in society as a whole. Involved in that process,
inevitably, were discussions about ordained leadership and its accessibility to
women. The fact that women very rarely get the chance to set an agenda and
stick to it, however, was in evidence with the Ecumenical Decade. Within
months of its inception the Lambeth Conference of 1988 declared a Decade of
Evangelism, to move the Anglican Communion and any partner churches that
wished to join in, from maintenance to mission. This other decade had the effect
of overshadowing the WCC decade and caused a considerable degree of
confusion in many minds, which probably detracted most from the decade
focused on women.

In 1995, as the United Nations held the Fourth Conference on Women in
Beijing, churchwomen from many different traditions were present raising
concerns about women's health, human rights, education, employment rights,
political and poverty issues. Hopes were raised that many aspects of women's
lives could be changed, provided vocal, articulate women could lobby those in
power long and loud enough. Many of the important issues discussed at

Beijing, including the international sex trade, the abduction of women in China and the growing gender imbalance in India caused by selective abortion of female foetuses, continue to make occasional headlines but have not been tackled in a strong and strategic way more than 12 years later.

Meanwhile, the last two decades of the twentieth century saw a steady stream of stories about denominations worldwide deciding to start ordaining women, all of which seemed to provide encouraging evidence that female clergy were reaching more new parts of the Church. The fresh possibilities for communication offered by the Internet, and the increased mobility of people between countries and continents, offered opportunities for women to share their stories of church life in all its ups and downs. They also made it possible for many more women living far away from higher education to take advantage of its opportunities, through forms of distance learning, and so to emerge as equally theologically competent practitioners alongside their male colleagues. Equal rights legislation in those countries with the longest history of women's ordination, even if this exempted the Church, still contributed to setting a new atmosphere within which maternity rights were much more widely recognized and church recruitment committees were alerted to the inappropriateness of asking certain questions of female candidates. The whole question of married women with children continuing in paid employment underwent a complete reversal in many developed societies during the last quarter of the twentieth century, as family budgets depended on both parents continuing to earn a wage. This slowly freed women clergy from some of the guilt previously heaped on them by those within the Church who expressed concern about the effect of their ministry on their families, while failing to offer the sort of practical support that might have been helpful.

This is not the whole story, though. Recent decades have also seen a number of worrying developments in the area of women's ordination. Despite the commemorations of those early pioneers of women's ministry which have been celebrated by the minority of contemporary church people who know their stories, much of the recent history of women in the Church tends not to be known and is little valued. For many younger women, both in the Church and beyond, the story of women's ordination is a finished work – or at least is in its final stages. They want to move on now, and are probably unaware of the complex and changing picture of partial acceptance and downright resistance spoken of in some parts of this book. Many of the arguments for women's ordination have been made and accepted, but the process of becoming a community of women and men in the Church is far from over, and involves layers of exploration and mutual listening that are only just becoming clear.

The origins and shape of this book

The origins of this book are found in a conference, Women and Ordination in the Christian Churches: International Perspectives, organized by the Lincoln Theological Institute for the Study of Religion and Society, which took place at the University of Manchester between 5 and 7 July 2006. The conference itself was the second stage of a longer-term research programme on women and ordination, beginning in 2000 with a four-year investigation of the Church of England's experience of ordaining women as priests since 1994. Following the publication of the research findings,[4] a discussion between Ian Jones and Professor Elaine Graham from the Department of Religions and Theology at Manchester generated a question about how far the Church of England's journey towards ordaining women might have been comparable to that of other Anglican provinces, or indeed to that of other denominations. In the original research it had been striking how far the Church of England's debate on women priests had been shaped not just by theological arguments but also (sometimes more importantly) by denominational culture and the wider position of the Church of England in society. For example, on one hand, women's acceptance as priests had been greatly helped by the fact that the first generation of women in priesthood were widely perceived to display qualities (compassion, openness and professional competence) that Anglicans had historically desired in their clergy above most other considerations. On the other hand, the fact that the 1992–94 ordination of women legislation was not a single-clause measure but permitted parishes to opt out of receiving a woman's ministry, arguably owed as much to the historic Anglican tendency to balance the competing interests of different church 'parties' as to any explicitly theological thinking on the nature of unity and communion. If the Church of England's journey towards ordaining women was shaped as much by history and culture as by theology, in what ways were the experiences of other churches also moulded by their own stories and contexts?

A second important dimension to the Anglican story made the need for sensitive comparisons particularly important: far from being conducted in isolation, the Church of England debate on women's ordination was constantly being informed by the wider church context. Women's ministry proved one (though not the most significant) sticking-point in the abortive scheme of union with an English Methodist movement which was already well advanced in its own plans for women's ordination by the time prospects of union collapsed in 1972.[5] A still more significant factor was the 1971 ordinations of two women by the Anglican Bishop of Hong Kong. This not only proved a critical spur for serious discussion of women's ordination to begin amongst English Anglicans but also generated a pan-Anglican debate on the nature of the Anglican Communion and the extent of provincial autonomy – a debate which still continues today. Subsequent events abroad also exerted considerable influence on the shape of the eventual legislation, not least in the inclusion of concessions for those opposed. Amongst a variety of motivations for these measures was a desire by English bishops to avoid a repeat of the sharp divisions which had occurred over the first ordinations of women in the Episcopal Church of the USA in the 1970s. At the same time, other ecumenical considerations – notably relations with Rome – clearly acted as a brake on Anglican exploration of women's ordination. Even after the decision to ordain women as priests in 1992 was taken, the international context continued to exert an influence on subsequent events. Anglican women and their supporters had long drawn encouragement and insight from women ordained elsewhere in the Anglican Communion and from those within other denominations. After the 1992 decision, opponents of women's priesting also began to develop an increasingly sophisticated nexus of international contacts (not least a network of traditionalist bishops travelling between provinces offering alternative episcopal oversight to parishes unhappy with their diocesan bishop's decision to ordain women). Key decisions have also increasingly been taken internationally: the Hong Kong ordinations of 1972 prompted an initial reaffirmation of the principle of provincial autonomy by Anglican Communion leaders. Since then, however, a growing impetus to develop a more systematic understanding of unity within the Anglican Communion has tended to push tensions over women's ordination and other issues 'upstairs' (or downstairs, or sideways, depending upon your theology of the Church) from provincial level to communion level, increasing the influence of bodies such as the Primates' Meeting (of Anglican archbishops) over local decisions. If the international context was so important for the Church of England's own journey towards women's full participation, this raised interesting questions as to whether the same was true for other denominations. Increasingly then, it seemed unsatisfactory to focus research and discussion at the purely national or denominational level without some consciousness of women and ordination in the Christian Church worldwide. This appeared even more important given the relative lack of extended comparative research on the topic. The conference from which this book arose was conceived in response to those needs.

In July 2006 nearly 70 women and men from more than a dozen different denominational backgrounds and seven countries gathered in Manchester to share insights into women's ordination around the world. Key questions for discussion included: how have national, denominational and ecclesial cultures shaped the different ways in which women's ordination is debated and/or enacted? What differences have women's ordained ministry, and debates on women's ordination, made in various church contexts? What 'unfinished business' remains (in both congregational and wider ministry) and how might this be addressed? How have Christians variously conceived ordained ministry including both women and men? How do ordained women and men work together in practice? What have been the particular implications for female clergy (and male clergy)? What distinctive issues are raised by women's entry into senior ordained/leadership positions? And how do episcopal traditions differ from non-episcopal ones in this respect? Though primarily dedicated to understanding women's ordination in the contemporary Church, the conference was deliberately multidisciplinary, attracting contributions from historians, theologians, sociologists and anthropologists. In particular, the planning team were keen to enable an exchange of insights between those working primarily in academic research and those working in mainly pastoral contexts, breaking down the somewhat artificial division often set up between 'theoreticians' and 'practitioners'. In fact, many of the conference participants straddled that divide in their own individual lives; amongst them were clergy engaged in postgraduate research, ordained university or theological college professors, and academics who were also active in the life of their denomination.

In producing this book, we have been keen to preserve the geographical, denominational and disciplinary breadth of the Manchester conference. As far as possible we have sought to achieve this through the original selection of papers delivered at the conference itself, though a few come from researchers who were prevented from attending through circumstances beyond their control. We are grateful for their continued commitment to the project. The contributions included here cover 11 countries and more than a dozen different denominations. Inevitably some traditions were more strongly represented in the original conference than others. A large number of submissions on the Anglican Communion meant that some had to be left out in the interests of balance. Conversely, the conference itself featured no paper from an Orthodox perspective, nor any contribution which ranged widely over the whole spectrum of Roman Catholic debate on women's ordination (though it was pleasing to hear several very enlightening papers on the experiences of the small group of Roman Catholic women who have been ordained *contra legem* since 2002). We therefore decided to seek additional material from Catholic and Orthodox perspectives, and are very glad to include here contributions from Catherine Gyarmathy-Amherd and Katerina Karkala-Zorba, both members of the Ecumenical Forum of European Christian Women. In a collection of this kind it is clearly impossible to cover every aspect of women's ordination; some of the more notable omissions and 'silences' are discussed further in the Afterword. However, we hope that this book reflects something of the diversity of experience of women and ordination, and goes some way to filling the present gap in the literature.

Ordering such a diverse array of papers into a coherent book has proved a challenging task. Rather than attempt to shoehorn the different chapters into an artificially tight thematic structure, and potentially thereby to negate the evident abilities of the contributors to cover more than one topic, the book is simply divided into three parts. These reflect the dominant disciplinary approach taken by each contributor – theological, historical, sociological – acknowledging of course that academic disciplines are themselves only useful constructs. The fact that this places perspectives from Central Europe alongside contributions from the USA, a Nigerian perspective alongside a view from the Pacific Islands, further serves to invite comparisons between the accounts.

Constructing a theological conversation

The book begins – rightly – with theology. The intention of Part 1 is not (as with so many books on the topic) to mount a systematic argument for or against women's ordination *per se*, but to review some of the major trajectories of debate in recent years and to subject some key ideas and assumptions to critical scrutiny. Anyone who has engaged with the debate on women's ordination at any level will be aware of how easily arguments from the Bible and the writings of the Patristic period are drawn into justifications for and against. This is vital of course: without a firm foundation in scripture and tradition it is questionable how 'Christian' any stance on women's ordination would be. The critical question thus becomes how Christian foundations are at work authoritatively in the Church today across centuries of historical change. In the opening essay of the collection, Frances Young tackles this question head-on, arguing that the ambiguity of the historical evidence about the origins of Christian ministerial order should lead us to treat straightforward arguments from precedent with suspicion. However, she goes on to assert that this need not leave us floundering in the dark: a proper understanding of the use of biblical 'types' in the Early Church opens up the possibility of an inclusive priesthood based on 'Christlikeness' which remains faithful to the core gospel vision.

As Mark Chaves has noted, a significant proportion of the denominations which only started to admit women into ordained ministry after the second half of the twentieth century, or in which debate still continues, have been those with a high theology of priesthood and an adherence to the threefold order of bishops, priests and deacons.[6] It is thus fitting that the next two contributions come from the Roman Catholic and Orthodox traditions. In the former, Catherine Gyarmathy-Amherd surveys official Roman Catholic teaching on women's ordination, with a particular focus on the period since Vatican II. She argues that whilst the official Roman Catholic position remains incontrovertibly against women's ordination, the spirit of several key documents and even of some recent pronouncements by high-ranking figures, holds open the possibility of conceiving a priesthood including both women and men. She is particularly attentive to discussions taking place in German-speaking contexts – an important context given the nationality of Pope Benedict XVI and his particular concern for the Christian foundations of Europe. Complementing Catherine Gyarmathy-Amherd's focus on Roman Catholicism, the following chapter, by Katerina Karkala-Zorba, reviews the theological foundations of recent discussions of women's ordination in the Orthodox churches – discussions which have resulted in the revival of a female diaconate in several branches of the Orthodox family. She returns to the hermeneutical question posed by Frances Young's essay: that of how faithfully to interpret the acts of Jesus for present-day contexts. Whilst noting that women have always figured prominently in the Orthodox tradition, Katerina Karkala-Zorba notes the urgent challenge to engage women in the life and structures of the Church, now that a growing number of them are studying theology. Her article also raises ecclesiological questions that are familiar to Anglican audiences: what questions are raised for a threefold understanding of orders when women may now be ordained to the diaconate but not to the priesthood or episcopate?

The final two contributions in Part 1 take a somewhat different theological approach as practical theologians bring scripture and tradition into critical conversation with contemporary educational and management theory. Whilst an important thrust of research and reflection on women's ordained ministry has been to emphasize the common grounds upon which women and men may be ordained or appointed as church leaders, the contributions by Ellen Blue and Rosie Ward explore the converse question: how far do women, because of their gender, have different experiences of, and perspectives on, ordained ministry to offer? From a mainline US Protestant perspective, Ellen Blue shares the results of an experiment in ministerial formation which brought together a group of exclusively female seminarians to reflect upon, and prepare for, the particular challenges they would face, as women, in their future ordained ministry. Without denying that male ordinands will also experience problems of their own, and without advocating a wholesale apartheid in theological education, Ellen Blue argues that dedicated educational opportunities for women ordinands are essential given the continued discrimination and marginalization that many ordained women face in their ministries. Ministerial formation and development for women is discussed from an English Anglican perspective by Rosie Ward. Faced with the question 'Do women lead differently?' she acknowledges that the jury is still out, and certainly on both doctrinal and empirical grounds there remains insufficient evidence to suppose that these differences are purely reducible to inherent 'femaleness'. Nevertheless, drawing on her own research and a wider body of literature on women in management, she argues that a combination of gender, personality and life experience may often result in women exhibiting a more empowering, collaborative and strategic leadership style than men. This chimes appropriately with the example of Jesus himself who, Ward asserts, embodies a 'power to' rather than 'power over' approach to authority.

Through the lens of history
Part 2 of the book adopts a historical perspective on women's ordination, with a particular focus on the experiences of pioneer women priests, ministers and pastors in their respective denominations. Rather than being of merely antiquarian interest, the five contributions in this section offer strong evidence for the importance of a sense of history in understanding the challenges facing today's women ministers and priests, and for appreciating the contextual factors influencing the shape of women's ordained ministry in different denominations and cultures. Moving in roughly chronological order, this section begins with two chapters located in the late nineteenth and early twentieth centuries: a period when many mainline Protestant denominations first began to reconsider the question of women's ordination. Ann Peart tells the story of Gertrude von Petzold, the first woman to be granted full ministerial status in the Unitarian Church in England, whilst Julia Pitman's study concerns Winifred Kiek, the pioneer female Congregationalist minister in early twentieth-century Australia. Without glossing over the contextual differences between the two accounts, there are some intriguing parallels between them. Both von Petzold and Kiek were foreigners (the former a Prussian settling in England, the latter an Englishwoman settling in Australia) whose training and ordination galvanized the debate on women's ministry in their adoptive countries. Their stories raise intriguing wider questions about the ways in which debates over women's ordination

and the experience of the first women ministers 'translate' from one culture to another. Additionally, both Kiek and von Petzold worked in denominations where pride in an enlightened attitude to women rubbed awkwardly against the practical reluctance of many congregations to accept a female minister. In both cases, too, policy on women's ordination was formulated *after* (rather than before) the first ordinations took place. However, a comparative perspective also helps to draw out important differences in the experience of these pioneers of women's ordained ministry: whilst von Petzold and her English contemporaries found themselves frequently constrained by wider cultural and denominational assumptions concerning appropriate roles and levels of education for women, Winifred Kiek and other women serving in colonial contexts found themselves comparatively unencumbered by such expectations. Nevertheless, Julia Pitman's chapter also reminds us of the degree to which – in the late nineteenth and early twentieth centuries – arguments for women's ordination were made on the basis of women's special contribution to ministry, rather than on the strict equality of the sexes.

This contrasts with the predominant tone of later twentieth-century debates, which often tended to turn around notions of equality.[7] This latter trend is well illustrated in Christina Odenberg's account of the journey towards women's ordination as priests and bishops in the Evangelical Lutheran Church of Sweden. In it, she disputes those who have suggested that women's ordination was foisted upon a sceptical church by a parliament committed to social equality. She nevertheless acknowledges the significance of a deep groundswell of public opinion which questioned why sexual equality could not also be manifested in the ecclesiastical sphere. Odenberg herself has served as parish priest, a member of the Church Assembly which debated successive refinements to the law, and subsequently as the first woman to be elected bishop in the Church of Sweden. Her account weaves personal experience in and around the larger historical story. Feminist scholars have often been particularly sensitive to the personal stories which lie at the heart of wider social and cultural shifts, and this is well-reflected in Odenberg's story, as well as those of Kiek and von Petzold.

Esther Mombo's essay gives a fascinating insight into the recent history of women's ordination within the continent of Africa, primarily within Anglicanism. She highlights the importance of ecumenical bodies, such as the All Africa Conference of Churches and the World Council of Churches, in bringing the debate about women's ordination onto the agenda of the Church over the last 40 or so years. The role of The Circle of Concerned African Women Theologians, a group to which she belongs, is highlighted for the way it promotes women's leadership and theological education. What emerges is a very diverse picture of women's ordination that varies greatly from Anglican province to province, with the issue often becoming a focus for power-struggles between opposing bishops. Meanwhile, theologically trained African women are finding themselves on the pastoral care front-line in questions of sexual violence, gender equality and the impact of HIV/AIDS. Esther Mombo contrasts the patriarchalism of central church structures with the strength of many women's organizations in the churches, and she calls on the Church to build future power relations based on community rather than hierarchy.

Part 2 ends with Angela Berlis's account of women's ordination within the Old Catholic churches of the Union of Utrecht, from the 1960s to the present day. In identifying the three phases of this process, from discussion to decision-making and then reception, she also considers the significance of conflict in church life. The author herself was one of the first women to be ordained to the priesthood in the Old Catholic Church, a tradition which provides an important ecumenical bridge between Anglicanism and Roman Catholicism, especially in continental Europe. Her study considers how women enter the threefold ministry and asks if the identity of the Old Catholic Church has changed because of this development. It explores the effect of the decision to ordain women on ecumenical relationships and weighs up the influence of cultural and societal changes on this process. Rather than resorting to extended episcopal oversight, as the Church of England has done, the Old Catholic churches have developed local solutions and established a varied pattern of 'reception' for women priests.

A sociological perspective

Part 3 of the book adopts a more sociological perspective whilst remaining attentive to historical and theological resonances. Here, many of the contributions examine the intersection of gendered identities with other modes of identity, among them race, sexuality, cultural heritage and family role, and how these may sometimes bolster, sometimes work against, the achievement of women's full participation in ordained ministry. In her analysis of US Protestantism (and in particular Episcopalianism), Adair Lummis focuses upon the changing relationship between concern for social justice and support for women's ordination. A passion for social justice, she argues, has given women and men 'strength to cut the path to the women's ordination, and the persistence to continue pruning the undergrowth'. However, as all gardeners know, the work of pruning and weeding is never-ending, and Lummis gives particular attention to identifying the sources of continued resistance; amongst them arguments concerning theology and church unity, the cultural conservatism of some US states, the downsizing of church women's organizations, and a sense of complacency that has seen the focus of social justice shift to other marginalized groups. Regarding the latter, Lummis argues that the two should not be regarded as mutually exclusive – indeed, she charts evidence that churches which display least concern for women's ministry often show a corresponding lack of concern for other marginalized groups.

As the statistical evidence in Lummis's chapter indicates, there has frequently been a strong relationship between opposition to women's ordination and theological conservatism. However, as Bolaji Bateye's study of Nigeria makes clear, this is not always the case. Despite the highly andro-centric nature of Yoruba society, Bateye notes how several women have emerged as influential leaders, with a strong sense of their anointing by God, amidst the 'new generation' of indigenized Pentecostal and charismatic churches rapidly growing in popularity. The presence of these female leaders also appears to have acted as an agent of change with regard to attitudes to gender amongst their Pentecostal and charismatic congregations. One of the most intriguing features of Bolaji Bateye's essay is the continued need to wrestle with the ambiguous legacy of colonialism: in some respects, African women greeted European missionaries as a source of liberation from a cultural system in which they were sometimes regarded as mere chattels, only to find that Western culture as it existed in the nineteenth century reinforced beliefs in the superiority of men over women. The indigenization of Pentecostal and charismatic Christianity into Africa (as in Nigeria) has provided an opportunity to re-examine the missionary legacy, further opening up the possibility of questioning inherited gender typologies, as this study shows.

A similar ambiguity over the colonial legacy is contained in Gwendoline Malogne-Fer's study of the Mâ'Ohi Protestant churches of French Polynesia, which charts the interplay between the extension of ordination to women and the gradual professionalization of the ministry. On the one hand, missionaries bequeathed a legacy of spiritual equality between men and women; on the other, the implantation of Protestant Christianity reinforced existing indigenous expectations that women's church work would be auxiliary to that of their husbands. As ordained ministry has progressively been opened up to women, this has challenged not only traditional assumptions about the woman's sphere of activity but also norms of family life and pastoral practice (according to which ministry was historically provided by the *couple pastorale* – a married male minister accompanied by his wife). As with Ann Peart's account of the first women ministers in Unitarianism, access to education has been a crucial issue for ordained women in the Mâ'Ohi Protestant Church, but here the boot is on the other foot: Protestant women pastors in the Pacific Islands have been *more* likely to have received a higher level of formal education than men. Whilst in some respects this has been a liberating force, in others a higher level of education has often increased the social distance between ordained women and their more traditional parish communities.

In many other contexts (such as the US case described by Adair Lummis) one might have expected the growth of a liberationist theological agenda to have furthered the cause of women's ordained ministry. However, here again (in another intriguing contrast) the effects have been ambiguous. Keen on rediscovering a more authentic Polynesian contextual theology, the (mainly male) Church's recent theological commissions have seized upon a precolonial heritage which privileges older, patriarchal culture and thereby risks further marginalizing women.

The observation that theoretical equality can sometimes be mitigated by dominant cultural or theological expectations is also made by Helen Cameron and Gillian Jackson, in their study of the experiences of senior women in the Salvation Army in the UK. Though leadership positions have formally been open to both women and men for over a century, few women, and even fewer married women, have been appointed to the most senior posts. As in Gwendoline Malogne-Fer's account of the Mâ'Ohi Protestant Church, the development of women's leadership in the Salvation Army has posed particular challenges to traditional assumptions about the respective roles of couples where both wife and husband are commissioned officers. There are signs that the historic tendency to treat couples as a single appointment (or with the husband's job taking priority) is beginning to break down. Cameron and Jackson's evidence suggests this is taking place only slowly, however, and will not progress without a more general shift in attitudes. The final contribution to the book, an exploration of women's ordination in the Anglican churches of the Caribbean by Evie Vernon, again includes consideration of changing family roles. In an account which draws heavily on oral testimony, her conclusion is upbeat: the first generation of Anglican women priests (ordained since 1996) have comparatively success-fully negotiated the demands of balancing family and ministerial duties, and (despite some opposition) have largely received a positive acceptance by their parishioners. Even so, it is still too early to tell what the long-term impact of their ordination will be.

Key intellectual and practical themes

Part of the richness of the conference from which this book was drawn was the interaction between academics and practitioners, and we hope that this has been transferred from the spoken to the written word. Not that the distinction between the academic and practitioner is hard and fast. One paper was given jointly by an academic and a clergywoman from the same tradition (Jackson/Cameron). Several participants have moved from local church ministry to academic work, and others combine both, so there is an inter-action within the lives of individuals as well as in the book as a whole.

This would no doubt be true of many fields of work and related academic disciplines, but it is very appropriate to a group of women talking and writing about leadership in the churches. Theology as an academic discipline is at its best when rooted in the praxis of the living people of God, and the leadership of women in the churches frequently gives rise to discussion about collaborative or integrative ways of working, which blur what some would wish to make into sharp boundaries.

This can be seen from the way in which themes, which are at once intel-lectual and practical, thread through the chapters.

What are women made of?
Underlying any questions about the appropriateness of certain roles and functions is a deeper question about the existential or ontological nature of women and men. If there is an existential difference, arising from our creation, it is possible that that difference makes us suitable for certain roles in life or precludes us from some others on the basis of our essential or created being.

Frances Young examines the question from an academic standpoint in the light of two writers, one from an Anglican and the other an Orthodox perspective. The two writers she considers, Ruth Edwards and Elisabeth Behr Sigel, rehearse what are by now fairly familiar arguments drawn from scripture and tradition that find a mutuality of woman and man in creation. Patristic sources as well as scripture argue against anthropomorphism of a kind that attributes gender to God, and therefore suggests that one human gender is more perfectly or solely capable of representing God.

By bringing them together, Young demonstrates that it is possible to develop a hermeneutic which is adequate to the task of describing genuine novelty in traditional churches. Though there have been instances of women in leadership, and though both scripture and tradition contain elements which are supportive of women's equality, the present situation in which mainstream Protestant churches by and large ordain women, and the argument is being raised in Catholic and Orthodox churches, is genuinely new. The hermeneutic, she suggests, is to discern the 'thrust' or 'heart' in both scripture and tradition, and to apply the same principles to the current situation.

Young's academic discussion comes to earth dramatically in the experience of women in leadership in the churches. While a woman may find openness and acceptance of her ministry in many contexts, she will never have to go far to find her very existence as an ordained woman called into question. As we will see, many, perhaps all church communities, include congregations or sections of culture, which are implacably hostile to the leadership of women.

The Salvation Army was founded by a husband-and-wife team and included gender equality in its founding documents, though as Cameron and Jackson make clear, it has largely failed to embody equality in the actual ministry of men and women. A strongly evangelical theology still questions the propriety of women seeming to exercise headship over men in church life, or in the home. This justifies co-leadership by married couples, exercised under the headship of the husband. Again, while perhaps unstated, this understanding seems to lie behind the injunction against a woman taking a senior position without consultation with (or permission from) her husband. The given reason for this may be a concern for the health of marriages, but, as the writers point out, it means that the marriage covenant 'trumps' the ministry covenant for women only.

Even where women are accepted as existentially capable of leadership, they may be put under pressure to hide their femininity and, in particular, to regard menstruation and pregnancy as potential barriers to ministry. Evie Vernon speaks of women feeling the need to dress in a gender-neutral way. She also mentions congregations' fear at the thought of a pregnant woman ministering, as if this flagrant demonstration of femaleness would cause the offence that could be avoided by a soberly dressed woman minister. Vernon triumphantly storms both these strongholds of prejudice. One of her inter- viewees celebrates the fact that she feels able to wear lipstick and high heels if that is an expression of who she is. In another lovely interview, a priest finds herself in demand to conduct a wedding whilst she is in the advanced stages of pregnancy, as a potential blessing to the marriage. This intriguing story explodes prejudice against women at so many levels that it would make a study in itself!

Fitting in

Questions about women's leadership are closely interwoven with the culture in which they are raised. This is a complex issue, as it needs to be recognized how culturally determined are the 'norms' against which the 'novelty' of women's leadership is set. The discussion includes church cultures as well as the wider norms of societies. Again, it is Frances Young who explores how closely the church structures, which form the basis for much of this discussion, are based on the Roman civic society in which they were developed. Who is to say that the same structures are relevant to the cultures of our own times?

Chaves' study[8] has demonstrated how churches' stands for or against women's ordination were partly determined by their view of the social mores of the nineteenth and twentieth centuries. In the early twentieth century, the discussion of women's ordination was set in the wider context of social reform, including women's equality and women's suffrage. Those churches which positioned themselves largely in opposition to shifts in the wider context became entrenched in their opposition to women's ordination or any kind of leadership over men, while those which recognized a challenge in the social changes soon passed resolutions to accept the ordination of women.

This had two other consequences in the lives of the churches. First, as churches aligned themselves with like-minded others, doctrinal differences widened into the liberal–evangelical split that we live with today. Second, the shifts in position suggested by resolutions to accept the ordination of women did not at that stage result in very many actual ordinations of women. That was to wait for further cultural change, spurred by second-wave feminism, during which the majority of middle-ground or liberal Protestant churches began to ordain women.

Ann Peart uncovers the irony of the position taken by Unitarians in the early nineteenth century. As a denomination, they supported the equality of women, for example, in access to education. Their attitudes to women preaching arose from the location of their membership in middle-class society, however, in which it was not considered respectable for women to speak in public. This would have associated them with the lower-class evangelical movements, in which women did take to the platform and the pulpit.

Perhaps a parallel today is the association between women's leadership and liberal or feminist ideas. Adair Lummis describes a nexus of liberal thought and activism within which support for women's leadership appears to sit. The issue arose, both in the nineteenth century and in the 1970s, from a general movement towards women's equality, as a matter of social justice. Ordained women are more likely to be active in other areas of social justice than ordained men.

The very connectivity of women leaders militates against their acceptance, for fear that they will push congregations to be more liberal than they would wish to be. For example, they might introduce inclusive language into worship, or feminist theology into their ministry. There is a distinct reluctance to use the word 'feminist' in the views represented in these essays. The assertion, 'Nevertheless I/we/she/they are not feminists' recurs sufficiently often to suggest that feminism is seen as a risky or extreme position from which it is important to distance oneself.

The situation is exacerbated when the wider unity of the Church is seen to be threatened by women's leadership. Lummis notes that there is more resistance in the Southern USA, similar, she says, to the attitude of countries in the 'South'. Churches with a strong international structure face difficulties in maintaining unity, especially when the churches of the South are demonstrably growing so much faster than those in the more liberal North. There is a real difficulty in balancing cultural respect with a challenge to inequality.

Perhaps because of the nature of the conference, the ecumenical question is not much raised, though it is prominent in many discussions of women's ordination. However, the Old Catholic Church specifically faces the issue in relation to the Roman Catholic Church. The view and hope expressed is that women's ordination has not changed the identity of the Old Catholic Church or its relations with the Roman Catholic Church.

Pulling up the ladder, or offering a leg-up

Within the churches which accept women's leadership, issues to do with relationships also arise. The pioneers in many cases have to develop their education and leadership for themselves. Some of this journey is rehearsed in Peart's article. Lummis also describes how leadership and organizational skills, developed in campaigns for women's rights, have been put to use in working for women's church leadership.

But complexities arise as women's leadership becomes more established. Women are not always supportive of each other, though the essays in this book do describe many situations where they are so. One of Evie Vernon's interviewees describes her experience at theological college. The arrogance of younger men was balanced by a wide age range among the women students, within which the experience of the older women strengthened the younger women.

Women's access to senior pastorates or positions is fraught with difficulty – the familiar 'stained-glass ceiling'. This is partly due to the need for sufficient women to gain experience at junior levels and 'get into position' for promotion. Lack of experience can also be used as a spurious excuse for failing to promote women. Jackson and Cameron discuss this in the context of the Salvation Army, where very few women have occupied senior positions, despite the long history of women's leadership.

In some instances, hostility to women's leadership comes from other women. These are not simply instances of women being 'their own worst enemy', but are complex interrelational issues. In the Salvation Army, for instance, married and single women have traditionally taken different career paths, and now eye each other uncomfortably as the situation changes.

The fascinating situation in the Polynesian Mâ'Ohi Protestant Church is described by Gwendoline Malogne-Fer. The church derives from the work of missionaries, but has developed within a Polynesian culture. Ministry is traditionally male, but as in many cultures ministers' wives were expected to share their husbands' ministries. The advent of women's ordination coincided with the professionalization of the clergy, and a new emphasis on academic training. At the same time, the Church was encouraged to contextualize and decolonize its own theology. The resulting tension seems to have isolated the ordained women from less well-educated male clergy, from clergy wives and from ministry itself, as many are in non-parochial positions.

Lastly, and perhaps most depressingly, the wider culture has changed. Lummis notes that it is harder now to gain financial support for women's issues, or to attract younger women to the movement. There is a perception that the battles have largely been won, and the campaign has moved on to other issues. This has enabled a backlash, which is expressed in several of the chapters.

Ellen Blue describes her experience in running a course specifically to prepare women for the difficulties they will face in ministry. The course itself is interesting and gains some significant reactions from its participants. Relevant to this discussion is the fact that she faces all kinds of hostility and opposition from women and men in running the course at all. They question the need for such a course these days, and accuse her of fomenting division rather than fostering cohesion.

Conclusion

This is the world in which women exercise church leadership now. We are experiencing the long-foretold backlash against feminism, and an astonishing (to those who have lived through the struggle for women's ordination and recognition in the last few decades) sense that the battle has been won, and all the necessary advances achieved.

The complexity of the situation confronting women church leaders and theologians is evident from these essays. There is still a tangle of cultural, postcolonial, scriptural and ecclesiological identity and expectation. These complicating factors need to be understood in their various contexts. We have no sword to cut through the knot, but must trace the strands as they interweave, and tease away at the toughest places, perhaps for many years to come.

There were two fascinating dynamics at the conference from which this volume comes. One was a continuous sense of discovery: a repeated, 'Wow – I didn't know that!' We have much to understand about each other, and we hope that this discussion does not end here. The intensity of the struggle within our churches and communities in many cases cuts us off from the solidarity that we could share simply by learning about each other's circumstances and resources.

The second dynamic was that the papers and discussion focused on practical matters, the realities of ministering or teaching or engaging in ecumenical debate. Some major underlying issues were not raised, or raised only in a narrow context. We did not debate the possibility of doing away with all our structures and creating a Ruether-like WomanChurch or a Fiorenza ekklēsia. Neither did we debate the justification of talking about leadership at all, nor the extent to which women in leadership introduce inclusive language or practices in worship. This was partly because we were practitioners. Janet Wootton has commented elsewhere that 'radical questioning ... is very hard from inside the power structures of a denomination. Clergywomen are, to some extent, least likely to rock the boat in which they are wrestling their way towards the bridge in order to take a hand at the controls.'[9] That is not a criticism of practitioners so much as a recognition of the particular focus that comes from within the traditions.

The editors hope that this book will achieve the dynamic of openness and discovery that marked the conference and that people's awareness and knowledge will be increased. They also hope it will contribute to the wider debates of feminist theology and ecclesiology.

Bibliography

Chaves, M., *Ordaining Women: Culture and Conflict in Religious Organisations* (Cambridge, MA: Harvard University Press, 1997).
Jones, I., *Women and Priesthood in the Church of England: Ten Years On* (London: Church House Publishing, 2004).
Parvey, C.F., *Ordination of Women in Ecumenical Perspective* (Geneva: WCC, 1980).
Wootton, J., *This is our Story: Women's Ministry in the Free Churches* (Peterborough: Epworth Press, 2007).

Notes

1   C.F. Parvey, *Ordination of Women in Ecumenical Perspective* (Geneva: WCC, 1980), pp. 9–10.
2   Parvey, *Ordination of Women*, pp. 18–19.
3   Parvey, *Ordination of Women*, pp. 60–64.
4   I. Jones, *Women and Priesthood in the Church of England: Ten Years On* (London: Church House Publishing, 2004).
5   The Methodist Church in Great Britain first ordained women two years later, in 1974.
6   M. Chaves, *Ordaining Women: Culture and Conflict in Religious Organisations* (Cambridge, MA.: Harvard University Press, 1997).
7   In this respect, Chaves's observation of the US context also appears to hold true for many other countries (Chaves, *Ordaining Women*, pp. 60–64).
8   Chaves, *Ordaining Women*.
9   J. Wootton, *This is our Story: Women's Ministry in the Free Churches* (Peterborough: Epworth Press, 2007), p. 95.

Part 1

Theological Perspectives

1

Hermeneutical Questions: The Ordination of Women in the Light of Biblical and Patristic Typology

Frances Young

At the core of controversies about the ordination of women are arguments about scripture and tradition. Too often, on both sides, there is a simple appeal to precedent, as if that settled the issue. This essay will begin by looking critically at these arguments, suggesting that it is impossible for either side to be convincing in the matter of historical reconstruction, and this must shift debate into the area of hermeneutics. How are scripture and tradition to be interpreted? How are we to justify novel developments in the continuing life of a body that seeks to be faithful both to its tradition and to its foundation documents?

The suggestion will be made that an adequate hermeneutic must discern the thrust or heart of the tradition and of the biblical teaching on which it rests. However, while this proves to affirm the gifts and leadership of women as well as men, and so has been convincing to the mainstream Protestant traditions, there remains a difficulty in arguing specifically for ordination to the priesthood as understood in Orthodox and Roman Catholic traditions. This problem is then met through a re-examination of typology. Historically typological argument has shaped the notion of priesthood, and it still figures significantly in arguments against the ordination of women. However, this has created a distortion in the way typology works, and has obscured the fact there exists a traditional typology which should justify the view that the non-inclusion of women in the ordained priesthood is an affront to the thrust or heart of the tradition.

1 Appealing to the past

Conservatives unite in appealing to the past – scripture having primacy for the conservative Protestant, tradition for the Roman Catholic or the Orthodox, especially the tradition of the Fathers. It is not therefore surprising that the comparatively recent report, *Women Bishops in the Church of England?* (2004) has a section about the emergence of the episcopate in the Early Church. This provides a handy example of what purports to be as balanced an assessment as is possible, so we will start with this document.

Earlier debates about the ordination of women to the priesthood or the diaconate revolved around similar historical arguments, *mutatis mutandis*, so this recent replay should be sufficiently representative.

The authors of the report speak from the outset of 'the ancient threefold order of ministry consisting of bishops, priests and deacons', which 'emerged in the first centuries of the Church's existence'. They acknowledge a variety of patterns in the New Testament, but then appeal to various scholars in support of a claimed ecumenical consensus, namely that expressed in the World Faith and Order Report of 1982, *Baptism, Eucharist and Ministry*. Although a number of the fourth- and fifth-century Fathers of the Church (such as Ambrosiaster, Jerome, John Chrysostom and Theodore of Mopsuestia) are quoted to show that they saw no great difference between the office of bishop and presbyter in the beginning, nevertheless the point is that they upheld the threefold order, accepting that a clear distinction emerged later – indeed a fourth-century writer who argued there was no distinction was condemned as a heretic. The report then appeals to the authority of Lightfoot for the claim that the origin of the episcopate belongs to the first century and is associated with St John. So the threefold order is said to be apostolic.

The next section of the report considers the role of the bishop in the patristic period, emphasizing that the bishop was the chief minister of the local church, with pastoral and priestly responsibilities. Further paragraphs show that the mon-episcopate emerged to ensure unity in the Church (and here long quotations from Ignatius and Cyprian are provided), that the bishop was regarded as the guardian of the apostolic tradition and the minister of ordination, and that leadership in mission was a key role. The report then turns to the development of the episcopal office, as the bishop comes to exercise oversight over more than one congregation in a particular locality, and presbyters become the local ministers of word and sacrament as delegates of the bishop. The history section continues with the emergence of metropolitans and patriarchs, and the primacy of the Bishop of Rome, followed by the specific history of ministry in pre- and post-Reformation England. Most of this is irrelevant to our argument here. It chiefly documents the long-term conviction of the Church of England that the threefold ministry is apostolic.

The chapter as a whole concludes that there is a convergence between the role of a bishop in the Church of England today and that of a patristic bishop; that this is not accidental but the fruit of a commitment to maintain historical continuity with the Early Church; but that there has nevertheless been change as the office adapted to changing circumstance, both within and beyond the patristic period. The question is then posed whether the ordination of women as bishops would simply be a further adaptation of the episcopal office to meet the circumstances of our time and our changed theological understanding of the relationship between men and women in the Church, or whether it would represent a fundamental break with the historic continuity of the episcopate which the Church of England has hitherto sought to maintain.[1]

Inevitably a report of this kind can provide only a summary account. Nevertheless the argument has a number of weaknesses. It ranges over a wide area and a period of more than 400 years, without being geographically or chronologically precise. Furthermore, historical accounts are always reconstructions on the basis of evidence which needs to be interpreted, and often the interpretation of the data is the key issue. Those engaged in these debates need to become more aware of the uncertainties involved in appealing to history.

Let me sketch some points where the history offered in this report can be regarded as contestable.

1. It is far from clear that the three orders were clearly differentiated from other roles in the early period. We have evidence from a number of sources that the tithes and offerings supported bishops, presbyters, deacons, subdeacons, readers, singers, door-keepers, deaconesses, widows, virgins and orphans.[2] Was the line between clergy and laity so clearly drawn as we assume?

2. Recent research suggests that the mon-episcopate was still contested in the third century, particularly in Rome![3] It is also worth asking why Ignatius protests so much about the importance of being in communion with the bishop to ensure unity. Probably it was because in the early second century that was not yet the situation, and he saw it as the solution to current disunity. The struggles of Cyprian's episcopate also suggest that a century later he too was trying to establish the authority of the bishop among competing charisms, and he could not assume it. The texts quoted are not evidence for an already existing situation.

These examples immediately alert us to the problems of interpreting the evidence. It is even more tricky when terminology remains the same though the reality has changed over time. Simply because the same language is being used, it is easy to assume continuity and read back into an earlier period a situation which is in fact later. The medieval prince-bishop has precious little in common, surely, with the *episcopos* referred to occasionally in the New Testament. It is vital to set the terminology in its initial social context, and then see how its connotations changed with the rise of different social parameters.

The terminology of *episcopos*, *oikonomos* and *diakonoi* comes from the household.[4] An ancient household was very different from the Western nuclear family unit: it would comprise the extended family of several generations, servants with their overseer or head steward, clients and tenants – perhaps 50 people all told. The Early Church met in houses, hosted by a patron, and familial language was adopted for the Christian family whose *pater familias* was God – they addressed each other as brother and sister, and the pastoral leader would soon be addressed as 'father' (that is, *papa* or pope). The person who organized everything was the 'overseer', God's steward, assisted by menservants and maidservants – hence the *episcopos* and the *diakonoi*, but it should not be assumed that men and women deacons would necessarily have the same functions, anymore than their household counterparts; in premodern societies some things are men's work, other things women's work. The elders in the family (*presbyteroi*) would have authority, as older people did in traditional societies – they would carry the communal memory; but they also needed material support because of their age, as did the older women, widows and orphans. In other words, it is quite possible to read 1 Timothy as a kind of 'household code' for the household of the Church, especially if we avoid importing ideas from later periods.

On the other hand, it is not unlikely that the earliest Christian communities modelled themselves on the Jewish synagogue.[5] Often the Jews in the Diaspora would also meet in households, the community would have a governing council of elders (*presbyteroi*), who would appoint an official (the *archisynagogos*) with assistants (*hyperetai*) to do the organization. The parallels are interesting, yet apart from the overlap of the elders, the terminology does not suggest direct borrowing – rather the members of the Church oscillated in their self-understanding between being family members and servants in God's household.

The sketch offered hints at the fact that presbyters were probably not identical with bishops in their origin – despite a century of scholarly consensus that there is little to distinguish the office of bishop and presbyter in the early period, the bishop eventually emerging out of a 'college' of presbyters. This challenge to the consensus is perhaps confirmed by some interesting later texts that suggest that the presbyters both appoint the bishop and form his advisory council. Presbyters, it seems, were the wise, elderly 'guardians of the tradition' as the persons with long memories; Papias's well-known comments about preferring the living and abiding voice to things written in books and so consulting the presbyters, who apparently belong to both the apostolic and the second generation of Christians, would appear to bear this out. Furthermore, as early as Ignatius, the presbyters are said to be in place of the *synedrion* (= sanhedrin or council) of the apostles, while the bishop presides in the place of God (just as a head secretary would act for his master in his absence), and *diakonoi* are entrusted with Christ's service; and, by the way, some similar texts from a later period add that the deaconesses are to be honoured as in the place of the Holy Spirit. So apostolicity is connected with the presbyters not the bishop, and the deacon rather than the priest is a type of Christ. The classic account of the origins and significance of the threefold order of ministry cannot be regarded as securely based.

We could go on to show how the household model would lend itself to development on lines parallel with state organization. Let me just indicate a few pointers: The phrase 'Caesar's household' was used for the civil service, and implicit in that terminology was the ancient cliché that the head of state was analogous to a *pater familias* writ large, while the head of a household was like a monarch writ small. Each ruler was ideally a beneficent and wise philosopher who sought the good of the domain over which he ruled. Such ancient ethical ideals were transferred to sketches of the good bishop. The very word 'diocese' is a word from Roman imperial governance. By the fourth century, ecclesiastical boundaries followed imperial subdivisions, and metropolitans emerged analogous to provincial governors. Thus the way in which ministry in the Early Church developed reflected its societal locus, and this can be further demonstrated by looking at parallels with municipal government at the city level: the emerging distinction between clergy and laity reflects the difference between officials and the plebs. History, far from supporting an unchanging structure, might instead pose the question of whether the Church should really maintain in a postmodern democratic society the sort of governance that emerged in societies that were monarchical, hierarchical and even feudal.

So far it would appear that my challenge to the historical argument might favour the argument for women's ordination. However, that would be to narrow its implications. The fact is that, faced with the appeal to history, those who would promote women's ordination counter it with their own search for precedent.

> Understanding why and how women, once leaders in the Jesus movement and in the early church, were marginalized and scapegoated as Christianity became the state religion is crucial if women are to reclaim their rightful, equal place in the church today. Jesus' message and practice were radically egalitarian in their day and constituted a social revolution that likely provoked his crucifixion. It is high time that the church, which claims to embody his good news to the world, stop betraying its own essential heritage of absolute equality.[6]

So Karen Jo Torjesen in her book, *When Women were Priests*, subtitled 'Women's leadership in the Early Church and the Scandal of their Subordination in the Rise of Christianity'. Importantly this book takes very seriously the social context of the Early Church, and it makes some significant historical observations, such as noting the effect of the Church's move from the quasi-private sphere of the house church to the public world of the city and empire: it would surely have been easier for women to have influence in the private sphere, and certainly women householders acted as patrons of Christian communities. It documents the gap between the patriarchal theories of society and the practical realities of women's position, as they ran households and even businesses. It rehearses the evidence for women's leadership in the Jewish synagogues of the Diaspora, and the many hints in the letters of Paul and other early Christian material that women played leadership roles in the mission of the Church, and were active as prophets and deacons. It acknowledges that women's leadership was contested – yet that is itself evidence that women were leaders. The distinction between clergy and laity starts to matter in the third century, she suggests, as the Church begins to emerge from the private sphere and ministry shifts into governance, modelling its offices on those of the municipality. The move from house to basilica in the fourth century is the final nail in the coffin of women's ministry, for the church accepted the general perception of society that for a woman to be prominent in the public sphere was a scandal.

There is much material here that is of historical interest, but as an argument from precedent it has the same problems as those we have already observed. The historical picture produced depends upon the interpretation of often ambiguous evidence – does the mosaic in the Roman church with its inscription *episcopa* really imply that Theodora was a bishop, or was she, as the standard account suggests, the mother of the ninth-century pope who built the church and buried her in the chapel?[7] Furthermore, it is by no means clear that a general argument for women's leadership can establish a precedent for women's ordination to the differentiated clergy that emerged later – indeed, the very argument advanced suggests that it was the emergence of distinct clerical orders which excluded women. So as in the former case, there are difficult issues about definition: what sort of bishops or priests are we talking about?

With some justification, defenders of women's ordination appeal to the many texts which do indeed show that there were deaconesses in the Early Church.[8] With less plausibility the argument is mounted that widows consti-tuted a ministerial order.[9] But in each case such argument is subject to the same objections. I have already pointed out that deaconesses almost certainly had different roles from deacons, just as menservants and maidservants have always done different jobs in the household. Widows probably did constitute some kind of order, though largely it would seem as the benefici-aries of charity – the evidence as usual is not straightforward; and it is hard to use it to justify the ordination of women as priests since it does not constitute a genuine precedent. Besides, one thing that is clear is that in the earliest period the Church repudiated temples, sacrifices and priests – the apologists boast of this rejection of current religious norms. In the New Testament the only person given the title of priest is Christ, though 'royal priesthood' is attributed to the Church as a whole. What the question about widows does do is to raise the issue of what is meant by 'ordination' – we have already noted that early on tithes supported a whole list of functionaries, and the line between clergy and laity was therefore not so clearly defined as later. Again, women clearly were patrons of house churches, but simply to put it in those deeply unfamiliar terms demon-strates the difficulty of reading the organization of the Early Church in ways that we easily recognize.

By now, I hope my first point is made. The argument from precedent, whether made for or against the ordination of women, is deeply problematic from the point of view of serious historical enquiry.

2 Interpreting scripture and tradition

There is a great irony in the current situation. The ordination of women is historically a novelty – that surely must be admitted in the light of my discussion so far. Yet it has been largely embraced by the churches of the Reformation, which owe their existence to a desire to reach back behind the accumulation of tradition to scripture as the norm;[10] whereas those churches, both Catholic and Orthodox, which have historically appealed to tradition over against scripture, and so have entertained the possibility of new developments, have treated tradition as fixed and refused to countenance a development with no precedent. Clearly hermeneutical issues lie at the very heart of the debate.

Some of the best advocates for women's ordination have not resorted to precedent, but rather have sought to discern the thrust of the biblical material or the living dynamic of the tradition. We will now examine two of these: one written from the Anglican position, the other from the Orthodox. We shall find considerable overlap, but more important is the fact that they are arguing in the same kind of way as the patristic authority, Athanasius. Faced with the challenge of Arius, that great Alexandrian patriarch in fact produced novel and original ideas – indeed, was accused of doing so by opponents; however, this he justified on the grounds that it represented the 'mind' of scripture and of tradition better than the text-slinging or verbal conservatism of the opposition.[11] In a similar kind of way the debate about women's ordination, I suggest, has provoked serious consideration of what is really at the heart of scripture and tradition.

2.1 An Anglican perspective

Ruth Edwards, of the Scottish Episcopal Church, provides the Anglican contribution in *The Case for Women's Ordination*.[12] Part I, called 'Foundations', focuses on the New Testament; Part II, entitled 'Developments', on tradition and the modern debate. Her context means that she has her eye both on those whose appeal is to certain texts of scripture, and on those who argue from tradition.

Firstly, then, we look at her treatment of scripture. As a lecturer in New Testament, she is meticulous about the background, both in the Graeco-Roman world, and in the Old Testament and early Judaism. She recognizes two strands in the latter: subordinationist and egalitarian, and so immediately engages with the hermeneutical question: what happens when parts of scripture point to different conclusions. This leads her to distinguish between general scriptural principles and more detailed culture-related prescriptions, and to seek appropriate ways of interpreting the Old Testament in the light of the New. However, she recognizes that even these principles are complex in their application and can produce differing outcomes. Chapters on 'Jesus and Women', on 'Paul: Misogynist or Feminist?' and 'Women in Ministry in the New Testament' then make what are now standard points: so (1) 'Jesus' attitude to women seems to have been unusually positive for a Jew of his period', yet 'the evangelists present some of Jesus' teaching as androcentric and the evidence suggests that he relied on men for public preaching and healing';[13] and (2) as posed, the question about Paul's attitude (misogynist or feminist?) is put in a way that is hardly fair – 'he wrote within the framework of ancient ways of thinking, which took for granted women's social and religious subordination'; yet, for the most part he was 'affirmative of women' and 'some passages seem to see the new life in Christ as superseding that subordination', even though others appear to endorse it.[14] (3) As for women's ministry, it is fruitless to look for precise precedents in the New Testament,[15] but the ideals of ministry in the New Testament suggest inclusion: spiritual gifts are given to all irrespective of gender; ministry is corporate and Paul's fellow-labourers are both male and female; the model for both men and women is Christ, and servanthood, for example, is possible for women as well as men.[16] This summary of her conclusions belies the careful exegesis of texts, the recognition that there is no clearly developed 'Church Order' in the New Testament, and the sensible acceptance of historical realities – of course the apostles were all men, given the social context! But my main observation would be that overall what informs the discussion is her search for the implications of scripture.

So we turn to her treatment of 'Developments'. There is a largely negative chapter on the Fathers, documenting their general tendency to subordinate women and the eventual suppression of women's ministry as deacons. A number of factors are offered in explanation: the general cultural ambience, the influence of subordinationist texts in scripture, resistance to heretical groups where women had leadership roles, and the developing ideal of virginity. This is followed by an equally negative account of the medieval period and the Reformation. The dramatically changing social situation is then sketched, and the challenges that this poses to the churches are identified. Quite apart from issues around traditional hierarchical structures and current democratic ideals, she asks, 'Can our doctrines of God, Creation, "Man", Sexuality, and Priesthood be rethought and reformulated, so as to make them intelligible to contemporary thinkers without destroying the traditional faith?'[17] This justifies four chapters in which the theological issues surrounding women's ordination are discussed. As in the case of scripture, so here too Ruth Edwards looks not for precedent but rather for the implications of the tradition.

The first of these chapters tackles images of God, and the assumption that only a man can represent a God conceived in essentially male terms. Examples from both scripture and tradition establish that feminine images of God have been used, but then the more important theological question about the status of images is broached. Neither scripture nor tradition encourages anthropomorphism – in fact, one could take this discussion a great deal further than Edwards does, offering a critique both of the tendencies of Western theology to project a superman onto the heavens by its theistic tradition, and of the feminist reaction in reclaiming the 'goddess' tradition, a critique which could easily be fuelled by the apophatic traditions of Eastern Orthodoxy and of medieval mysticism. The deep thrust of the Christian tradition is opposed to any idea that God can be reduced to the concepts of the human mind or the limitations of creaturely experience, and the Fathers were quite clear that it was inappropriate to attribute gender to God. The implication of the tradition is by no means found in the idea that only a man can represent God.

The next discussion argues for the essential equality of male and female before God, tackling the argument that God created men and women different – maybe equal but certainly not interchangeable – and so women should not be ordained but stick to their own roles. This leads into treatment of contentions about authority and priesthood. Both discussions involve appeals to scripture – Genesis and the Pauline epistles in particular, but much of the discussion here also revolves around the impossibility of documenting real differences between men and women, and the actual capability of women to fulfil all the roles required of the various orders of ministry. Again, however, the implications of scripture and tradition are drawn out: collegiality of men and women in the Body of Christ might sum up the nub of Edwards' arguments. Furthermore, she affirms the importance of novelty in the history and life of the Church:

> What matters is whether a change is consistent with the principles of truth as revealed to us through scripture, reason, and the on-going life of the Church. ...[W]omen's ordination ... is simply doing things a new way in accordance with the Spirit's continuing guidance and to meet the needs of the Church in present-day society... Women's ministry should ... be seen as a natural consequence of the Gospel message, comparable to the admission of uncircumcised Gentiles to table-fellowship, carried out despite Jesus' original command not to go to the Gentiles (Mt. 10.5).[18]

So she concludes with seven guiding principles derived from what I shall call the 'hermeneutical interaction' of scripture, tradition, reason and experience:

- the real equality of the sexes
- the complementarity of the sexes
- Christian ministry as service rather than the exercise of domination
- priesthood and ministry as belonging to the whole people of God
- women and men as equally 'representing' humanity
- women and men as equally 'representing' God
- all ministry as by God's grace, not by right.

I have summarized this book at some length, partly because it enables us to survey the range of arguments that have been in play over the issue of women's ordination, but also because it is interesting hermeneutically. The very distillation of principles from what I have called the 'hermeneutical interaction' of scripture, tradition, reason and experience allows for a kind of logic to emerge that creates new insight out of the very fabric of what is received, ensuring continuity and faithfulness to the tradition and its foundation documents, whilst fostering change and development. This is more important than the fact that in detail one might disagree with some of the interpretations offered along the way. But it is time to compare this with our Orthodox representative.

2.2 An Orthodox perspective
Elisabeth Behr-Sigel, aged 94 in the year 2000, was associated with the great twentieth-century thinkers of the Orthodox diaspora in the West such as Meyendorff, Bulgakov and Endokimov. She has become an important

theological writer in her own right, one who interprets the tradition while 'discerning the signs of the times', as one collection of her essays is entitled.[19] Another is entitled *The Ministry of Women in the Church*.[20] As collections of essays produced for different occasions these works contain considerable overlap, and my exposition will dip in and out of different discussions. Behr-Sigel confesses that on the matter of women's ordination to the priesthood she has shifted position and moved further than most Orthodox could, partly as a result of being involved in ecumenical dialogues about the position of women in the Church. While constructively critical of the Western feminist movement, she has also been insistent that the Orthodox Church must come to terms with modernity. But what she evidently sought to do in these essays, is to tease out the implications of the tradition, which includes scripture.

With some passion she insists that tradition should be 'living':

> As for the argument from Tradition brandished about without discernment, it has always seemed to me not only insufficient but also offensive to the Church and the Spirit that is at work in her. This argument denies to both any creativity or capacity to adapt to new situations – without, of course, denying the essentials... [It implies] that the future of the Church is nothing more than its past indefinitely repeated. The whole history of the Church reveals, however, that even though the life of the Church is continuity, it is also dynamism and creativity. Authentic faithfulness to Tradition is creative and requires each generation to respond to new needs and challenges according to the dynamic of Tradition. Faithfulness to Tradition is the work of the Spirit in the Church, raising the heavy dough of humanity.[21]

So she seeks within tradition for the new possibilities now discernible, acknowledging that much in the past has been coloured by archaic taboos.

Overlapping with Edwards, though in a different style, she provides a sensitive treatment of the classic gospel stories which depict Jesus relating to women as persons,[22] and discusses the Pauline material,[23] suggesting that the gospel had to be inculturated, so that the injunctions we find negative are not surprising, but they should be put into the context of his great vision of the Church – the Body of Christ with its *koinonia* of persons. Like Edwards, she points to Gal. 3.27-8, and speaks of the 'already and not yet'. However, she sees the Fathers in a very different light from the picture common among Western feminists: for she sketches how they affirm the common vocation of all the baptized, women and men, and 'the ontological unity within the distinction of persons in the humanity of man and of woman'. She offers quotations: Basil insists that 'the woman possesses, just as the man does, the privilege of having been created in the image of God. Both their natures are equally honorable.' Gregory of Nazianzus proclaims: 'The same creator for man and for woman, for both the same clay, the same image, the same death, the same resurrection.' She affirms that the Fathers' 'egalitarianism is situated in the eschatological perspective of the completeness of the end of time when genital sexuality will be transcended'.[24] She insists that it is not gender differentiation that matters but rather the redemption of *anthropos* – humanity.[25] While she admits that the Fathers were men of their own time, influenced inevitably by cultural stereotypes, she also highlights the other side: Maximus wrote that 'the division male-female... was added later and without any relation to the divine archetype'.[26] This whole tradition is developed at length in Chapter 2 of *The Ministry of Women in the Church*.

Furthermore, Behr-Sigel celebrates the contribution of women to the life of the Church over the centuries, drawing attention to women saints, and also to the way in which women contributed to keeping the Church alive in communist Russia.[27] She affirms that

> All through the centuries, Christian women have been baptized, chrismated and invested with the fullness of the royal priesthood; they have confessed their faith in Christ, endured martyrdom, evangelised, prophesied and attained the heights of holiness in the life of consecrated virginity as well as in married life.[28]

She stresses the priesthood of the whole people of God:[29] together men and women 'have the vocation of being the kings and priests of the creation, of being the celebrants of the cosmic liturgy'.[30] She insists that Orthodox women are conscious of participating in the royal priesthood of the laity, knowing that they are called to holiness, to deification not only in the life of the world to come but also here and now.[31] For Orthodoxy, Christ alone is the high priest and all priesthood derives from him. As members of the Body of Christ all participate in the priestly offering of worship.[32] She quotes 'an Orthodox spiritual master' on the subject of the offertory prayer:

> At this moment, we pray for the whole creation; consecrating all men and women as well as the whole world to God. We carry out the office of priest so that our priesthood might be the ministerial priesthood delegated by the Church or the 'royal priesthood' that scriptures attribute to all believers.[33]

But this priesthood also extends into daily life. This kind of intuition, she suggests, may explain why the problem of women priests has not become so acute for the Orthodox Church as for other churches.

Orthodox men and women, she states, feel that the structure of the Church is essentially a communion of love and prayer, rather than a pyramid of powers.[34] As is typical of Orthodox theology, the Trinity becomes a crucial principle:

> The idea of human vocation as Trinitarian life is but a germ in the patristic interpretation of Genesis 1.26, but it has been developed more extensively in modern Russian religious thinking ... In the new community whose womb is the Church, men and women are called to

grow and develop together, being oriented towards each other, not
against each other or in competition. Men and women are to have
many-sided relationships of friendship, of conjugality, according to the
criteria of reciprocal service and mutuality. Such relationships reflect the
communion-in-distinction of the Son and the Spirit as they do the
common work of actualising the Father's will.

Humankind may not be God, but is, as a whole, in God's image and oriented
towards the divine likeness. One more quotation may sum up her position:

> Grounded on the bedrock of the scriptures and washed of all the disfig-
> uring historical deposits, the ecclesial tradition proclaims the unity of
> humanity and the equality of man and woman as persons in the image
> of the personal God, of the God who is One in three persons.[35]

Behr-Sigel thus distils the essence of the tradition, finding more seeds that
are positive than Edwards, who tends to set the positive aspects of scripture
against the realities of Church history. Nevertheless, she too is acutely aware
of the 'doublespeak' about women and their place. The thing that most
differentiates her work from anything we have previously looked at is her
focus on Mary, the Mother of God, and here the doublespeak becomes
particularly acute. She notes Endokimov's surprise that 'in Church history,
the spectacular development of the veneration of the Mother of God was
accompanied by a growing and concomitant scorn for Mary's sisters who
were condemned to silence and relegated to an inferior place in the ecclesial
community'.[36] She acknowledges the fact that the idealization of Mary as
virginal mother has presented women with an impossible ideal, suggested
that Mary has nothing in common with ordinary women and so encouraged
their identification with unredeemed Eve. Besides this, particularly in the
West, Mary has provided a model of obedience and submission, so
contributing to women's subjugation. However, Behr-Sigel takes note of a
subtle change in the papal document *Mulieris dignitatem*: now Mary has
become a symbol of the mystery of women. Femininity no longer implies
imperfection: 'as the new Eve, Mary is "the new beginning of the dignity of
woman, of all women, of every woman"'. Yet this document reaffirms the
impossibility of ordaining women to the priestly ministry, and it does so
'precisely from the sublimated femininity which defines women, that was
magnified in Mary and through her in all women'.[37] She goes on to note a
parallel effect in some recent Orthodox theology, as 'the idea of a particular
relationship between "the feminine", of which Mary is the archetype, and
the Holy Spirit' is pushed quite far. Priesthood is associated with Christ, and
so distinguishable from this privileged association of women with the Holy
Spirit. We are back with the arguments based on women's essential difference
from men, already addressed by Edwards.

   Behr-Sigel's own exploration of Mary leads to quite other conclusions. But
I shall incorporate her observations later in the discussion. For the issue now
raised is the question of typology, and typological arguments have been partic-

ularly significant in the whole debate. So it is to typology and its hermeneutics that we now turn.

3 The ordination of women in the light of biblical and patristic typology

None of the arguments reviewed so far establish any grounds for ordination of women to priesthood as such. One of the reasons why post-Reformation churches have found it easier to make the move is their insistence on the priesthood of all believers, understood in an individualistic way, as a scriptural doctrine. Ministers are easily treated as having a functional role, proper to the ordering of the Church and representative of the priesthood of the community, but not ontologically different from any other believer. The specific connotations of priesthood, as distinct from presbyterate or eldership, came into the tradition through typology. Hence its fundamental significance.

Typology is multifaceted. Within the Bible itself we find stories which are told in ways that mirror one another: Elijah and Ezekiel bear the marks of a new Moses, the stories of Abraham 'typify' the exodus and bear the impress of Israel's story.[38] For early Christianity the important thing is the implicit notion that past narratives foreshadow, or prefigure, future events. In the New Testament such typology pervades the gospel narratives: Jesus brings manna in the desert as he miraculously feeds the crowds, and as the blood of the Passover lamb saved the Israelites from the angel of death, so Christ's blood saves from death and the devil. But it was not just events that became 'figures'. In the Epistle to the Hebrews, the covenant, the Temple and the whole sacrificial system is reinterpreted as fulfilled in Christ. Another kind of typology emerges in early Christian preaching as biblical characters become 'types' of virtues to be imitated, the most obvious example being Job, who typifies patience against the odds. Though the association of presbyters and deacons with priests and Levites is already found earlier (*I Clement*), the key moment for church order comes in the third century with Cyprian, who inherited and developed the tradition that saw persons of the Old Testament as prophetic prefigurations of Christ, while persons in the Church may become what we might call 'postfigurations'.

Cyprian[39] speaks of Christ being prefigured in the priest Melchisedek: so, in Genesis, 'the image of sacrifice clearly constituted in bread and wine is already present proleptically. Fulfilling and completing this reality, the Lord offered bread and the cup mixed with wine'. As Melchisedek prefigures, so the eucharistic president postfigures:

> For if Christ Jesus our Lord and God himself is the High Priest of God the Father and first offered himself as a sacrifice to the Father, and commanded that this take place in his memory, that priest indeed truly functions in the place of Christ who imitates that which Christ did, and consequently offers a true and complete sacrifice in the Church to God the Father ... the Lord's passion is the sacrifice we offer.

Once this move was made, almost inevitably typology validated virtually indiscriminate transfer of features from priests of the old covenant to priests of the new. Priestesses were not a feature of what we might call 'Old Testament' religion – they were associated with those fertility rites from which the prophetic tradition sought to distance Israel. Furthermore, scripture excluded from priesthood anyone with a blemish or impurity, and archaic taboos put women into that excluded category. This is the origin of so many of the arguments for women not being admitted to the priesthood.

The hermeneutics of typology, therefore, has to be faced. It is the crucial issue. What I want to suggest is that the claim that no woman can be a type of Christ is an extraordinary misunderstanding of the dynamics of typology. Even Cyprian regards anything in creation as potentially a type of Christ, and the one who puts on Christ in baptism is a living type of that new creation in Christ, humanity refashioned in God's image. Above all, the martyrs are types of Christ, expressing 'to the fullest the common vocation of all Christians to live typologically the *passio* of Christ'.[40] There were in Cyprian's time famous women martyr-saints. There is nothing to stop a woman being a type of Christ, then; gender is irrelevant. It is simply not the point of comparison. Types of Christ are like ikons – they represent not as literal portraits, but as symbols that bear the presence of Christ. The eucharist is not something like a passion-play with the priest acting out the role of Christ at the Last Supper. The Body of Christ is the gathered Church, and the whole sacrament is a representation of the one perfect and sufficient sacrifice made by the priest Christ in offering his own body for the sins of the whole world.

But so far the argument simply challenges the 'literalizing' of typology in terms of gender representing gender. I now wish to offer a positive typological argument for including women among those who may act as priests at the eucharist, an argument I have not seen used before but which builds on the Catholic understanding of Mary as type of the Church and on Behr-Sigel's discussion of the role of the Theotokos in the Church's life.

Behr-Sigel graphically describes the omnipresence of Mary, the birth-giver of God, in Orthodox devotion and liturgy. Like many others she emphasizes the difference between Orthodox veneration, in its existential and poetic dimensions, and the dogmas of the Roman Catholic Church; but even more important is the point that the 'basis and meaning of Mary's glorification' is to be found in the fact that she is inseparable from her Son – mariology is anchored in christology. 'Her glory reflects on all humanity, and the Mother of God reveals mankind's highest vocation.'[41]

> Mary is never considered alone, outside her specific vocation in the history of salvation. In this history, the one God in three Persons is the real actor but in Mary, he associates his creature with the great play ... 'God is come among men; He who cannot be contained is contained in a womb ... For God empties himself, takes flesh, and is fashioned as a creature ...' [42]

In the person of a woman, a human mother, Mary represents humanity associated with the accomplishment of God's loving plan ... From the often expressed Orthodox point of view, Mary remained in intimate solidarity with all mankind ... Because of her faith Mary became God's first co-worker.[43]

Thus Mary's willing consent is a key element in Orthodox understanding – she is the 'type' of one who responds to God, and so of every believer.[44]

This notion can be filled out further, and shown to be deeply within the tradition, through Verna Harrison's study of Gregory of Nyssa:

Notice that an essential feature of Mary's virginity and also that of the Christian soul is receptivity to God. Her purity and integrity open a place within her where God can enter, where Christ can be formed, and from which he can come forth ... Mary's receptivity is intrinsic to her creaturehood; like all human persons, as Gregory understands them, she lives by participation in God ... For Gregory the virginal soul, like Mary, receives the entrance of God and brings forth Christ, though spiritually not physically.[45]

Mary is a type of every believer, man as well as woman.

So to return to Behr-Sigel: 'Mary brings to God the willing agreement of all humanity.'[46] In her Dormition, 'believers are called upon to contemplate the glorification of all creatures at the end of time when all things will be accomplished'; Mary here anticipates the end for which all 'mankind' was created, and 'we participate through faith in this end while still groaning in the labor pains of the new creation's birth'.[47] So Mary is 'the image and personification of the spirit-bearing Church, the womb of the new humanity ... She is the archetype and the guide of those men and women who aspire to give birth to Christ in their hearts'.[48] Behr-Sigel concludes that 'in the Orthodox vision Mary is not seen mainly as the model for women or as the archetype of womanhood in the banal or sociological meaning of the term'. Rather the 'signification of Mary is both unique and universal, both cosmic and eschatological'. 'It is of no small consequence, however, that this new creation, having Mary as its human root, has a woman's face'.[49] Mary is a figure of the Church, of the Body of Christ, of which men and women both are members.[50]

So it is that Behr-Sigel argues that the priesthood of the Church could properly be represented by a man or a woman. But I suspect we can go further. For in the Orthodox Feasts and their ikons there is much that appears to place Mary in a priestly role. Many show her in the *orans* (praying) position: at the Ascension she is there *orans* at the centre of the group of the Apostles; in the *Deesis* she leads the saints of the New Covenant in intercession, as John Baptist leads those of the Old Covenant. Leading the Church in intercession is surely a priestly role. Could it not further be said that this priestly role is expressed symbolically in the feast and ikon of her presentation in the Temple, Mary becoming typologically the archetypal high priest who enters the Holy of Holies? The hymnography of these feasts celebrates Mary as the Ark of the Covenant, the place of God's presence, the Temple of the Holy Spirit and the Tabernacle of the Word of God. So she mediates God to the world in Christ, as the living Temple. She is all-holy, her purity from contamination making possible the incarnation, and so our purification. Again we may speak of a priestly role. In the preface to the original French edition of Behr-Sigel's book, Anthony Bloom wrote:

> Twice Mary had a properly priestly ministry: once when she carried her son who was destined to be sacrificed to the Lord, and once when, at the foot of the cross, she completed the offering by uniting her will, in heroic abandoning of self, to the will of the heavenly Father and to that of the Son of God who by her had become the Son of Man and the sacrificial Lamb.

If it can be acknowledged that Mary has a priestly ministry, then through that typology priesthood can surely not be withheld from women, particularly when it is set in the broader context of Mary's role as 'type' of the Church.

If this argument has the potential to be convincing with respect to the Orthodox tradition, so too with respect to Roman Catholicism, as is argued by John Wijngaards in *The Ordination of Women in the Catholic Church*.[51] He traces the notion of Mary's priesthood within tradition, citing medieval precedents and indicating that recent Roman theology, which contrasts the apostolic-Petrine tradition with the marian tradition, is responsible for excluding this. This explains the position of Pope John Paul II:

> The fact that the blessed Virgin Mary, Mother of God and Mother of the Church, received neither the mission proper to the apostles nor the ministerial priesthood clearly shows that the non-admission of women to priestly ordination cannot mean that women are of lesser dignity, nor can it be construed as discrimination against them. Rather it is to be seen as the faithful observance of a plan to be ascribed to the wisdom of the Lord of the Universe.[52]

John Wijngaards provides some justification for regarding this as contrary to earlier tradition which honoured Mary as the priest *par excellence*.

I refrain from summing up my methodological conclusions at length. I simply underline the main point – we need a hermeneutic that eschews the notion of finding precedents, while discovering that living tradition which remains in continuity with the past but ever seeks renewal by following through the logic of its transcultural instincts. With respect to the ordination of women, the heart of the tradition points beyond discrimination, while typology, so far from suggesting that only a male priest can represent Christ, in fact points to the Christ-likeness of every saint, woman or man, as well as offering a specific typological model for women in the priesthood of Mary. I end with a celebration from the Orthodox tradition:

Let us praise, O faithful believers, the one who is the glory of the universe, the gate of heaven, the Virgin Mary, the flower of the human race and the birth-giver of God. She is the heaven and the temple of God; she has destroyed the boundaries of sin; she is the liberation of your faith.[53]

Bibliography

Behr-Sigel, E., *The Ministry of Women in the Church*, trans. Stephen Bigham (Crestwood, NY: St Vladimir's Seminary Press, 1999; previously Oakwood publications, 1991; original French, Paris: Editions du Cerf, 1987).
Brandenburg, H., *Ancient Churches of Rome from the Fourth to the Seventh Century*, (Turnhout, Belgium: Brepols, 2005).
Burtchaell, J.T., *From Synagogue to Church: Public Services and Offices in the Earliest Christian Communities* (Cambridge: Cambridge University Press, 1992).
Church of England, *Women Bishops in the Church of England? A Report of the House of Bishops Working Party on Women in the Episcopate* (London: Church House Publishing, 2004).
Edwards, R. *The Case for Women's Ordination* (London: SPCK, 1989).
Fiorenza, E.S., *Jesus: Miriam's Child, Sophia's Prophet* (London: SCM Press, 1994).
Fishbane, M., *Biblical Interpretation in Ancient Israel* (Oxford: Clarendon Press, 1985).
Harrison, V. ,'Gender, Generation and Virginity in Cappadocean Theology', *JTS* (new series) 47 (1996), pp. 38–68.
Lampe, P., *From Paul to Valentinus: Christians at Rome in the first Two Centuries*, ed. Marshall D. Johnson, trans. Michael Steinhauser (London: Continuum, 2003).
Laurance, J.D, *'Priest' as Type of Christ. The Leader of the Eucharist in Salvation History According to Cyprian of Carthage* (New York: Peter Lang, 1984),
Mitchell M.M. and Frances M. Young (eds), *Cambridge History of Christianity: Origins to Constantine* (Cambridge: Cambridge University Press, 2007), 'Rome', pp. 397–412.
Plekon, M. and S.E. Hinlicky (eds), *Discerning the Signs of the Times: The Vision of Elisabeth Behr-Sigel* (Crestwood, NY: St Vladimir's Seminary Press, 2001).
Thurston, B.B., *The Widows: A Women's Ministry in the Early Church* (Minneapolis, MN: Fortress Press, 1989).
Torjesen, K.J., *When Women were Priests: Women's Leadership in the Early Church and the Scandal of their Subordination in the Rise of Christianity* (San Francisco, CA: HarperCollins, 1993).
Wijngaards, J., *The Ordination of Women in the Catholic Church: Unmasking a Cuckoo's Egg Tradition* (London: Darton, Longman & Todd, 2001).
Young, F., 'On Episkopos and Presbyteros', in *JTS* (new series), 45 (April 1994), pp. 142–8.
——, *The Theology of the Pastoral Letters* (Cambridge: Cambridge University Press, 1994).
——, *'Presbyteral Ministry in the Catholic Tradition or Why Shouldn't Women be Priests?'* (London: Methodist Sacramental Fellowship, 1994).
——, *Biblical Exegesis and the Formation of Christian Culture* (Cambridge: Cambridge University Press, 1997).

Notes

1 *Women Bishops in the Church of England? A Report of the House of Bishops Working Party on Women in the Episcopate* (London: Church House Publishing,

2004), pp. 64–5.

2 E.g. *Apostolic Constitutions*, II.25.

3 Peter Lampe, *From Paul to Valentinus: Christians at Rome in the first Two Centuries*, ed. Marshall D. Johnson, trans. Michael Steinhauser (London: Continuum, 2003); see 'Rome' in Margaret M. Mitchell and Frances M. Young (eds), *Cambridge History of Christianity: Origins to Constantine* (Cambridge: Cambridge University Press, 2007), pp. 397–412 for references to subsequent discussion.

4 The following paragraphs draw upon my previous work, which see for detailed references: 'On Episkopos and Presbyteros' in *JTS* (new series), 45 (April 1994), pp. 142–8; *The Theology of the Pastoral Letters* (Cambridge: Cambridge University Press, 1994), pp. 97–121; *Presbyteral Ministry in the Catholic Tradition or Why Shouldn't Women be Priests?* (London: Methodist Sacramental Fellowship, 1994).

5 See e.g. James Tunstead Burtchaell, *From Synagogue to Church: Public Services and Offices in the Earliest Christian Communities* (Cambridge: Cambridge University Press, 1992).

6 Karen Jo Torjesen, *When Women were Priests: Women's Leadership in the Early Church and the Scandal of their Subordination in the Rise of Christianity* (SanFrancisco, CA: HarperCollins, 1993), p. 7.

7 Hugo Brandenburg, *Ancient Churches of Rome from the Fourth to the Seventh Century* (Turnhout: Brepols, 2005).

8 John Wijngaards, *The Ordination of Women in the Catholic Church: Unmasking a Cuckoo's Egg Tradition* (London: Darton, Longman & Todd, 2001) provides access to the evidence.

9 See e.g. Bonnie Bowman Thurston, *The Widows: A Women's Ministry in the Early Church* (Minneapolis, MN: Fortress Press, 1989).

10 There is, of course, a conservative tradition among Protestants which argues against the ordination of women on two grounds: (1) the Pauline texts prohibiting women to speak or have headship over men, and (2) the supposed order of creation established in Genesis. See discussion of Edwards below – she tackles these 'literalist' arguments.

11 for further discussion, see Ch. 2 in Frances Young, *Biblical Exegesis and the Formation of Christian Culture* (Cambridge: Cambridge University Press, 1997).

12 Ruth Edwards, *The Case for Women's Ordination* (London: SPCK, 1989).

13 Edwards, *The Case for Women's Ordination*, p. 49.

14 Edwards, *The Case for Women's Ordination*, p. 69.

15 Edwards, *The Case for Women's Ordination*, pp. 81–2.

16 Edwards, *The Case for Women's Ordination*, pp. 82–3.

17 Edwards, *The Case for Women's Ordination*, p. 130.

18 Edwards, *The Case for Women's Ordination*, p. 182.

19 Michael Plekon and Sarah E. Hinlicky (eds), *Discerning the Signs of the Times: The Vision of Elisabeth Behr-Sigel* (Crestwood, NY: St Vladimir's Seminary Press, 2001).

20 Elisabeth Behr-Sigel, *The Ministry of Women in the Church*, trans. Stephen Bigham (Crestwood, NY: St Vladimir's Seminary Press, 1999).

21 Behr-Sigel, *The Ministry of Women in the Church*, pp. 18–19.

22 Plekon and Hinlicky (eds), *Discerning the Signs of the Times*, Ch. 8; Behr-Sigel, *The Ministry of Women in the Church*, pp. 61–4.

23 Behr-Sigel, *The Ministry of Women in the Church*, pp. 64–72.

24 Plekon and Hinlicky (eds), *Discerning the Signs of the Times*, pp. 116–17.

25 Plekon and Hinlicky (eds), *Discerning the Signs of the Times*, pp. 101–2; Behr-Sigel, *The Ministry of Women in the Church*, p. 55.

26 Behr-Sigel, *The Ministry of Women in the Church*, pp. 43, 46.

27 Plekon and Hinlicky (eds), *Discerning the Signs of the Times*, Ch. 10.

28 Behr-Sigel, *The Ministry of Women in the Church*, p. 116.

29 Behr-Sigel, *The Ministry of Women in the Church*, p. 8.

30 Behr-Sigel, *The Ministry of Women in the Church*, p. 42.
31 Behr-Sigel, *The Ministry of Women in the Church*, p. 135.
32 Behr-Sigel, *The Ministry of Women in the Church*, p. 140.
33 Behr-Sigel, *The Ministry of Women in the Church*, p. 168.
34 Behr-Sigel, *The Ministry of Women in the Church*, p. 122.
35 Behr-Sigel, *The Ministry of Women in the Church*, p. 122.
36 Behr-Sigel, *The Ministry of Women in the Church*, p. 36.
37 Plekon and Hinlicky (eds), *Discerning the Signs of the Times*, p. 106.
38 A range of different kinds of typologies is traced in the Hebrew Bible by Michael Fishbane, *Biblical Interpretation in Ancient Israel* (Oxford: Clarendon Press, 1985), pp. 35–79; for further discussion see Young, *Biblical Exegesis*, pp. 192–201.
39 Cyprian, Epistle 63.14, 17. My discussion of Cyprian owes much to John D. Laurance, '*Priest*' *as Type of Christ. The Leader of the Eucharist in Salvation History according to Cyprian of Carthage* (New York: Peter Lang, 1984), though he should not be held responsible for all the conclusions drawn. The following paragraphs draw upon my (unpublished) lecture *Presbyteral Ministry in the Catholic Tradition*.
40 Laurance, '*Priest*' *as Type of Christ*, pp. 193–4.
41 Behr-Sigel, *The Ministry of Women in the Church*, p. 189.
42 Behr-Sigel, *The Ministry of Women in the Church*, p. 192, quoting from the liturgy for the Feast of the Annunciation.
43 Behr-Sigel, *The Ministry of Women in the Church*, pp. 193–4.
44 Cf. Behr-Sigel, *The Ministry of Women in the Church*, p. 60.
45 Verna Harrison, 'Gender, Generation and Virginity in Cappadocean Theology', *JTS* (new series), 47 (1996), pp. 38–68.
46 Behr-Sigel, *The Ministry of Women in the Church*, p. 77.
47 Behr-Sigel, *The Ministry of Women in the Church*, p. 198.
48 Behr-Sigel, *The Ministry of Women in the Church*, p. 207.
49 Behr-Sigel, *The Ministry of Women in the Church*, p. 210.
50 Plekon and Hinlicky (eds.), *Discerning the Signs of the Times*, p. 112.
51 John Wijngaards, *The Ordination of Women in the Catholic Church: Unmasking a Cuckoo's Egg Tradition* (London: Darton, Longman & Todd, 2001). (This book I found on the conference bookstall; I was intrigued to find that I had been anticipated in making this argument.)
52 From his *Apostolic Letter on Reserving Priestly Ordination to Men Alone*, quoted by Elizabeth Schüssler Fiorenza, *Jesus: Miriam's Child, Sophia's Prophet* (London: SCM Press, 1994), p. 163.
53 Behr-Sigel,*The Ministry of Women in the Church*, p. 206.

2

The Ordination of Women in the Roman Catholic Church

Catherine Gyarmathy-Amherd

Introduction

When asked to write this chapter I did not realize what I was getting involved in. I am not a professional theologian but a laywoman who feels the Roman Catholic Church is her spiritual home yet has also viewed some recent developments with growing concern. I am also a woman with significant ecumenical experience: not only do I live a mixed marriage with a (Hungarian) Protestant husband but I also look back on eight years of co-presidency of the Ecumenical Forum of European Christian Women. These years of collaboration with lay women, theologians and female pastors from different confessions, all actively involved in their churches, opened new horizons and also led me into a closer analysis of the position of women with regard to ordination within the Roman Catholic Church.

Looking back

The Roman Catholic Church's relationship with women has a long and painful history (although it is not alone amongst Christian denominations in this respect). St Paul's words in 1 Cor. 14.34-35 and 1 Tim. 2.12 have long provided the grounds by which women have been allotted a 'place' in Church and society. Teachers of the Church have commented that women 'can neither teach nor testify' (Augustine of Hippo), are 'in a state of subjection' and thus 'cannot receive the sacrament of Order' (Thomas Aquinas) and 'should be married in veils that they might always be submissive and humble to their husbands' (Isidor of Seville).[1] A variety of other philosophers and writers throughout history have promoted a negative picture of women by denying them their dignity as human beings and branding them as inferior to men, thus hiding the 'genius of women under a bushel'.[2] Two Dominican friars were responsible for one of the most misogynistic documents of all: the fifteenth-century *Malleus Maleficarum*, the handbook of the Early Modern European witch-craze.

Yet despite all this, women *were* visible in the Church. Jesus was accompanied by women from his birth until his death; women were the first to meet him on

Easter morning. He talked with women, healed them and sent them out with his message. We have the testimony of many women martyrs in early Christian times: out of the 14 auxiliary saints,[3] three are women: Barbara, Catherine and Margaret. Such imposing women as Catherine of Siena, Teresa of Avila and Thérèse of Lisieux have been proclaimed doctors of the Church (though only in 1970 and 1997 respectively). In the medieval period, abbesses were influential figures in European monasticism. Women were also managers of large households, offered their services to the sick and needy and travelled to the four corners of the earth as missionaries.

In spite of these testimonies of faith, responsibility and involvement, women were hardly visible in the recorded life of the Church for many centuries. In the encyclical *Casti Nubii* (1930, paras 26–8) the stereotype of the submissive and obedient woman, the woman as a childbearer was cemented. However, by the Second World War (but especially since the late 1960s), Western society was undergoing rapid change and calls grew for greater consideration of women's rights. Besides the particular struggle for recognition of the rights of women, women also found themselves at the forefront of the wider movement for human rights for all. Today we find women as heads of national governments, taking parliamentary seats, occupying senior management positions and working as professors in higher education. In many countries, greater opportunities than ever are available to women both in their working and domestic lives. However, the rise of women was also a challenge to many in society and in the churches. Radical feminism has certainly nurtured (and continues to nurture) deep anger, contempt and resentment against Christianity, the Bible, the Church and everything related to them. However, it also challenges Christian women to reflect upon their position and their relationship to Church and society.

The road to renewal

By the 1950s, many theologians were beginning to feel that renewal of the Church was necessary. New forms – such as vernacular liturgy and the westward-facing celebration of the Mass – were openly discussed as possibilities. Dialogue with other churches became an important matter of concern.[4] Pope John XXIII (1958–63) sensed that great social transformations in values and culture demanded that the Church scrutinize the signs of the times and interpret them in the light of the gospel (this sentiment is expressed in the conciliar document *Lumen Gentium*, November 1964). From the Second Vatican Council which followed (1962–65), several key documents have particular implications for women. The first, *Pacem in Terris* (1963, 15, p. 3), asserted that 'Human beings have the right to choose *freely* the state of life they prefer and therefore to set up a family with equal rights and duties for both man and woman and also the right *to follow a vocation* to the priesthood or the religious life' (italics mine). The Pastoral Constitution on the Church (*Gaudium et Spes*, 1965, 'The Church in the Modern World'), urged all Catholics wherever necessary to undertake with vigour the task of renewal and reform.

Expectations were further raised by Pope Paul VI's statement to the Vatican Study Commission on the Role of Women in Society in 1975: 'it is evident that women are meant to form part of the living and working structure of Christianity in so prominent a manner that perhaps not all their potentialities have yet been made clear'. More widely, women's consciousness was raised, and many set out to search for their own way to live their faith and to find their own spirituality in the light of the gospel, with the intention (through their experience of life and faith) of contributing to the renewal of the Church.

Women and ministry: priesthood and diaconate

Through these developments, the call for women's ordination was, and is, a response to the proclamation of the full Christian personhood of all Catholics, women included. Vatican II spoke of the participation of the laity, of collegiality, of the Church as the People of God. From this, many women began to feel that some amongst them would experience the call to priesthood, as had Catherine of Siena, Teresa of Avila, Thérèse of Lisieux and Edith Stein (Sr Teresa Benedicta of the Cross) before them. Indeed, the question of women as priests had already been raised in advance of the Vatican Council. In 1962 the Swiss Catholic laywoman Gertrud Heinzelmann addressed the Preparatory Commission of the Council with a petition demanding the equality of the sexes in the Church and access to the priesthood for women. Heinzelmann pointed out that through their faithfulness, their deep religious desires, their service in child-rearing and their charitable engagement, women constituted an important support for the Church.[5] In making this petition public, she triggered a worldwide discussion. In the coming years, more and more books, articles and doctoral dissertations,[6] written by both men and women, theologians and laity appeared on the question of women's ordination. A new generation of feminist theologians grew up, and the question of the ordination of women was fast becoming a central issue. These women could count on the solidarity of a considerable number of lay women, male theologians and lay men. A further factor influencing the growing consideration of, and demand for, women's ordination was that women were already working as ordained ministers, first in many Protestant churches and subsequently in the Anglican Communion, and proving themselves equal to the task.

Thus Rome found itself increasingly confronted with demands and rising expectations from women: sentiments which did not accord with traditional teaching on the sacraments, particularly regarding priestly ordination. Indeed, the period since the 1970s has seen the issuing of several new encyclicals and declarations relating to the role of women in Church and society. We shall now examine these in greater depth.

First, in October 1976, the Vatican published the *Declaration on the Ordination of Women* (*Inter Insigniores* (AAS69/1977)) with the aim of silencing once and for all discussions over the issue. Two particular arguments against women's ordination were put forward here: first, that Jesus only called men as apostles; second, that only a male minister can truly represent Christ at the eucharist. The document also made reference to the New Testament (Pauline) images of Christ as the bridegroom and the Church as his bride. From this image, the subordination of woman to man has frequently been adduced. Contrary to the original intention, however, discussion was not curtailed but intensified, emphasizing the growing polarization between 'traditional' and 'liberal' camps in the Roman Catholic Church.

The same arguments appear again in the second important text: *Mulieris Dignitatem* (On the Dignity and Vocation of Women, AAS 80, 1988). Drawing on Genesis 1 (the creation of man and woman and their relationship), it stated that human beings reach unity through the integration of the masculine and feminine. Women are again defined with reference to motherhood, the married woman being the consecrated woman. Single women are not considered at all. Again the spousal image is used: 'The bridegroom is the one who loves; the bride is loved. It is she who receives love, in order to love in return' (22). *Mulieris Dignitatem* is particularly interesting because it deploys a biblical understanding often cited by feminist theologians to enhance the theological understanding of womanhood, yet at the same time uses it to set clear limits on women's sphere of activity. Indeed, the document essentially repeats traditional understandings of the male character of priesthood: the 'no' to priesthood is further underlined by the document's citation of canon law, para. 1024, which reads: 'a baptized male alone receives sacred ordination validly'.

However, the still-prevailing opposition to ordaining women is not uniquely based on such theological and traditional thinking. We know that its roots are also to be found in strongly emotional sensitivities about women and sexuality expressed both by society in general and by many men in particular. As in all the monotheistic religions, the negative images associated with the priesthood of women are often derived from pagan rites (idolatry is thus adultery and prostitution). As Uta Ranke-Heimann has comprehensively shown, women are still sometimes seen as unclean where taboos persist over menstruation. Although modern biological and medical knowledge have changed attitudes, according to Mary Grey 'the model of sexuality is still strongly a male, patriarchal model'.[7]

A further development came in 2004, with the publication of a *Letter to the Bishops of the Catholic Church on the Collaboration of Men and Women in the Church and in the World*, prepared by the Congregation for Doctrine of the Faith and written by its then head, Cardinal Joseph Ratzinger. The document opens with the following words: 'The Church, expert in humanity, has a perennial interest in whatever concerns men and women and "….is called today to address certain currents of thought which are often at variance with the authentic advancement of women"' (Introduction/para. 1). In fact this document reaffirms all the arguments from *Mulieris dignitatem*. Initially it appears to engage positively with feminist theology but in reality does quite the opposite. For example, the document states that women should be present in the worlds of work, society and politics, with access to positions of responsibility 'which allow them to inspire the policies of nations and to promote innovative solutions to economic and social problems' (13). Quite correctly, it also calls for the just valuing of women's work within the family (13). Women are not solely defined by marriage, and there is discussion of single and childless women, since 'motherhood can find norms of full realisation also where there is no physical procreation' (13). Having said that, motherhood remains a key referent for women's identity, and there is a reassertion of the notion that the woman lives 'for the other' and is 'the helper' (6). There is criticism of the idea that the liberation of women entails criticism of holy scripture (3), but also a suggestion that, by calling for their rights, women make themselves adversaries of men (2). Indeed, it also suggests that proclaiming the liberation of women from biological determinism risks minimizing the difference between physical attributes (sex) and cultural elements (gender) (2). The letter's final chapter focuses on the relationship between Church and women. Mary is taken as the model of femininity to which the Church should aspire: ready to listen and welcome believers. 'In this perspective one understands how the reservation of priestly ordination solely to men does not hamper in any way women's access to the heart of Christian life. Women are called to be unique examples and witnesses for all Christians of how the Bride is to respond in love to the love of the Bridegroom' (16).

Thus the *Declaration*, *Mulieris Dignitatem* and the *Letter to the Bishops* were all intended to quell discussion about the issue of women in ministry, yet they have been accepted by some and criticized by others, and the discussion goes on. Many women gladly accept the role of motherhood/womanhood portrayed in these documents because it is their choice. Just as many, however, deplore the documents' regression to a traditional image of women which does not correspond to their vision of life. What is certain is that the documents have failed to stem the debate. New publications, conferences and meetings on the subject appear all the time.[8] In response, such 'disobedience' has incurred sanctions: women religious who speak up at conferences have either had to comply with the rules or are threatened with expulsion from their order. Both male and female theologians have been ejected from university chairs for writing in favour of women's ordination, or (in some countries) have been turned down from posts in theological colleges or not accepted for pastoral work in parishes (among them, Sr Joan Chittister, Professor Silvia Schoer and, much earlier, Professor Hans Küng).

The debate

Yet the teachings of the *Constitution on the Church in the Modern World* (1965) and the cultural movement towards a fairer valuation of women awakened in many women a new consciousness of their potential. This new consciousness gave many Catholic women, but also many women from other churches, a new self-respect and a new sense of responsibility in the

Church. Women have come a long way within the Church. Today we see them serving at all levels in parishes and schools, in caring for the elderly, serving as hospital and prison chaplains, studying theology and teaching in universities. The call of women to full personhood has also prompted a new consideration of what personhood means for men, for an analysis of the relationship between men and women, and last (but not least) for structural reform of the Church. It is in this context that the ordination of women has become a highly important issue.

Looking at the Catholic Church today, several main streams of opinion on women's ordination can be made out. On the one hand, there is a large corpus of Catholics who do not contest the teachings of the Church and are deeply concerned about the demands of more liberal voices. They can be particularly irritated by the views of liberal and feminist theologians. However, they are not to be identified with the ultra-traditionalist Catholicism of Monsignor Lefèbvre and his followers, who explicitly reject Vatican II not only on the liturgical level but also on the level of doctrine (a position eventually resulting in excommunication by Pope John Paul II in July 1988). Rather, most Catholics are 'traditionalist' with a small 't': undogmatically conservative, institutionally loyal and active in the historic lay voluntary organizations. A second, more diffuse, group of Catholics takes little interest in questions about women and ordination. They are churchgoers, but are not greatly involved in theological dialogue and dispute. A third group may be characterized as 'liberal Catholics' who – in spite of many reservations – are determined to be faithful to Jesus Christ, to his teachings and to Christian values, and wish to preserve the spiritual and cultural heritage of Vatican II. This group is composed of both men and women, theologians and lay people, and profess a Church of witness, community and ministry. Equality between women and men is an important issue, and so advocacy of women's ordination assumes a prominent place in their activities. At the same time, documents such as *Inter Insigniores, Mulieris Dignitatem,* the *Letter to the Bishops,* the *Letter to Women* and *Ordinatio Sacerdotalis* have arguably signalled a general shift away from the spirit of Vatican II. According to the Church of Rome, these statements should have meant an end to discussion. However, the question remains: did Rome seriously expect full obedience in this respect? Did it believe that in spite of wider social and political developments (notably the increasing equality of men and women in human rights and the guarantee of freedom of expression) further debate on women's ordination could be silenced? As the disputes of the last decade have shown, quelling debate was impossible, leaving Rome to resort to the more traditional tool of sanctions against opponents. In recent years, the most significant reaction to this development has been the illegal ordination of several women both as priests, deacons and bishops; in Austria in 2002, France and Canada in 2006 and Switzerland and the USA in 2007.[9] All have been excommunicated. Many Catholics (notably laypeople and activists sympathetic to Christian feminism) have felt a sense of solidarity with the *contra legem* ordinations, but they have questioned the decision to bypass canon law. Some accuse the women and their supporters of ultra-feminism, of putting their own desires before those of the Church and of unbridled egotism. However, I think, given the women's longstanding commitment to the Church, a more sympathetic assessment is required, always remembering that ordination is not indulging in an ego trip, but is (in the words of Soline Vatinel) 'replying to an urgent call of the Spirit, often reluctantly, and sometimes the response will cost a great deal'.[10] As Karl Rahner has commented, 'it is almost of greater importance to perceive such gifts of the Spirit on their first appearance, so that they may be furthered and not choked by the incomprehension and intellectual laziness, if not the ill-will and hatred, of those around them, ecclesiastics included'.[11]

In the 1990s the shift away from the values of Vatican II prompted protests and actions throughout the world. In 1996 the movement Wir sind Kirche (We are Church) began its work. Today, active in many countries and on three continents, it is pledged to work for a 'sisterly-brotherly' Church. The members of this network are Catholics with a deep commitment to the values of Vatican II and fully support, among other things, the ordination of women. Initially the church authorities were ready to listen to the requests, but today, unfortunately, the dialogue is stalled. While in Switzerland the Church has refused to enter into dialogue with both the campaigning platforms Tagsatzung Basel and Luzerner Manifest (similar in profile to Wir sind Kirche), in Austria representatives of Wir sind Kirche have been recently received by the Nuncio Mgr Edmond Farhat, who promised to arrange a meeting with the Congregation for the Doctrine of the Faith.[12]

Although the question of women and priesthood has often taken centre-stage, a related (though distinct) debate surrounds the ordination of women to the diaconate. In 2001 an official notification was issued reminding bishops that women have not been admitted to the diaconate. This was prompted by (and primarily addressed to) German-speaking bishops who had taken the step of beginning the formation of women for diaconal service. Confrontation was intensified still further in 2004 with the publication of the *Letter to the Bishops of the Catholic Church on the Collaboration of Men and Women in the Church and the World* (May 2004). From these, Rome's fears are evident: ordaining women to the diaconate is seen as automatically entailing their ordination to the priesthood. On one level, this refusal to consider the ordination of women as deacons is a denial that both women's professional know-how and their vocation to ordained ministry are equal to those of their male counterparts. However, on another level the prohibition on ordaining women to the diaconate has practical implications: ordaining women as deacons would go some way to easing the pastoral situation in many countries. In Switzerland, for example, some parishes no longer have their own priest but are led by pastoral workers – women amongst them – who take day-to-day pastoral charge of a parish but cannot administer the sacraments. Whilst the Orthodox Church (particularly in Greece) is reviving the traditions of the Early Church in consecrating women deaconesses (Rom. 16.1), the Latin Church continues to refuse to countenance the restoration of the diaconate to women.

Liberal theologians, working within the Church, men and women alike, call the Church to remember that the constitutions of Vatican II encourage all

believers to share in the mission of Christ. They question the narrow interpretation of the scriptures which suggests that because Jesus called only men as
apostles, and because priests are the successors of the apostles, only a male priest
can adequately represent Christ at the eucharist. What particularly angers
feminist theologians and many lay women is the fact that biblical texts such as
Romans 16, which clearly show women serving the young Church, are not interpreted in the same strict way as texts referring to Jesus and the apostles. In
Romans 16, Paul describes Junia (sometimes called Julia) as an apostle, and
greets Phoebe as a deacon.

The sacrifice involved in submitting to ordination has become particularly
acute in the secularized West, where the role and social construction of
priesthood has changed dramatically in recent decades. The challenge facing
those who take on some aspect of the priestly task is well-illustrated by the
recent *Directory on the Ministry and Life of Priests*, issued by the Congregation
for the Clergy in 1994[13] and directed at priests of the Church of the Latin Rite.
(This document – in management jargon one could call it a job-description –
runs to 56 pages, and the reader is left feeling overwhelmed by the expectations
placed upon the clergy.) It is hardly surprising that many young men, in spite
of a deep sense of vocation, consider themselves unable to cope with such
rigorous requirements and ultimately choose not to be ordained. At the same
time, Marcel Vincent OP speaks of a widespread 'desacralization and declericalization of priesthood', adding that in some parts of the world, the shortage
of clergy is so serious as to demand a new type of priest: woman or man,
married or celibate. In a recently published study of 1,400 pastoral assistants
in German-speaking parts of Europe, Professor Paul Zulehner (Vienna), has
spoken of a corresponding clericalization of the laity, who increasingly perform
work for which they are not formally empowered.[14] At parish level, many
accept this development in practical terms, although according to Professor Leo
Karrer of the University of Fribourg (Switzerland) it means that lay theologians
engaged in church and pastoral work feel themselves in the role of foreign
workers, who are tolerated but restricted in their tasks. The Swiss experience
detailed by Professor Karrer is similar to that in Austria and Germany. In both
pastoral and theological terms, this situation is ultimately unsustainable.

However, the issue of women's ordination cannot and should not be linked
to declining numbers of clergy. Instead, it should be regarded as a challenge to
adopt new perspectives, search for new approaches and seek the full integration
of women into the ministry of the Church. Professor Walter Kirschläger of the
University of Lucerne, in a lecture in Lucerne on 26 October 2006, has called
for renewed vision and engagement by the whole Church in order to find
creative ways of achieving the equality of women and men. Kirschläger asserts
that for the Catholic Church to retain its freedom, it must not only support the
promotion of human rights in society as a whole but also implement them
within the Church. Sandra Mazzolini, in her article 'The Ecclesiological Model
and Ministry', similarly urges the Church to greater creativity in discovering new
models of church life. Whilst considering all aspects of church life, this includes
a specific focus on ministry and ways in which it might respond to the changed
social context in which women and men find themselves today – notably the

way in which recognition of women's civil and political rights have also exerted a profound influence on women's identities.[15]

Human rights

Quite apart from the obvious questions of theology, ecclesiology and tradition, the whole debate on women's ordination is, in addition, a debate about human rights. In the aforementioned *Directory on the Ministry and Life of Priests*, para. 17 speaks of the 'temptation of democratism'. 'Democratism' (the creation of the word is symptomatic of how difficult members of the hierarchy have found the concept of democratic rights) is considered one of the most pressing dangers of the day because 'it leads to a denial of the authority and capital grace of Christ and distorts the nature of the Church, and, moreover, 'damage[s] the hierarchical structure willed by Jesus'. However, as Marie Thérèse Van Lunen Chenu has pointed out, the Universal Declaration on Human Rights has already been adopted (almost word for word) in Vatican II's *Gaudium et Spes* (29): 'Any kind of social or cultural discrimination in basic personal rights on the grounds of sex, race, colour, social conditions, language or religion, must be curbed and eradicated as incompatible with God's design.' Further impetus has come from secular political sources.[16] In a report to the parliamentary Assembly of the Council of Europe of the Committee on Equal Opportunities of Women and Men entitled 'Women and Religion in Europe', the authors write: 'the religious stereotyping of women's character and role is not compatible with our modern understanding of gender equality and equal opportunities for women'.[17] A recent dissertation on 'The Equality of Women in State and Church: A Problematic Area of Conflict' has highlighted the tension women experience in attempting to maintain their loyalty to the Church whilst facing discrimination on grounds of sex and exclusion from ordination (amounting to a further exclusion from a profession).[18] Thus on two levels, the Church finds itself in a difficult position on the question of women's rights: internally, there is a tension between the vision expounded in *Gaudium et Spes* and the current reality. Externally, a parallel tension exists between the Church's own selective handling of human rights and the more generalized defence of human rights by the UN and European Union.

Ecumenism

Both the Orthodox and Roman Catholic churches often stress that women's claims to ordination are potentially damaging to relationships with other denominations. Yet this issue cannot be made responsible for the stagnation in ecumenism in recent decades. Other issues, such as intercommunion, the apostolic succession and papal infallibility also impede dialogue between the churches. Many women in both Catholicism and Orthodoxy object to being treated as scapegoats and made to feel responsible for the growing difficulties of ecumenical dialogue. They also feel greatly concerned when the issue of women's ordination is used as a tool to hinder collaboration between the World Council of Churches (WCC), the Conference of European Churches (CEC) and the Bishops' Conference of Europe,[19] which has been so fruitful for many years, and continues in the form of the *Charta Oecumenica* (Guidelines for the growing Cooperation among the Churches in Europe, signed and presented in Strasbourg, on 22 April 2001). The aforementioned bodies carefully omit open discussion about the issue when working in joint programmes. Here and there, however, the issue flares up, the Catholic side[20] repeating its refusal to ordain women, the Protestant side[21] advocating equal rights for women, including access to ordination. However, women's ordination is often not the primary cause of division: one recent 'ecumenical thunderstorm' in Switzerland was provoked not by the question of women as priests but by Rome's recent reaffirmation of the Catholic Church as the one, true Church of Christ.

Re-scrutinizing the signs of the times[22]

On 13 August 2006 many Catholics tuning in to a broadcast interview with Pope Benedict XVI on Bayerische Rundfunk (ARD), ZDF, Deutsche Welle and Vatican Radio were surprised to find Benedict allowing himself to be addressed by German journalists on the question of women's ordination – not least since open discussion of this issue has been banned by the Vatican for at least 30 years. The Pope reminded his audience that there was a legal inhibition (canon law 1024) to the ordination of women, but then he continued:

I believe that women themselves, with their energy and strength, with their superiority, with what I'd call their 'spiritual power', will know how to make their own space. We will have to try and listen to God so as not to stand in their way but, on the contrary, to rejoice when the female element achieves the fully *effective* place in the Church best suited to her, starting with the Mother of God and with Mary Magdalen.

[Aber ich glaube, die Frauen selber mit ihrem Schwung und ihrer Kraft, mit ihrem Uebergewicht so zusagen, an ihrer Würde, an ihrer geistlichen Potenz sich einen Platz zu verschaffen wissen und wir wollen versuchen, auf Gott zu hören, dass wir den auch nicht behindern, sondern uns freuen, dass das Weibliche in der Kirche, wie es sich gehört – von der Muttergottes und von Maria Magdalena an – seine *kraftvolle* Stelle erhält'.][23]

It is interesting to compare the German original with the English translation (taken here from the Vatican Radio website). Despite its flaws the former is strong and spontaneous, while the English version (in translating '*kraftvolle*' as 'effective' rather than 'powerful') offers a more conservative interpretation of the German original. Could the words of Pope Benedict be considered as a sign of readiness to reopen the dialogue?

Rescrutinzing the signs of the times is just as necessary in these days as it was in 1965. Life within the Church, but also in society, has undergone enormous changes since Vatican II, the increased prominence of women being only one of the visible signs. Both Church(es) and society have to acknowledge that the patriarchal system is no longer unassailable and is progressively being replaced by the post-patriarchal structures. It would be high time for a new dialogue since the current polarization of views is affecting not only the Church but also all the people of faith. The Church should not be a place for dispute but a place for reconciliation, where problems can be peacefully resolved. Women want to be Church! They wish to share the work in the vineyards of God as empowered partners using prophetic and ministerial talents, to live their charisms to the full.

Bibliography

Vatican papers (accessed at: http://www.vatican.va)

Encyclical on Christian Marriages (Casti Connubii), Pius XII (1930).

Code of Canon Law (Codex Juris Canonici) (1983).

Decree on the Churches of the Eastern Rite (Orientalium Ecclesiarum), Paul VI (November 1964).

Dogmatic Constitution on the Church (Lumen Gentium), Paul VI (November 1964).

Pastoral Constitution on the Church in the Modern World (Gaudium et Spes), Paul VI (December 1965).

Declaration on the Ordination of Women (Inter Insigniores) (AAS69), Paul VI (1977).

Letter to the Bishops of the Catholic Church Regarding Certain Aspects of the Church (Communio, Communionis notio), John Paul II (1992).

Apostolical Letter on the Ordination to the Priesthood (Ordinatio Sacerdotalis), John Paul II (1994).

Letter to Women (AAS86), John Paul II (1995).

Apostolical Letter on the Dignity and Vocation of Women (Mulieris Dignitatem) (AAS80), John Paul II (1998).

Letter to the Bishops of the Catholic Church on the Collaboration of Men and Women in the Church and the World , Congregation for the Doctrine of the Faith (2004).

Catechism of the Catholic Church (Libreria Editrice Vaticana, 1993) (new English edn 2000).

Encyclical Letter to the Bishops, Priests and Deacons, Men and Women, Religious and All Lay Faithful on Christian Love (Deus Caritas est), Benedict XVI (2006).

Books, articles and lectures

Ahlers, S., *Gleichstellung der Frau in Staat und Kirche – ein problematisches Spannungsverhältnis* (Münster: LIT, 2006).

Arana, M.J. and Salas, M., *Mujeres Sacerdotas, porqué no?* (Madrid: Publicaciones Claretianes, 1994) (accessed at http://www.womenpriests.org/sp/aran_sal/ara_cont.asp).

Council of Europe, doc. 10670 (Strasbourg, September 2005), *Women and Religion in Europe*.

Cullmann, O. and Karrer, O., *Einheit in Christus: Evangelische und Katholische Bekenntnisse* (Zurich: Zwingli, 1960).

Daly, M., 'A Built-in Bias', *Commonweal* (January 1965) (accessed at www.ministryforwomen.org).

Ertel, W., and G. Forster (eds.), *Wir sind Priesterinnen: Aus aktuellem Anlass: Die Weihe von Frauen 2002* (Düsseldorf: Patmos, 2002).

Grey, M., 'The Ordination of Women – Seeking a New Approach', lecture to the Annual General Assembly of Catholic Women's Ordination, London (7 May 2002) (accessed at www.ministryforwomen.org).

Halkes, C., *'Gott hat nicht nur starke Söhne': Grundzüge einer feministischen Theologie* (Gütersloh: Güthersloher Verlagshaus, 1982).

Heimbach-Steins, M., 'Menschrechte der Frauen, Universaler Anspruch und kontextbezogene Konkretisierung', *Stimmen der Zeit*, August 2006, pp. 546–61.

Heinzelmann, G., *Frau und Konzil – Hoffnung und Ewartung* (Zurich: Verlag der Staatsbürgerin, 1962).

Hunt, M., 'Feminist Ministries in a Discipleship of Equals', keynote address, Call to Action, Milwaukee, WI, 3–4 November 2006 (accessed at www.ministryforwomen.org).

Hurka, H.P., 'Gerechtigkeit ist das Kennzeichen des Reiches Gottes' (Austria, 14 October 2006) (accessed at www.wir-sind-kirch.at).

Kasper, W., *Wegweiser Oekumene und Spritualität* (Freiburg: Herder, 2007).

——, 'Oekumene im Wandel', keynote address, General Assembly of the Congregation for the Promotion of Christian Unity, 13 November 2006, also appearing as: 'Strittige Fragen über Grundlagen und Ziel der Oekumene', *Stimmen der Zeit*, 1 (January 2007), p. 9.

Kässmann, M., 'Was folgt auf das "Jahrhundert der Oekumene"' Otto-Karrer Lecture 2005, *Orientierung*, 4 (28 February 2006), p 45.

Kirchschläger, W., 'Ohne Einschränkung durch Geschlecht und Lebensstand – zu biblischen Grundlagen kirchlicher Dienste', lecture, Lucerne, 28 October 2006.

Küng, H., and G. Lohfink, 'Keine Ordination der Frau?', *Theologische Quartalsschrift* (1977).

Küng, H., 'Women's Ordination and Infallibility', *The Tablet* (16 December 1995).

Lauer, R., 'Women and the Church', *Commonweal*, 20 (December 1963), pp. 365–8 (accessed at www.ministryforwomen.org).

Mazzolini, S., 'Modello ecclesiologico e ministero', *Annali di Studi Religiosi*, 7 (2006), pp. 281–303.

Neues Aemterverständnis in der Kirche, Schweiz (Lucerne: Katholischer Frauenbund, 1999).

Nöknek (is) teremtette, Romania Magyar Pax Romana (Csikszereda: Status Kiado, 2006).

Prüller-Jagenteufel, V., 'Kraft der Weihe', *Diakonia*, 33.5 (2002), pp. 369–72.

Rahner, K., *Mission and Grace*, vol. 2 (London: Sheed & Ward, 1964).

——, *The Charismatic Element in the Church* (New York: Herder & Herder, 1964).

——, 'Priestertum der Frau', *Stimmen der Zeit*, 105.5 (May 1977), pp. 291–301.

Raming, I., 'The Exclusion of Women from Priesthood' (Metuchen, NJ: Scarecrow Press, 1973) (accessed at www.ministryforwomen.org).

Fiorenza, E. Schüssler, *Der vergessene Partner* (Düsseldorf: Patmos, 1964) (accessed at www.ministryforwomen.org).

——, 'The Twelve', in A. and L. Swidler (eds), *Women Priests* (New York: Paulist Press, 1977), pp. 114–21 (accessed at www.ministryforwomen.org).

Ranke-Heinemann, U., *Eunuchs for Heaven: The Catholic Church and Sexuality* (London: André Deutsch, 1990) (accessed at www.ministryforwomen.org).

Swidler, A., 'The Male Church', *Commonweal* (24 June 1966), pp. 29–44 (accessed at www.ministryforwomen.org).

——, *Women in a Man's Church* (New York: Paulist Press, 1972) (accessed at www.ministryforwomen.org).

van Lunen Chenu, M.T., 'Human Rights in the Church: Non-Rights for Women in the Church', in *Human Rights: The Christian Contribution* (Paris: 1998) (accessed at www.ministryforwomen.org).

Vatinel, S., opening speech of the Ordination of Catholic Women conference, Australia, 2002 (accessed at www.ministryforwomen.org).

Vincent, M., 'Catholic Women Ordained Priests: Alternatives', *Les Réseaux des PARVIS*, 18 (2003) (accessed at www.ministryforwomen.org).

Zulehner, P., *'Ortsuche': Umfrage unter Pastoralreferentinnen und Pastoralreferenten im deutschsparchigen Raum* (Ostfildern: Schwabenverlag, 2006).

Notes

1 For a review of statements concerning women made by the Church Fathers and their medieval successors, see www.womenpriests.org

2 Quoted from another source by John Paul II in a letter 'To Women' (AAS 87, addressed to the fourth World Conference in Beijing, 1995) (this and most subsequent texts referenced have been accessed in electronic format – see Bibliography for details).

3 This group of 14 saints called upon as helpers includes St Catherine of Alexandria, St Barbara and St Margaret of Antioch.

4 O. Cullmann and O. Karrer, *Einheit in Christus: Evangelische und Katholische Bekenntnisse* (Zurich: Zwingli, 1960).

5 G. Heinzelmann, *Frau und Konzil – Hoffnung und Ewartung* (Zurich: Die Staatsbürgerin, 1962); G. Heinzelmann, 'We Won't Keep Silence any Longer: Women Speak out to Vatican II', *Commonweal* (5 October 1962), pp. 504–8 (accessed at www.ministryforwomen.org).

6 E. Schüssler-Fiorenza, *Der vergessene Partner* (Düsseldorf: Patmos, 1964), p. 96 (accessed at www.ministryforwomen.org); C. Halkes, '*Gott hat nicht nur starke Söhne':_Grundzüge einer feministischen Theologie (*Gütersloh: Güthersloher Verlagshaus, 1982) (accessed at www.ministryforwomen.org); K. Rahner, *Mission and Grace*, Vol. II (London: Sheed & Ward, 1964); M. Daly, 'A Built-in Bias', *Commonweal* (January 1965) (accessed at www.ministryforwomen.org).

7 U. Ranke-Heinemann, 'Female Blood: The Ancient Taboo and its Christian Consequences', in *Eunuchs for Heaven: The Catholic Church and Sexuality* (London: André Deutsch, 1990), pp. 12–17 (accessed at www.ministryforwomen.org). M. Grey: 'The Ordination of Women – Seeking a New Approach', lecture to the Annual General Assembly of Catholic Women's Ordination, London, 7 May 2002 (accessed at www.ministryforwomen.org).

8 A. Swidler, *Women in a Man's Church* (New York: Paulist Press, 1972) (accessed at www.ministryforwomen.org); H. Küng 'Women's Ordination and Infallibility', *The Tablet*, 19 December 1995; M.J. Arana and M. Salas, *Mujeres sacerdotas, porqué no?* (Madrid: Publicaciones Claretianes, 1994) (accessed at http://www.womenpriests.org/sp/aran_sal/ara_cont.asp).

9 For more, see ordinations: www.virtuelle-dioezese.de and www.romancatholicwomenpriests.org, and also (in print) W. Ertel and G. Forster (eds), *Wir sind Priesterinnen: Aus aktuellem Anlass: Die Weihe von Frauen 2002* (Düsseldorf: Patmos, 2002) (which had to be withdrawn at the order of Cardinal-Archbishop Friedrich Wetter of Munich) and V. Prüller-Jagenteufel: 'Kraft der Weihe', *Diakonia*, 33.5 (2002), pp. 369–72.

10 S. Vatinel, opening speech of the Ordination of Catholic Women Conference (OCW), Australia (2002) (accessed at www.ministryforwomen.org). Soline Vatinel is not a member of the *contra legem* group.

11 K. Rahner, *The Charismatic Element in the Church* (New York: Herder & Herder, 1964), pp. 42–83.

12 www.wir-sind-kirche.at, Zeitung Nr. 55/Oktober 2007, visit with Nuncio Mgr Edmond Farhat; www.luzerner-erklärung.ch: letter to nuncio Mgr Francesco Canalini, 2 November 2006.

13 Published by Libreria Editrice Vaticana.

14 P. Zulehner, '*Ortsuche': Umfrage unter Pastoralreferentinnen und Pastoralreferenten im deutschsparchigen Raum* (Ostfildern: Schwabenverlag, 2006).

15 S. Mazzolini, 'Modello ecclesiologico e ministero', *Annali di Studi Religiosi*, 7 (2006), pp. 281–303.

16 M.T. van Lunen Chenu, 'Human Rights in the Church: Non-Right for Women in the Church' in *Human Rights: The Christian Contribution* (1998) (available at: http://www.ministryforwomen.org); C. Booth, 'A Catholic Perspective on Human

Rights', the Tyburn Lecture, published in *The Tablet* (21 June 2003), pp. 4–7 (available at www.ministryforwomen.org).

17 Council of Europe, Doc. 10670 (September 2005), *Women and Religion in Europe*, paras 15–17.

18 S. Ahlers, *Gleichstellung der Frau in Staat und Kirche – ein problematisches Spannungsverhältnis* (Münster: LIT, 2006).

19 The WCC includes almost all Orthodox, Protestant, Anglican and Old Catholic Churches, along with many independent churches worldwide. The CEC covers the same constituency within Europe. The Council of European Bishops Conferences is specifically Roman Catholic.

20 Cardinal Walter Kasper, Oekumene im Wandel, Keynote, General Assembly of the Congregation for the Promotion of Christian Unity, 13 November 2006: 'Strittige Fragen über Grundlagen und Ziel der Oekumene', *Stimmen der Zeit*, 1 (January 2007), p. 9.

21 M. Kässmann, bishop of the Evanglische-Lutherische Landeskirche, Hannover, Otto-Karrer Lecture 2005: 'Was folgt auf das "Jahrhundert der Oekumene"', *Orientierung*, 4 (28 February 2006), pp. 44–6 (45).

22 *Gaudium et Spes* (4) lays down that the Church has a duty to scrutinize the signs of the times.

23 www.oecumene.radiovaticana.org/en1/Articolo.asp?c=91054 (accessed 1 October 2007: emphasis mine).

3

The Ordination of Women from an Orthodox Perspective

Katerina Karkala-Zorba

Equality in Jesus

'There is neither Jew nor Greek, there is neither bond nor free, there is neither male nor female' (Gal. 3.28)

Probably there is no other text used in so many ways in matters of equality as this passage of the letter of Saint Paul to the Galatians. And probably it is also the most misunderstood text. In fact, in our understanding, the full meaning of the text is to be found if one continues the reading: 'for all are one in Christ Jesus' (Gal. 3.28). It is in the person of Jesus that we all become united, that we all get the same rights, the same duties and are equal. But this equality is more than just an equal partition of rights; it is a fully recognized equality of the two parts in comparison: Jew and Greek, bond and free, male and female.

It is in the same sense that we might understand the description by Saint Paul of the different gifts or talents which are accorded to everyone, as we can read in his letter to the Romans:

> But having different gifts, according to the grace which has been given to us, whether it be prophecy, let us prophesy according to the proportion of faith; or service, let us occupy ourselves in service; or he that teaches, in teaching; or he that exhorts, in exhortation; he that gives, in simplicity; he that leads, with diligence; he that shows mercy, with cheerfulness. (Rom. 12.6-8).

No gift is inferior to another, precisely because they all are given by God.

The Orthodox Church identifies itself as the church where the living continuity is summed up in the notion of tradition. In that sense tradition means something 'more concrete' then just the passing over of the faith from our foremothers and forefathers to us.[1] In fact tradition is only valid if it is still a source of life for the descendants. It is the living tradition of the Church, 'the ever-new, personal and direct experience of the Holy Spirit in the present, here and now'.[2]

Men and women in the Church

In the Orthodox Church women are present in various forms: we find women on the icon wall, as on the walls of the church. We also find examples of many Holy Mothers and women from the Early Church and the Church of the first millennium, all the martyrs and great martyrs like Saint Catherine, Saint Marina, simple nuns in the monasteries, abbesses, but also other women who are leading the way ahead in front of us. All those women are not mere fictions, but they come to life in the midst of the liturgical event, as also in the life of every one, either as name-patronesses and name-patrons or as saints, as we celebrate them every day in the feast calendar of the Orthodox Church. There are many other feasts in the year which remind us of the contribution of women in the plan of the salvation of God, like the feast of the myrrh-bearers (second Sunday after Easter) or the feast of the Samaritan woman (fourth Sunday after Easter). Among all the holy women and men, Mary, the Mother of God, has a very special place: she is the *Panaghia*, the All-holy. She is the prototype for the spiritual perfection of the human being,[3] the new Eve, who restores in herself the whole creation. She is the deaconess of salvation,[4] who wants to bring us nearer to Jesus.

Women take an important role in the life of the Church. They are usually the ones who connect the family to the ecclesiastical life and also keep it alive. They have in their hands the preparation for the sacraments (baptism, marriage, burial, eucharist, etc.) especially concerning the traditional rituals. On very special prayer days, one will see almost only women in the church, for example, during the *Chairetismoi* (greetings) to Mary, sung on Friday, during the Great Lent, together with the *Akathistos Hymnos* to Mary. It is the same for the prayers of intercession sung during the 15-day period before the Dormition of Mary.[5]

Still today in the Orthodox Church, women are the ones who dare to make the link to the Church and to bring their families closer to God in that way. For many people, women were the initiators of their spiritual life – their mothers, grandmothers, godmothers, elder sisters, etc. Women are also necessary for the future, as the initiators of faith in family life, in school and in general in secular society. But in order to guarantee this, it is more than urgent to facilitate the active participation of younger women in the life of the Church.

Leading positions and hierarchy in the Church

Today we tend to misunderstand and misinterpret the functions and roles of the hierarchy in the Church: even the Archbishop or Patriarch in the eucharistic synaxis is '*primus inter pares*' (the first among equals). The priest cannot fulfil his work, or celebrate the liturgy if the people of God are absent, since the liturgy in its very meaning is the work (*ergon*) of the people (*laos*), of men and women. Today in Greece men and women are studying theology and sometimes there are even more female students than male. But it is important to know that for the Orthodox Church theological studies are not equal to the preparation to priesthood. This is also the case for men who are studying theology. For both male and female lay theologians, the normal professional occupation would be to become a teacher in religious education. In some cases it would be possible to have a job in the offices of the diocese.

The fact that more and more women are studying theology demonstrates a new challenge for the Orthodox Church, namely to give those women the opportunity to exercise their profession in the framework of the local Church. And if it cannot be through ordination, then other forms of involvement have to be created.

The challenges of modern society are faced in various ways in the Orthodox Church. The Synod of the Church of Greece is working in different committees, in order to face the needs of the Orthodox Christians in Greece, who form about 97 per cent of the population. Those committees deal with themes such as pastoral work, Christian education and youth, marriage, family and demographic issues, ecology, European affairs, bioethics and women's issues.[6]

The ministry of deaconesses and the question of women's ordination

The Orthodox Church recognizes the ordination of women deacons. It is a ministry very well known not only in the Early Church but also in the Byzantine period. In 1954 Professor Evangelos Theodorou wrote his thesis on 'The "Ordination" or "Laying on the Hands" of the Women Deacons',[7] stating that 'the ordination of deaconesses was the unique type of ordination of women in the Church'.[8] Theodorou is clear about the fact that the deaconesses were ordained by the same ordination (*cheirotonia*) as deacons and other orders of the higher clergy, such as deacons, presbyters and bishops, because their ordination took place 'within the altar area and before the altar table, during the Divine Liturgy',[9] while the 'laying-on the hands' (*cheirothesia*) was practised for the so-called lower clergy, such as cantors, readers and subdeacons. The tasks of the deaconesses were works of Christian love: providing hospitality for women, visiting sick, afflicted and needy women, always in conjunction with the bishop. They also practised missionary, catechetical and teaching ministry among women. They were the connecting link between the clergy and lay women and they were responsible for the spiritual guidance of women. Many deaconesses exercised their duties in monasteries. During the liturgical service the deaconesses were responsible for the women attending the services and led their participation in singing. Theodorou states further that the deaconesses, 'doubtless ... entered the altar area' and 'stood next to the male deacons'.[10] They further had the duty of bringing the Holy Eucharist to sick women at home and preparing women and children for baptism.

In the twentieth century there have been different attempts to revive the ministry of deaconesses in the Orthodox Church. In Russia this has been the case from the beginning of the century, with Bishop Stefan of Mogilev, Mother Ekaterina of Lesna, Archpriest Aleksii Maltsev and Bishop Evlogy. The ministry of Mother Maria Skobtsova, newly recognized as a saint, for sick and needy people, shows that she had the same tasks as the deaconesses of the Early Church.[11]

Bishop Nektarios of Aegina, today recognized as a new saint, ordained a nun to the ministry of deaconess in the year 1911. There are witnesses that there have been more nuns in monasteries in Greece ordained as deaconesses.[12]

All this shows that the restoration of deaconesses is not a new question for the Orthodox Church. In our day, besides E. Theodorou, there have been other attempts to raise the question. We will refer to the Interorthodox Consultation of Rhodes in 1988, which tried to adapt the ministry to the cultural and social situation of today.[13]

The Greek American Orthodox theologian and psychologist Kyriaki Karidoyanes FitzGerald has published her work on women deacons in the Orthodox Church,[14] referring to the 'Identity of the Deaconess', the 'Witness of Women Deacon Saints', the 'Charism of Women Deacons' (according to the rite of the Apostolic Constitutions and to the Byzantine ordination), 'the Issue of Ordination' and the 'Decline'. She concludes with a chapter 'Towards the Restoration of the Order of Women Deacons' and a commentary on 'Women Deacons: Ecclesial Memory of Spiritual Opportunity?' For FitzGerald, it is a calling of the Lord that 'enables the Church, through the presence of the Holy Spirit, to respond to the pastoral needs at hand'.[15]

In the year 2004 the Synod of the Church of Greece discussed the issue of 'The Role of Women in the Institution of the Church and the Revival of the Ministry of Deaconesses'. Metropolitan Chrysostomos of Chalkida, Chairman of the Special Commission of the Synod on Women Issues, introduced the theme in front of the Synod and concluded that 'a first step for the revival of the ministry of deaconesses could be the ordination of selected nuns'.[16] The question whether 'only unmarried women and widows would be allowed to the ministry of deaconesses',[17] remains open. This would lead to inequality, since married male deacons can be ordained in the Orthodox Church.

The ongoing question of the ordination of women also still remains open. As we have seen, the ordination of deaconesses is known as a *cheirotonia*, i.e. an ordination, as for other ordinations. But according to the tradition of the Orthodox Church there is no case known where a deaconess has been ordained to the ministry of priest or bishop.[18]

We may state here that the Orthodox Church knows no limits in its expression of the true faith and witness. This is true also for the question of the ordination of women.[19]

Elisabeth Behr-Sigel, an Orthodox theologian from France, has worked intensively on the subject of the role of women in the Church. In different publications, she has treated the subject of 'The Ministry of Women in the Church'[20] and 'The Ordination of Women in the Orthodox Church'.[21] Until the end of her lifetime (she died in 2005 at the age of 98 years) Behr-

Sigel identified the ordination of women as an important issue in ecumenical dialogue.[22] For her, the question of the ordination of women is not brought from outside to the Orthodox Church but has now become an internal issue. She never contented herself by simply saying that 'the Orthodox Church does not know the ordination of women into the ministry of priesthood', but has always faced the challenges of our time.

Inter-Orthodox consultations on the issue

Different meetings have taken place in the last 40 years on a local, European and international level. Often those meetings are as an answer to the challenges of the ecumenical movement to the Orthodox Church. So we see that several of those meetings have been organized in cooperation with the World Council of Churches.

The first Consultation of Orthodox Women took place in 1976 in Agapia, Romania, on the theme 'The Role of Orthodox Women in Church and Society'.[23] At this inter-Orthodox meeting the need for active roles for women in the parish, as well as the need for theological education, was underlined. The importance of family life, like the affirmation of female monastic life, the support for the special gifts of women in social justice and pastoral care, the need for theological training and the reinstitution of the diaconate were among the primary subjects of this consultation. Other issues were the opening of minor orders such as subdeacons to women and the facilitation of proper liturgical translations.

Another pan-Orthodox consultation took place in 1988 in Rhodes and had as its theme the 'Role of Women in the Orthodox Church and the Question of the Ordination of Women'.[24] It was significant because it stressed the point on the theological discussion of gender and ordination. The gender typology and complementarity Eve/Mary and Adam/Christ, the apostolic succession, the incarnation and priesthood of Christ and the male as priestly icon of Christ were some major aspects of the discussion in Rhodes. Though it concluded that women cannot be ordained priests, it called for a fuller participation of men and women in the unity and service of the Church. It proposed the reinstitution of the female diaconate and the minor orders, such as reader or teacher.

It is in this direction that the final text of the conclusions of the consultation went. The text underlines the need for a fuller participation of women in the life of the Church, following their special gifts, underlining the 'importance of the actual work which women are undertaking at the parish level today, but often without sufficient support and encouragement from the leadership of the Church'.[25] Those tasks are stated in the same text: among others, education at all levels, pastoral counselling, church administration and participation in decision-making bodies at all levels, social work, arts (iconography, music), youth work, representation in the ecumenical movement and publications and communication.

Another important step was taken in 1990 in Crete, under the theme 'Church and Culture'. The keynote speakers at this conference addressed human sexuality, ministry and participation/decision-making in the Church. Several thought-provoking discussions ensued, involving topics such as sexism, female 'uncleanness' and sacraments, prayer and language, family planning, the utilization (or lack thereof) of educated and competent women within the Church, lay ministries including the diaconate, ecumenism, and most importantly, renewal of our spirits and minds as we look ahead to the future.

Other meetings took place in Kerala, India, in 1990; in Geneva in 1992 ('Feminine Images and Orthodox Spirituality'); and in 1994 ('Women in Dialogue – Wholeness of Vision' and 'Feminist and Orthodox Spiritualities'). In 1994 a meeting was also convened in Livadia (Greece) on the theme 'Orthodox Women in a United Europe'. More than 200 delegates discussed the different ways in which Orthodoxy can contribute to Europe in matters of 'ethos', but also in helping women to embody new roles in the modernized world. Global issues were discussed, but not the question of the priesthood of women. The recommendation of Rhodes for the restoration of the female diaconate was not taken into consideration.

In 1996 two other meetings took place: in France (Vendée) 'Men and Women in the Church'; and in Syria (Homeira) the first Antiochian women's convention.

The most important meetings, however, were in 1996 in Damascus and 1997 in Istanbul under the general title 'Discerning the signs of times?'[26] with the aid of the World Council of Churches, who included both consultations in the framework of the Decade of Churches in Solidarity with Women.[27] The conference in Damascus discussed, among others, themes of equality of men and women in Christ, theological education, communication, spirituality and parish life. The consultation in Istanbul was supported by the Ecumenical Patriarch Bartholomew I, and very interesting discussions took place on themes such as the diaconate, the liturgical life, theological education, spirituality and prayer. The conference urged women to take action and to sustain our communities at the parish level. The participants of this meeting also met with the Armenian Patriarch Karekin II, and were encouraged by the decision of the Armenian Apostolic Church to ordain women to diaconal ministry.

Towards the active participation of women today

Today women do play an important role in the Orthodox Church. They are the most active members among the lay people of the Church. They are often the initiators and bearers of faith in our secularized globalized society. Probably in the near future we will all have to focus not on the issue of 'male or female priesthood' but on the need to find people to become pastors in an ever-changing world. And there we have to follow the example of Jesus, who did not distinguish between men and women; who did dare to discuss theological issues with the Samaritan woman; who visited the house of Mary and Martha; who showed himself as the resurrected Lord first to women. And it is for men and women that the Son of God came to the earth.

Today the issue of the ordination of women tends to divide and torment different sides in the ecumenical movement and local and national churches. Would it not be more fruitful instead of finding arguments pro or contra the ordination of women to argue for more active participation of all lay people, men and women, in the Church today? If for secular and political movements the role of women has changed significantly in the past century, it seems that the Church, though teaching a liberating equality among all believers, does not practise its teaching.

If we therefore continue to argue for the ordination of women today in the Orthodox Church, as deaconesses or for other ministries as well, it could finally break the chain of a church always trailing behind political and cultural developments. A true feminist theology has to go beyond the demands and achievements of the feminist movement of today. It has to bring into being the words of the Apostle: 'There is neither male nor female, for all are one in Christ Jesus' (Gal. 3.28). This goes in the same direction as our Lord prayed for us: 'that [we] all may be one' (Jn 17.21). As Father Alexander Schmemann wrote:

[The] priesthood is Christ's, not ours. Not only have none of us, men or women, any 'right' to it, but it is emphatically not one of the human vocations analogous, even if superior, to all others. The priest in the Church is not 'another' priest, and the sacrifice he offers is not 'another' sacrifice. It is forever and only Christ's priesthood and Christ's sacrifice, for in the words of our Prayer of Offertory, 'it is Thou who offerest and Thou who art offered, it is Thou who receivest and Thou who distributest ...' And thus the 'institutional' priesthood in the Church has no 'ontology' of its own. It exists only to make Christ Himself present, to make His unique Priesthood and His unique Sacrifice the source of the Church's life and the 'acquisition' by men of the Holy Spirit. And if the bearer, the icon, and the fulfiller of that unique priesthood is man and not woman, it is because Christ is man and not woman ...[28]

The Early Church understood very well how to interpret the symbolic character of Jesus's actions in the world. Today we need to look again at those symbolic acts and interpret them for the revival of the Christian faith today. If Orthodox women, together with men, long for a more active participation in the Church, it is because of their wish to serve the Church in our society today. And women are still playing an important role in nourishing their families, their partners and friends with the light of faith. It is a very important question that the Orthodox Church has to answer today, for how long still women will 'keep on lighting the oil-lamps in their homes'.[29]

Bibliography

Arjakovsky-Klépinine, H., *Mère Marie Skobtsov – Le sacrement du frère* (Paris: Le sel de terre, 2001).
Behr-Sigel, E. and Ware, K., *The Ordination of Women in the Orthodox Church*, Risk Book Series No. 92 (Geneva: WCC Publications, 2000).

Behr-Sigel, E. 'L'Ordination des femmes: Un point chaud du dialogue oecuménique', *Contacts*, 195 (2001), p. 236.
——, 'The Life of Maria Sktobtsova – An Orthodox Nun', *MaryMartha*, 4.2 (1996), p. 18.
——, *The Ministry of Women in the Church* (Redondo Beach, CA: Oakwood, 1991). (French original: *Le Ministère de la femme dans l'église* [Paris: Cerf, 1987]).
Breaban, C., Deicha, S. and Kasselouri-Hatzivassiliadi, E. (eds), *Women's Voices and Visions of the Church, Reflections of Orthodox Women* (Geneva: WCC Publications).
Chrysostomos, Metropolitan 'The Role of Women in the Whole Institution of the Church, Revival of the Institution of the Deaconesses', in: www.ecclesia.gr.
FitzGerald, K.K. (ed.), *Orthodox Women Speak: Discerning the Signs of the Times* (Brookline, MA: Holy Cross Orthodox Press, 1999).
——, *Women Deacons in the Orthodox Church, Called to Holiness and Ministry* (Brookline, MA: Holy Cross Orthodox Press, 1999).
Gioultsi, E., Ἡ Παναγία, Πρότυπο Πνευματικῆς Τελειώσεως [*The Panaghia, Ideal of spiritual fulfilment*] (Thessaloniki: P. Pournara, 2001).
Hackel, S., 'Mother Maria Skobtsova: Deaconess Manquée?' *Eastern Churches Review*, 1.13 (1967), pp. 264–6.
——, *Pearl of Great Price: The Life of Mother Maria Skobtsova 1891–1945* (London: Darton, Longman & Todd, 1981).
Hopko, Thomas, *Women and the Priesthood* (New York: St Vladimir's Orthodox Press, 1999).
Karkala-Zorba, K., 'As Long as Women Keep on Lighting Oil-Lamps in their Homes...', in C. Breaban, S. Deicha and E. Kasselouri-Hatzivassiliadi (eds), *Women's Voices and Visions of the Church, Reflections of Orthodox Women* (Geneva: WCC Publications).
——, 'The Role of Women in the Orthodox Church Today', *MaryMartha*, 5.1 (summer 1996–97), pp. 3–8.
Limouris, G. (ed.), *Ecumenical Patriarchate: The Place of the Woman in the Orthodox Church and the Question of the Ordination of Women, Inter-Orthodox Symposium, Rhodos, Greece, 30 October – 7 November 1988* (Katerini: Tertios, 1992).
Mariia Mat', *Mother Maria Skobtsova, Essential Writings*, trans. Richard Pevear and Larissa Volokhonsky (Maryknoll, NY: Orbis, 2003).
Schmemann, Protopresbyter A., 'Concerning Women's Ordination: A Letter to an Episcopal Friend', in *St Vladimir's Theological Quarterly*, 17.3 (1973), pp. 239–43.
Tarasar, Constance J. and Irina Kirillova (eds), *Orthodox Women: Their Role and Participation in the Orthodox Church, Report on the Consultation of Orthodox Women, Agapia, Romania* (Geneva: WCC Publications, 1977).
Theodorou, E., Ἡ 'Χειροτονία' Ἡ 'Χειροθεσία' τῶν Διακονισσῶν, [*The 'Ordination' or 'Laying-on of Hands' of the deaconesses*], PhD thesis, Athens, 1954.
——, 'The Institution of Deaconesses in the Orthodox Church and the Possibility of its Restoration', in G. Limouris, *Ecumenical Patriarchate: The Place of the Woman in the Orthodox Church and the Question of the Ordination of Women* (Katerini: Tertios, 1992), pp. 207–38.
——, Ἡρωΐδες τῆς Χριστιανικῆς Ἀγάπης, [*Heroines of Christian Love*] (Athens: Apostoliki Diakonia, 1949).
——, 'Οἱ διακόνισσες στήν ἱστορία τῆς Ἐκκλησίας' [Deaconesses in the History of the Church], in G. Limouris (ed.), *Ecumenical Patriarchate, The Place of the Woman in the Orthodox Church and the Question of the Ordination of Women* (Katerini: Tertios, 1992), pp. 185–208.
Ware, T. (Bishop Kallistos of Diokleia), *The Orthodox Church* (London: Penguin, 1997).
——, *The Orthodox Way* (New York: St Vladimir's Seminary Press, 1995).

Notes

1 Cf. Timothy Ware (Bishop Kallistos of Diokleia), *The Orthodox Church* (London: Penguin, 1997), pp. 195ff: 'Holy Tradition, the Source of the Orthodox Faith'.
2 Bishop Kallistos Ware, *The Orthodox Way* (New York: St Vladimir's Seminary Press, 1995), p. 8.
3 Eftichia Gioultsi, 'Η Παναγία, Πρότυπο Πνευματικῆς Τελειώσεως [*The Panaghia, Ideal of spiritual fulfilment*], (Thessaloniki: P. Pournara, 2001), p. 202.
4 Katerina Karkala-Zorba, 'The Role of Women in the Orthodox Church Today', *MaryMartha*, 5.1 (summer 1996–97), pp. 3–8.
5 The Feast of the Dormition of Mary is celebrated on 15 August each year. The feast commemorates the repose (dormition, Greek '*koimisis*') or 'falling-asleep' of the Mother of Jesus Christ. It also commemorates the translation or assumption into heaven of the body of the *Theotokos* (God-bearer).
6 For the committees of the Holy Synod of the Church of Greece, see www.ecclesia.gr.
7 Evangelos Theodorou, 'Η 'Χειροτονία' 'Η 'Χειροθεσία' τῶν Διακονισσῶν, [*The 'Ordination' or 'Laying-on of Hands' of the deaconesses*], PhD thesis, Athens, 1954; E. Theodorou, Ἡρωΐδες τῆς Χριστιανικῆς 'Αγάπης, [*Heroines of Christian Love*] (Athens: Apostoliki Diakonia, 1949).
8 E. Theodorou, 'The Institution of Deaconesses in the Orthodox Church and the Possibility of its Restoration', in G. Limouris (ed.), *Ecumenical Patriarchate, The Place of the Woman in the Orthodox Church and the Question of the Ordination of Women* (Katerini: Tertios, 1992), pp. 207–38, p. 225.
9 Theodorou, 'The Institution of Deaconesses', p. 213.
10 Theodorou, 'The Institution of Deaconesses', p. 223.
11 Hélène Arjakovsky-Klépinine, *Mère Marie Skobtsov – Le sacrement du frère* (Paris: Le sel de terre, 2001); Elisabeth Behr-Sigel: 'The Life of Maria Sktobtsova – An Orthodox Nun' in *MaryMartha*, 4.2 (1996), p. 18; Sergei Hackl, *Pearl of Great Price: The Life of Mother Maria Sktobtsova 1891–1945* (London: Darton, Longman & Todd, 1981); Sergei Hackl, 'Mother Maria Skobtsova: Deaconess Manquée?' *Eastern Churches Review*, 1.13 (1967); Mariia Mat', *Mother Maria Skobtsova, Essential Writings*, trans. Richard Pevear and Larissa Volokhonsky (Maryknoll, NY: Orbis, 2003).
12 Theodorou, *The 'Ordination'*, p. 95.
13 Cf. Conclusions of the Consultation Report, VIII: 'The Diaconate and "Minor Orders"', in Limouris (ed.), *Ecumenical Patriarchate*, p. 31.
14 Kyriaki Karidoyanes FitzGerald, *Women Deacons in the Orthodox Church, Called to Holiness and Ministry*, (Brookline, MA: Holy Cross Orthodox Press, 1999).
15 FitzGerald, *Women Deacons*, p. 198.
16 Metropolitan Chrysostomos, 'The Role of Women in the Whole Institution of the Church, Revival of the Institution of the Deaconesses', paper presented before the Holy Synod of the Church of Greece on 8 October 2004 (see www.ecclesia.gr).
17 Chrysostomos, 'The Role of Women in the Whole Institution of the Church', Ch. 3.
18 Evangelos Theodorou, 'Οἱ διακόνισσες στήν ἱστορία τῆς 'Εκκλησίας', [Deaconesses in the History of the Church], in Metropolis von Dimitrias, Φύλο καί Θρησκεία 'Η θέση τῆς Γυναίκας στήν 'Εκκλησία, [Gender and Religion, The Position of the Woman in the Church] (Athens: Indiktos, 2004), pp. 185–208.
19 Thomas Hopko, *Women and the Priesthood* (New York: St Vladimir's Orthodox Press, 1999).
20 Elisabeth Behr-Sigel, *The Ministry of Women in the Church* (Redondo Beach, CA: Oakwood Publications, 1991).
21 Elisabeth Behr-Sigel and Kallistos Ware, *The Ordination of Women in the Orthodox Church*, Risk Book Series No. 92 (Geneva: WCC Publications, 2000).
22 Elisabeth Behr-Sigel, 'L'Ordination des femmes: Un point chaud du dialogue oecumé-

nique', in: *Contacts*, 195 (2001), p. 236.

23 Constance J. Tarasar and Irina Kirillova (eds), *Orthodox Women: Their Role and Participation in the Orthodox Church, Report on the Consultation of Orthodox Women, Agapia, Romania* (Geneva: WCC, 1977).

24 G. Limouris (ed.), *Ecumenical Patriarchate, The Place of the Woman in the Orthodox Church and the Question of the Ordination of Woman*, Interorthodox Symposium, Rhodos, Greece, 30 October to 7 November 1998 (Katerin: Tertios Publications, 1992).

25 Limouris (ed.), *Ecumenical Patriarchate*, p. 30.

26 Kyriaki K. FitzGerald (ed.), *Orthodox Women Speak: Discerning the Signs of the Times* (Brookline, MA: Holy Cross Orthodox Press, 1999).

27 The decade was convened in 1988 and ended in 1998 with the General Assembly of the World Council of Churches in Harare. (See also www.wcc-coe.org).

28 Protopresbyter Alexander Schmemann, 'Concerning Women's Ordination, a Letter to an Episcopal Friend', in *St Vladimir's Theological Quarterly*, 17.3 (1973), pp. 239–43, p. 243.

29 Katerina Karkala-Zorba, 'As Long as Women Keep on Lighting Oil-Lamps in their Homes ...', in C. Breaban, Sophie Deicha, E. Kasselouri-Hatzivassiliadi (eds), *Women's Voices and Visions of the Church, Reflections of Orthodox Women* (Geneva: WCC Publications), pp. 115–24, p. 115.

4

Should Theological Education be Different for Clergywomen? Doing 'Women's Work' in a Mainline Protestant Seminary

Ellen Blue

Introduction

In this essay, I argue that because the lived professional experience of male and female pastors differs, there is a need for specialized theological education for women and substantial benefit in including coursework specifically for them. Admittedly, danger exists when we legitimize different treatment based on gender; it is precisely such differentiation that has prevented equal access to the pulpit. Nevertheless, both the content and pedagogy of traditional theological education leave women unprepared to deal with resistance to their presence in ministry.

I will discuss a cross-disciplinary class, 'Issues for Women in Christian Ministry', which I taught in autumn 2003 and again in 2005 as a faculty member at Phillips Theological Seminary in Tulsa, Oklahoma. Phillips is affiliated with the Christian Church (Disciples of Christ), a relatively progressive denomination in the USA. We have students from many denominations, with more United Methodists than any other kind. I also bring to this topic over a dozen years of experience as an ordained United Methodist and the knowledge born of having been a seminary student who graduated and went out to live as both a pastor and a woman.

Although men were not barred from my theological classes, only women enrolled. Anecdotal evidence indicates most 'women's courses' in US seminaries attract at least one man, as did my own women's history class. Therefore, I will not only explore how a specialized curriculum helped prepare women pastors, but also briefly consider the related, but not identical, topic of how our unusual, all-female, 'separate space' contributed to that goal.

Discussion

The course was designed as practical theology to help meet real-life challenges in the pastorate. One objective was to identify special gifts women might bring to specific tasks such as preaching, designing liturgy, reflecting theologically, counselling, administering church business, exercising leadership and maintaining healthy relationships while serving a church. The major focus was making students more confident that they could identify and cope with the gender-related problems women face in performing these tasks.

An overarching goal was helping students form their identities as women ministers.[1] A dozen ordained guest speakers visited the class each semester, and letting students hear the stories of women who had successfully created such self-identities contributed to that goal. Each ordained female faculty member served as a guest for a session about her area of expertise, and I recruited active pastors, making sure all the students' denominations were represented. All guests had served in the local church, some for over 25 years.

Each began by recounting some of her journey in ministry. While many kinds of learning are enhanced by the inclusion of relevant stories, Elizabeth Tisdell[2] maintains that feminist pedagogy in particular is 'about stories, both personal narratives and public stories, and their use in education'. Stories 'give context, provide examples, touch our hearts, and put a human face on the rational world of ideas'. Another scholar asserts 'the content of women's studies, not just the pedagogy, is particularly influential; indeed, in feminist pedagogies, it is hard to separate content from process'.[3] Surely, when the content concerns identities that female ministers construct for themselves and the ways in which they construct them, this is especially true.

After the guest made her presentation, the students asked her questions. In *Women's Ways of Knowing*, Belenky et al.[4] observe that 'connected knowers' are able to 'develop procedures for gaining access to other people's knowledge'. Although students could not participate in syllabus construction (a hallmark of feminist pedagogy), because speakers' schedules required booking them months earlier, students shaped each class by choosing what to ask. At the penultimate gathering, a panel of clergywomen addressed students' questions, some of which we had been considering all semester. By quizzing each guest about certain topics (pastoral authority and family issues), the students helped determine themes for the course.

In 2003 the class drew 12 students, and in 2005, 14.[5] Early sessions were devoted to introducing ourselves and to my introducing the students to feminist ideas about interpreting scripture and doing theology. Throughout the semester we occasionally spent time developing a 'hermeneutic of suspicion' toward problematic scriptural passages, like the story of Lot's daughters, blamed in the text for their father's drunken, incestuous abuse of them after their mother dies.

My pedagogical method included using documents from my own pastorates. A lecture on feminist theology I had delivered to a gathering of laypeople could have been reworked into a class lecture. Instead, I left it as it was, explained the circumstances in which it was delivered, and let the class gain not only the information it contained but also observe how I had packaged a controversial topic for lay people. For a session on liturgy, I led a ritual I had used with several women's gatherings. The final class was a worship session based on the Lucan story of the bent woman (13.10-17), using a sermon I had preached in two congregations.

Before the 2003 class, one student had taken one course in feminist theology; otherwise, students had no training in feminist critique or women's studies. The 2005 class was similarly unfamiliar with feminism. In 2003 one woman was deeply suspicious of feminism, though I did not know this until she expressed a change of heart after hearing me lecture on the existence of women who are both Christian and feminist, and after reading Sarah Lancaster's *Women and the Authority of Scripture*.[6]

Our preaching text was Carol Norén's *The Woman in the Pulpit*.[7] Regarding worship, we used Marjorie Procter-Smith's *In Her Own Rite*.[8] For counselling, we read a *Journal of Feminist Studies in Religion* article I wrote about working with parishioners who had suffered intra-family abuse and clergy sexual misconduct.[9] The class on 'Sexual Harassment/Misconduct' drew on Peter Rutter's excellent volume, *Sex in the Forbidden Zone*,[10] and Marie Fortune's film, *Not in My Church*,[11] about a sexual predator who uses his pastorate to take advantage of women, destroying their careers and self-esteem.

Along with contributing her specialized knowledge, each guest discussed what to wear in the pulpit. Simple for men, who wear suit and tie for informal services, or robe and stole for formal ones, the issue is far more complex and 'loaded' for women. Even if a woman wears a robe, without good advice, she may order one which will never fit correctly because it is cut for a man. Stoles may be too long and too wide at the shoulders. Unless specially ordered, clerical robes come with pocket slits, not pockets. Since most women's clothes have no pockets, a slit grants access to nothing helpful. Where to stash tissues or breath mints may seem trivial, but it is crisis-inducing to discover immediately before a pastor performs her first baptism that she has no place to put the battery unit for a lapel microphone. Although they affect competency in leading worship, most female students never hear these issues addressed and may make a sizable investment in a problematic robe. Each guest brought her robe and stoles, and over the semester, the students saw what no stores stock – a wide variety of vestments designed for women's bodies.

We used Catherine Wessinger's anthology of essays on women's leadership in various mainstream denominations as a history text, since the past progress within a particular group inevitably impacts on women ordained there today. As it happens, 2006 marked the 50th anniversary of full clergy rights for Methodist women in the USA. Our founder, John Wesley, licensed women to preach, but their licences were revoked not long after his death in 1791 and access to pulpits was intermittent in Methodism. The process is historically complicated, but women did not have full connexion – ordination that equals the status of ordained males – in the Methodist Church in North America until 1956.

At a 2006 celebration, a male bishop in North Carolina told the assembly, 'We have passed the time for any [congregation] ... to object to a pastoral appointment because the appointee is female. Fifty years is long enough. Be ready. It's that simple' (Hand 2006, p. 7). Alert readers will recognize that he made these remarks precisely because all churches are *not* ready – they have *not* found 50 years long enough to reconcile themselves to the idea.

The United Methodist Church (UMC) provides a good example of how mainstream American Protestantism has handled women's ordination. We are not the most progressive, but neither are we among the slowest. Our stated, albeit unrealized, goal is 'open itinerancy', where any pastor, regardless of race or gender, could be appointed to any congregation. Because the UMC is connexional, clergy are not hired by congregations free to select whom they will – and avoid whom they won't – as pastor. Full ordination makes ministers itinerant; we are guaranteed a church, but agree to serve wherever we are sent by the bishop. Career paths are determined by a hierarchy which is still overwhelmingly male, though we have made inroads. Fifteen of the 50 active US bishops are female.[12] Most bishops have appointed a woman to their cabinets, giving several dozen other women input into decision-making. Much of the fiercest resistance to women occurs at the congregational level.

Data for 2005[13] reveal that of 29,563 local church appointments in US UMC churches, 26 per cent are filled by women. These 6,850 women are concentrated below the stained-glass ceiling, as associate pastors or as senior pastors of small churches. While 25 per cent of senior pastors of the smallest churches (less than 200 members) are women, only 5 per cent of senior pastors of churches with more than 1,000 members are female. Along with the reality that women in small churches make less money and enjoy fewer benefits, analyst Craig This[14] listed other effects. Almost half the delegates to major conferences where policy is set come from churches with more than 1,000 members; 10 per cent come from the smallest churches where most women serve. It is these delegates who are assigned to serve on national boards and commissions. He notes that appointment as District Superintendent and election as bishop are related to large-church service. '[T]o have access to these avenues of vocational advancement and influence in the decision-making life of the church, it follows that ordained women must be better represented as senior pastors', he said, arguing that the UMC must 'groom' women for large congregations. It seems obvious that grooming women for large congregations involves making them successful in smaller ones.

Awareness of the imperative for success should not make us ignore the coin's other face – the impact of failure on individual clergywomen's lives. Every student I teach hears me state that the primary task of a pastor is to stay sane in the pastorate. The class laughs, but I am serious. Local congregations have the means, opportunity, and sadly sometimes the motive, to destroy their pastor's mental, spiritual and emotional health. Staying sane and spiritually healthy is a prerequisite to any kind of ministry, and it is, in and of itself, a major act of ministry to the congregation.

For clergywomen, sanity and spiritual health must be pursued more intentionally, since being made to feel unwelcome at least part of the time seems inevitable. For example, in Katherine Paisley's first congregation, in rural Tennessee, 'My very existence was confrontational to their understandings of life and the Church. I didn't actually have to do anything to be confrontational, just showing up on Sunday morning to preach did it.'[15] I am acquainted with a woman whose church was deliberately burned down a few days after she first served eucharist, and a woman in her sixties who received a barely veiled rape threat after a student pastors' meeting at her seminary where she prayed aloud.

Miriam Therese Winter *et al.* compiled comments from hundreds of women about their extreme discomfort in churches; some had left, but others remained, even while seeking spiritual nourishment elsewhere – hence, their title, *Defecting in Place*.[16] (This was also a text for our class.) Footnotes reveal many of the women were clergy. Mark Chaves wrote in 1997 that only about half of the denominations in the USA had granted full clergy rights to women, and that 'conflicts over women's ordination have become more harsh and contentious over time'.[17] His research into the policies of 103 denominations made him conclude that the decision to ordain women is more a function of a denomination's desire to make a statement about liberalism in a larger sense than of its recognition that individual women deserve equal opportunity. Hence, he says, formal recognition of the right of women to minister may be only 'loosely connected to on-the-ground congregational practice'.[18]

My own metaphor for ministry is 'midwifing'. We midwife the birth of souls, and the primary soul birth each of us has to attend to is our own. When people use the phrase, 'being born again', to refer to something that occurs instantaneously, I point out that being born is a very long process. Labour is painful, messy and hazardous to both mother and child. No wonder clergy burn-out is common.

It is good news that women's enrolment hovers around 50 per cent at mainline seminaries. Yet women continue to leave the local pastorate in much greater numbers than men, which explains why percentages of women pastors do not increase as rapidly as seminary statistics predict.[19] Furthermore, most men who leave the pastorate leave the ministry, while most women retain ordination and adopt another form of ministry, like chaplaincy or teaching. Such women have not misinterpreted their calls or become newly disenchanted with Christianity – they have found the local church too hostile a place in which to thrive spiritually or professionally. Zikmund *et al.* say women leave 'because they have terrible experiences in the parish as women';[20] their title, *Clergy Women: An Uphill Calling*, conveys how difficult pastoring often feels to females.

Knowing ahead of time about likely difficulties, and having access to information about how other women have addressed them and assurance that other women have survived them, cannot but help to enhance new clergywomen's abilities to cope with the shadow side of parish ministry. My students recognized this. A 2005 student wrote, 'I have a deeper awareness about inappropriate behavior from male colleagues and church officials … [It] has sent warning bells off in my mind when I see patterns of behavior that previously I would not have seen as dangerous. I feel better equipped to protect myself'.[21] A Colombian student said it allowed her 'to encounter God beyond gender and to become aware of the maleness of the world, my vocabulary, my environment and in my internalized understanding of God as a man' and 'provided me with the strength to face strategically the world ahead of me'.[22] A graduating senior concluded, 'This was the single most important class I took at PTS.'

Other comments on anonymous evaluations included: 'It will contribute to my personal and professional growth for years to come'; 'I learned much in respect to what I am going through as female clergy'; 'The conversations with women in ministry were life-giving'; and 'I felt safe in ... asking women's questions.' Several insisted it should be required for all female students.

Indisputably, my class was a positive educational experience for all who took it, no matter what their denominational affiliation. It occasioned what one of my female colleagues called a 'tsunami' at Phillips. Even male faculty commented often about good things they heard, including a remark that it was 'raising the bar' for the whole seminary. Nevertheless, on more than one occasion, I found myself forced to justify the existence of the course. Interestingly, feminist theology had been offered recently and both feminist and womanist theology offered since, with no objections. In liberal seminaries, the idea that female scholars draw upon their particular social locations and find they have some different things to say about God has become acceptable.

Yet my class – which called into question the idea that the actual doing of ministry is the same for women – raised challenges. Some were minor: in the student common-room, a woman asked, 'Is this going to be a lot of male-bashing?' I responded that I do not do much male-bashing; in fact, I rather like men. It occurred to me only later to wonder whether she thought male-bashing would have been a good or a bad addition. Surprisingly, I also encountered serious objection. Much centred on a man and a woman on the staff. They were not chauvinists, but rather particularly dedicated to inclusiveness; it was their desire for equality of treatment that caused their concern.

The man told me that some male students were 'uncomfortable' because the course made the seminary 'too woman-oriented' and they felt 'excluded'. Females are a bare majority of students (53 per cent), but our President, Vice-President for Academic Affairs/Dean and Associate Dean – i.e. all persons with authority over academics – are male. In 2003 five of six tenured faculty were male. In 2005 the woman had retired, so five of five were male. Just one 'women's class' was offered. Frankly, it was difficult for me to understand how it made men feel excluded. When speaking about objections to inclusive language, I often maintain: 'If I say, "You're standing on my foot and it hurts", it is ludicrous to respond, "No, it doesn't hurt", or "Well, it shouldn't hurt."' I do not wish to discount men's complaints. Nonetheless, as Bell *et al.* note in 'Teaching in Environments of Resistance': 'In contrast to traditional liberal curricula and pedagogies, critical, feminist, and antiracist pedagogies are designed to disrupt the canon of the academy in order to bring about social change.'[23] Disruption and change make people uncomfortable. Yet doing away with all discomfort is neither the best pedagogical goal nor strategy. Objections must be evaluated for legitimacy.

The woman who voiced objections was one of our guests. Even during her presentation, she expressed concern about the existence of a class entitled 'Issues for Women in Christian Ministry' which did not assuage men's discomfort with women's enlarging roles. 'How are men going to learn if we don't teach them?' she enquired. 'Who will educate the men?' She asked whether I couldn't have named the class 'Gender Issues in Ministry', so men would have felt 'more invited'. Her assumption that women are responsible for making men feel welcome in seminary, to the point that offering one class to address women's needs was problematic, struck me as what is sometimes called a 'Wendy' reaction (after the responsible older sister in the story of Peter Pan). Attentiveness to the feelings of men distracted her from the truth that seminaries have long been and still are male bastions. A 2003 study at a Presbyterian school showed examining post-ordination careers 'misses the full story of how talented women who seek to become ordained are often discouraged even before they finish their seminary preparation' and 'things appear to be even worse for women than studies of ordained clergy reveal'.[24]

Clearly, some of the same arguments apply to the existence of a practical theology class for and about women which would apply to affirmative action – giving preference in hiring or school admissions to minorities. Enlightened folk realize that one critical need of women, as for men of colour, is to be mainstreamed, to be treated no differently simply because one is in the minority in a particular setting, and that benefits would surely accompany true colour-blind and gender-blind education. On the other hand, having levelled the playing field (with a decision to ordain women) does not negate the fact that all the runners in this race do not start from the same place. Some must still run much further than others. I find a theological rationale for affirmative action – and women's courses – in the story of Zacchaeus in Luke's gospel (19.1-10). The dishonest tax collector, upon having an encounter with Jesus, declares he will repay everything he gained by fraud four times over. I contend those who have held power unfairly, simply because of sex or race, are obligated not just to open the doors to the excluded, but also to work twice – or four times – as hard on behalf of minorities to redress the wrongs that have resulted from white and/or male dominance. This may even include giving up one's 'earned' place in the hierarchy or one's comfort with the status quo.

So, in response to the implicit question I have raised – is there a place in the seminary for consideration of uniquely women's issues? – I offer an unqualified 'yes'. Since the classes were all female, I also asked students to comment on how that affected learning. By citing their observations, I am not here proposing an answer to, but simply pointing toward, a related question: Is there also room for separate learning space for some groups? (A thorough discussion, beyond the scope of this essay, would address logical follow-up questions: Which groups? And who decides which groups?)

A severe critic of academia's sexism, Gloria Steinem, speaks positively about her all-women's college, because she learned that women can do everything.[25] Hillary Rodham Clinton believes studying at Wellesley was advantageous, because all organizations had female presidents, vice-presidents, and so on, and women had immense opportunities to learn political and leadership skills.[26] In recent decades, controversy has surrounded the desire of some black parents in urban areas to create all-black schools for their children. Leontine Kelly, the UMC's first African-American woman bishop, recounts how her siblings chose an all-black high school over an integrated one, and her own transfer from an integrated college to an all-black institution, in order to be leaders in extracurricular organizations.[27]

On the other hand, my students and I could easily see the problematic nature of Mary Daly's adamant refusal to allow men into some classes. Her refusal led, or contributed to, her loss of a tenured position at Boston College.[28] Yet it is not just legal issues but ethical ones as well that make me loath to mandate exclusion of anyone because of their sex.

While several of my students thought hearing a male viewpoint might have been good in a few instances, all of them maintained that overall, the one-sex classroom with which we were gifted proved helpful. One said, '[H]aving males in the class might shift the emphasis to changing their understanding and thus ... distract from ... an opportunity for the females to address issues.' I echo her assertion that we needed all our time; of all my classes, this is the one where I most desired more time. Several students commented that they wished the course could extend into a second semester. The student initially suspicious of feminism wrote: 'I noticed a definite difference ... I felt more comfortable in learning ... [W]omen could discuss their stories without fear of condemnation ... I've gained a lot of courage ... in my process of becoming a minister.' Indeed, many spoke of increased confidence about their calls.

In a voluntary signed evaluation, with permission to quote, one of the school's brightest students deemed it 'a notch above my other classes. Why? Is it ... a content that is totally relevant to me as the person I am? ... Is it because we are all women, and there is just a chemical in the room that says something powerful?' She concluded both reasons applied.[29] Others mentioned the ability to 'brin[g] out into the open, thoughts that may have been "silenced" before', and to 'wrestle with issues involved in being called to a vocation that has traditionally been preserved for males ... When dealing with difficult topics, I felt that the common ground we could claim as women helped us to work through these issues – from anger or angst to some sort of resolution'. One said: 'As a group, we can more deeply empathize with each other – thus we learn on a different level than just merely "instruction".' Another noted:

We all speak the same language; there is so much already given that we can talk with great understanding ... I wouldn't want all classes to be all-female, but to be able to openly and freely discuss issues for women in ministry, to be understood, to be awakened is a gift ... What has been *so* beneficial is the *profound* awareness of *how long* women have been considered secondary (or less). There's a *deep* knowing (and grieving) of this fact. (italics hers)

Still another spoke of the extraordinary 'level of insight and knowledge [the class] provides'.

Gender makes a difference in how interpersonal relationships are conducted, and the relationships one has as a pastor are no exception to this. Moreover, not every aspect of relationships can be put into words. The student comments contain acknowledgement that learning resulted from simply being in the room with powerful ordained women and noticing on conscious and unconscious levels the way in which they spoke and carried themselves and related to me and to each other. Comments like these reflect intuitive awareness of the different kinds of knowledge and ways of knowing which feminist pedagogy honours, and which I believe women on the journey to professional ministry need as a part of their training.

Conclusions

Our mission at Phillips, as at most mainline seminaries, is to prepare women and men for ministry. If churches hope to retain more gifted women in the pulpit, then women should receive better preparation for the gender-specific situations which they are likely to encounter in ministry. Consider the issue of authority. Undeniably, young male ministers may encounter problems with authority, but they are not exactly the same problems which young or even middle-aged or older women may encounter. Whatever congregants may say to young men about their sermons, it is probably never, 'I liked your little talk.'

The author of a 2003 essay on 'en-gendering' a theology of women's call to ordained ministry says both 'institutional barriers and interior predicaments' afflict women in unique ways as they are 'authoring and being authorized in their calls'. Many are 'caught off-guard' and 'blind-sided' by the gendered problems and 'ill-prepared' to face them.[30] I would enquire how women who have been educated as though they will encounter no differences in ministry purely as a result of their gender could be anything but 'ill-prepared' to face such differences when they occur. If the life of ministry is not the same for women as for men – and numerous studies and overwhelming anecdotal evidence suggest that it is not – then why should preparation be identical?

At the first class session I asked each student to recall the very first time she saw a woman in the pulpit. Each had a very clear memory – except the one student who *still* had never seen one – and most had had that first experience only within the last few years. None had ever seen more than a handful of women preaching or leading worship. The ease with which men find male preachers to emulate is still not duplicated for women. Until there are enough successful women pastors to provide role models outside the academy for all our women students, and so long as many experiences in ministry remain gender-related, it seems necessary to me to have aspects of ministerial training which are gender-related, as well. Progress cannot be achieved by pretending that differences in the lived experiences of women and men called to ministry do not exist.

As a last comment, I would note that one thing I did not foresee was the profound effect the class had on our guests. Most articulated regret that there had not been a similar class during their ministerial preparation. They also profited from the opportunity to tell their stories to the women who would follow where they have led. One student wrote, 'The class was exposed to history in the making ... My sense is that this ... was the first opportunity presenters ever had to articulate their faith journeys as clergy women. If this alone had been the only reason to meet, it would have been enough'. I concur.

Bibliography

Alsgaard, E., 'Memories and Dreams: 4 Clergywomen Reflect on Their Calling', *Circuit Rider*, 30.3 (May/June 2006), pp. 24–6.

Belenky, M. Field, Clinchy, B. McVicker, Goldberger, N. Rule and Tarule, J. Mattuck, *Women's Ways of Knowing: The Development of Self, Voice, and Mind* (New York: Basic Books, 1986).

Bell, S., Morrow, M. and Tastsoglou, E., 'Teaching in Environments of Resistance: Toward a Critical, Feminist, and Antiracist Pedagogy', in M. Mayberry and E. Cronan Rose (eds), *Meeting the Challenge: Innovative Feminist Pedagogies in Action* (New York: Routledge, 1999), pp. 23–46.

Blue, E., 'When Feminist Theology Becomes Practical Theology; Some Reflections on its Use in the Pastorate', *Journal of Feminist Studies in Religion*, 17.2 (autumn 2001), pp. 131–42.

Chaves, M., *Ordaining Women: Culture and Conflict in Religious Organizations* (Cambridge, MA: Harvard University Press, 1997).

Clinton, H. Rodham, *Living History* (New York: Simon & Schuster, 2003).

Craig, J. (comp.), *The Leading Women: Stories of the First Women Bishops of The United Methodist Church* (Nashville: Abingdon Press, 2004).

Finlay, B., *Facing the Stained-Glass Ceiling: Gender in a Protestant Seminary* (Lanham, MD: University Press of America, 2003).

Gargiulo, M., *Not In my Church*, produced by M. Fortune and J. Anton, Center for the Prevention of Sexual and Domestic Violence, Seattle, Washington, Michi Pictures, 1991.

Hand, D.M., 'Western North Carolina Conference' *Newscope*, 34.25 (23 June 2006), p. 7.

Hayes, E., 'Creating Knowledge about Women's Learning', in E. Hayes and D.D. Flannery (eds), *Women as Learners: The Significance of Gender in Adult Learning* (San Francisco, CA: Jossey-Bass, 2000), pp. 217–45.

Hayes, E. and Flannery, D.D., *Women as Learners: The Significance of Gender in Adult Learning* (San Francisco, CA: Jossey-Bass, 2000).

Hitchcock, J., 'Forced Retirement', in *Arlington Catholic Herald*, 1999 (accessed 16 December 2003 at http://www.catholicherald.com/hitch/99jh/jh990819.htm).

Lancaster, S. Heaner, *Women and the Authority of Scripture: A Narrative Approach* (Harrisburg, PA: Trinity Press, 2002).

'Mary Daly Ends Suit, Agrees to Retire' (accessed 16 December 2003 at http://www.bc.edu/bc_org/rvp/pubaf/chronicle/v9/fl5/daly.html).

McDougall, J.A., 'Weaving Garments of Grace: En-gendering a Theology of the Call to Ordained Ministry for Women Today', *Theological Education*, 39.2 (2003), pp. 149–65.

Norén, C.M., *The Woman in the Pulpit* (Nashville, TN: Abingdon Press, 1991).

Procter-Smith, M., *In Her Own Rite: Constructing Feminist Liturgical Tradition* (Nashville, TN: Abingdon Press, 1990).

Rutter, P., *Sex in the Forbidden Zone: When Men in Power – Therapists, Doctors, Clergy, Teachers, and Others – Betray Women's Trust* (New York: Fawcett Crest, 1989).

'Statistics', *Wellsprings: A Journal for United Methodist Clergywomen*, 11.1 (winter 2003), pp. 32–9.

Steinem, G., *Revolution from Within: A Book of Self-Esteem* (Boston, MA: Little, Brown, 1992).

This, C., 'Clergywomen in Local Churches', *The Flyer*, 37.2 (April–June 2006), pp. 8–9.

Tisdell, E., 'Feminist Pedagogies', in E. Hayes and D.D. Flannery, *Women as Learners: The Significance of Gender in Adult Learning* (San Francisco, CA: Jossey-Bass, 2000), pp. 155–83.

Wessinger, C. (ed.), *Religious Institutions and Women's Leadership: New Roles Inside the Mainstream* (Columbia, SC: University of South Carolina Press, 1996).

Winter, M.T., Lummis, A. and Stokes, A., *Defecting in Place: Women Claiming Responsibility for Their Own Spiritual Lives* (New York: Crossroad, 1995).

Zikmund, B. Brown, Lummis, A.T. and Mei Yin Chang, P., *Clergy Women: An Uphill Calling* (Louisville, KY: Westminster John Knox Press, 1998).

Notes

1   I use the term 'women ministers' advisedly, understanding the negative effects of linguistically distinguishing part of a group as other ('male nurse', 'black doctor'), but also understanding the negative effects of expecting the experience of a woman in ministry to be identical with that of a male.

2   E. Tisdell, 'Feminist Pedagogies', in E. Hayes and D.D. Flannery, *Women as Learners: The Significance of Gender in Adult Learning* (San Francisco, CA: Jossey-Bass, 2000), pp. 155–83, p. 157.

3   Hayes and Flannery, *Women as Learners*, p. 243.

4   M. Field Belenky, B. McVicker Clinchy, N. Rule Goldberger and J. Mattuck Tarule: *Women's Ways of Knowing: The Development of Self, Voice, and Mind* (New York: Basic Books, 1986), p. 113.

5   In 2003 all were white women pursuing ordination in the United Methodist Church, the Christian Church (Disciples of Christ), the Presbyterian Church USA or the United Church of Christ. (A recent graduate, a Wiccan pursuing Unitarian Universalist ordination, audited.) In 2005, 11 were white, one was black, one Latin American (Colombian) and one of mixed ancestry; the UMC, the DOC, the UCC, the Presbyterian and the National Baptist churches were represented.

6   S. Heaner Lancaster, *Women and the Authority of Scripture: A Narrative Approach* (Harrisburg, PA: Trinity Press, 2002).

7   C.M. Norén, *The Woman in the Pulpit* (Nashville, TN: Abingdon Press, 1991).

8   M. Procter-Smith, *In her Own Rite: Constructing Feminist Liturgical Tradition* (Nashville, TN: Abingdon Press, 1990).

9   E. Blue, 'When Feminist Theology Becomes Practical Theology; Some Reflections on its Use in the Pastorate', *Journal of Feminist Studies in Religion*, 17.2 (autumn 2001), pp. 131–42.

10   P. Rutter, *Sex in the Forbidden Zone: When Men in Power – Therapists, Doctors, Clergy, Teachers, and Others – Betray Women's Trust* (New York: Fawcett Crest, 1989).

11   M. Gargiulo, *Not in My Church*, Produced by M. Fortune and J. Anton, Center for the Prevention of Sexual and Domestic Violence, Seattle, WA, Michi Pictures, 1991.

12   One of 19 active bishops in the UMC Central Conferences (those outside the USA) is female; she serves in Germany. The UMC has had 21 female bishops; four of them

are retired and one is deceased (Jo Ann McClain, Office of the Council of Bishops, personal communication 7 July 2006).

13 *The Flyer* is published by the UMC's General Commission on the Status and Role of Women. Some data come from Craig This (emails to author, 6 July 2006).

14 C. This, 'Clergywomen in Local Churches', *The Flyer*, 37.2 (April–June 2006), pp. 8–9.

15 E. Alsgaard, 'Memories and Dreams: 4 Clergywomen Reflect on their Calling' *Circuit Rider*, 30.3 (May/June 2006), pp. 24–6, p. 25.

16 M.T. Winter, A. Lummis and A. Stokes, *Defecting in Place: Women Claiming Responsibility for their Own Spiritual Lives* (New York: Crossroad, 1995).

17 M. Chaves, *Ordaining Women: Culture and Conflict in Religious Organizations* (Cambridge, MA: Harvard University Press, 1997), p. 185.

18 Chaves, *Ordaining Women*, p. 5.

19 B. Kohler, Assistant General Secretary, General Board of Higher Education and Ministry, UMC, personal communication, 8 March 2004.

20 B. Brown Zikmund, A.T. Lummis and P. Mei Yin Chang, *Clergy Women: An Uphill Calling* (Louisville, KY: Westminster John Knox Press, 1998), p. 117.

21 Heather Nygard-Scherer, email to author, 3 July 2006.

22 Lizette Merchan, email to author, 4 July 2006.

23 S. Bell, M. Morrow and E. Tastsoglou, 'Teaching in Environments of Resistance: Toward a Critical, Feminist, and Antiracist Pedagogy', in M. Mayberry and E. Cronan Rose (eds), *Meeting the Challenge: Innovative Feminist Pedagogies in Action* (New York: Routledge, 1999), pp. 23–46, p. 23.

24 B. Finlay, *Facing the Stained-Glass Ceiling: Gender in a Protestant Seminary* (Lanham, MD: University Press of America, 2003), p. 118.

25 G. Steinem, *Revolution from Within: A Book of Self-Esteem* (Boston, MA: Little, Brown, 1992), pp. 118-49.

26 H. Rodham Clinton, *Living History* (New York: Simon & Schuster, 2003), p. 29.

27 J. Craig (comp.), *The Leading Women: Stories of the First Women Bishops of The United Methodist Church* (Nashville, TN: Abingdon Press, 2004), pp. 141–3.

28 J. Hitchcock, 'Forced Retirement', *Arlington Catholic Herald* (1999) (accessed 16 December 2003 at http://www.catholicherald.com/hitch/99jh/jh990819.htm); 'Mary Daly Ends Suit, Agrees to Retire' (accessed 16 December 2003 at http://www.bc.edu/bc_org/rvp/pubaf/chronicle/v9/fl5/daly.html).

29 Sheri Curry, evaluation, autumn 2003.

30 J.A. McDougall, 'Weaving Garments of Grace: En-gendering a Theology of the Call to Ordained Ministry for Women Today', *Theological Education*, 39.2 (2003), pp. 149–65, pp. 149, 154.

5

Doing Leadership Differently? Women and Senior Leadership in the Church of England[1]

Rosie Ward

Introduction

One key question which was asked when women were priested in the Anglican Church was 'will women lead differently?' Indeed, some people had argued for women priests on the basis that they would bring a different kind of leadership and ministry into the Church. The same question, do women lead differently? is being asked again about women archdeacons and bishops. What difference will it make to have a number of women archdeacons, and ultimately bishops, in the Church?

Much has been written on the subject of women in leadership in the past few years, but there is little that is specifically Christian. This essay explores issues of leadership style and appropriate biblical leadership. It starts from the observation that the New Testament sees no division by gender of spiritual fruit (character) or spiritual gifts (gifts, talents and 'roles'), and that Jesus is the leader whom all leaders must follow, both men and women. It also explores how women's entry into senior leadership positions will enhance the Church by the addition of the experiences and gifts which they bring.

What is leadership?

Some women would avoid the term 'leader', because it has been associated with particular styles of leadership. Fifteen or 20 years ago, one reaction to a dominant style of leadership in the Church and other spheres was to replace it by facilitation, epitomized in the phrase: 'We won't have a leader.' Emerging churches sometimes speak of having no designated leader, or of shared leadership, but even a group with no designated leader will still be led.

There are many definitions of leadership, most of them about how leaders influence others and seek to go somewhere. The definition I am using has been developed over a number of years in the Arrow Leadership Programme, an 18-month programme for younger leaders: 'Christian leadership is a servant-oriented relational process whereby those who lead, under God's leadership, using their God-given capacity, seek to influence others towards a kingdom-honouring goal.'[2] This emphasizes both relationships and goals, the servant attitude of the Christian leader, and the skills and competencies needed for leadership.

Different roles for women?

Leadership for women is complicated by questions which men never face. All women have to think about what it means to be a woman in ministry; whatever church we belong to, our leadership is a challenge to nearly 2,000 years of male leadership. One encouragement to me is the evidence of women in diaconal and presbyteral roles in the Early Church, and increasing insight into what caused their gradual disappearance, which means that recent developments are more of a restoration of what was lost than an innovation.

Before considering whether women lead differently I want to see what the Bible says, if anything, about different gifts or roles for women. How do evangelical women respond to arguments about so-called 'headship', which limit leadership to men? For evangelicals, this is the starting-point for discussing women's ministry, rather than arguing from the perspective of justice or equality.

In the last decade or so, some evangelical churches have placed an increasing emphasis on male–female difference, in so-called 'biblical feminism' promoted by the Council for Biblical Manhood and Womanhood (CBMW) through the Danvers Statement. This argues that 'distinctions in masculine and feminine roles are ordained by God as part of the created order'.[3] The CBMW material has influenced some churches on a variety of levels: one denomination in the USA has abolished the office of deaconess, and elsewhere women have been removed from the position of elder. It has made it difficult for some evangelical women aspiring to authorized ministry. This sort of thinking also lies behind the view of some conservative evangelicals in the Church of England.

In response I would argue that there is no biblical doctrine of what constitutes 'masculinity' and 'femininity' in scripture, and almost nothing about gender differences as part of the original created order. The male dominance mentioned in Gen. 3.16 is generally understood to be a prediction of how male sinfulness would manifest itself after the Fall, rather than a prescription for male behaviour. We can see this lived out both in the Old Testament and in the whole of society.

Jesus came to reverse the effects of the Fall, and while he chose 12 men to be his inner core of disciples, he is not shown to have had any tendency to see women as different in kind to men. When the crowds commend Jesus's mother, he draws attention to the importance of faith rather than of child-bearing. In many places he makes it clear that gender is irrelevant to the concerns of the kingdom of God. At Pentecost the Spirit is poured out on both men and women, fulfilling the prophecy of Joel. Paul's discussion of spiritual gifts makes no suggestion that these are not given as the Spirit wills to both men and women.

Where there do appear to be limitations on the role of women in ministry in Paul's writings, many recent commentators have demonstrated that these are not as they may seem at face value, but relate more to particular circumstances than to all women for all time. The 'headship' argument rests mainly on the Greek word *kephale* in 1 Cor. 11.2-26 and Eph. 5.21-33, though the latter relates to the home rather than the church. Some of those who wish to restrict women's leadership back up their references to New Testament texts by arguing that the eternal subordination of Christ to the Father in the Trinity implies the subordination of women to men. There is, however, plenty of material refuting the idea that *kephale* means 'head' in the sense of having authority over, and the 'subordination' argument.[4]

Nowhere do the scriptures command us to develop our awareness of ourselves as males or females; rather, Jesus' teaching and the teaching of Paul's epistles are intended to apply to all followers of Christ equally. If men and women are called to exemplify the fruit of the Spirit of Gal. 5 then men rather than women may find such things as gentleness or self-control a challenge! While God gives people different gifts to equip them for different roles, there is no suggestion in scripture that God gives some gifts only to men and others only to women.

Biblical leadership

What has always made Christian leadership different has been that we model our leadership on Jesus, the one who came not to be served but to serve. Jesus presents us with a model to follow: a model of humility not ego, of service not status, someone who knew who he was, who had a clear vision of what God wanted him to do, who modelled what he taught, who equipped others to lead, who embodied love and warmth and who was vulnerable. None of these things is gender-specific, although the vulnerability of Jesus may be more of a challenge to men than to women.

Sadly, Christian leadership has not always looked like this. Too easily power, ambition and self-seeking have affected the Church as much as other spheres of leadership. While some women have rejected the idea of leadership altogether, the solution for bad leadership is not to have no leadership but to have good leadership.

There are some conundrums around Christian leadership which are not easily resolved: if power is made perfect in weakness, how are we meant to handle our strengths? When Jesus speaks of suffering, and the world speaks of success, what is the appropriate response of a Christian leader? How do women follow Jesus's model of self-sacrifice when some do not have a 'self' to sacrifice? As those who have been excluded from many areas of leadership, how may women struggle and argue for their gifts to be used, but still do this in the spirit of Christ? How do women maintain godly ambition yet avoid self-seeking ambition?

The matter of 'selfhood' has been discussed in Christian feminist writing since Valerie Saiving's article 'The Human Situation: A Feminine View' was published in 1960.[5] She and others have suggested that some women have been socialized to give up so much of themselves that nothing remains of their own uniqueness. This 'sin of hiding' or of resignation, of not using one's gifts or trying to accomplish anything significant, may be a particular temptation for women. This area needs further exploration.

Some women have questioned the concept of 'servant' leadership, seeing this as a male construct, because the term 'servant' is redolent of women's service to men. However 'servant leadership' also seems to be gaining in currency to denote an effective relational style of leadership at which women excel.

Research on women and leadership

In a recent book on leadership, Tom Peters entitles one chapter 'Meet the New Boss: Women Rule!' He argues that women constitute a woefully neglected source of leadership talent and that they bring gifts which current business needs. Peters concludes that 'accelerating the movement of women into leadership roles is a ... strategic imperative ... of the highest order'.[6] He draws on the work of two women who have researched women and leadership, Helen Fisher and Judy Rosener. They have concluded that women and men have different gifts, and that women bring to leadership such talents as emotional sensitivity, empathy, a penchant for long-term planning, a gift for networking, a desire to reach consensus and a collaborative leadership style. Rosener, writing in 1990, was one of those who sparked the current debate about women as leaders.[7] She surveyed the way women came to break the glass ceiling in organizations, and found that the first female executives adhered to many of the 'rules of conduct' that spelled success for men. When a second wave made its way to the top, they adopted some of those same styles and habits but also drew on the skills which they had developed from their shared experiences as women. This is important in relation to women trying to break the stained-glass ceiling. Fisher's book *The First Sex* argues from an anthropological basis that women's gifts of cooperation, patience, intuition and 'web'-thinking are ideal for twenty-first-century leadership, and that working collaboratively with men, women will 'change the world'.[8]

An important British piece of research in a similar vein is by Susan Vinnicombe of Cranfield Business School. Her analysis of the leadership styles of a number of male and female managers concluded that the majority of male leaders were traditionalists (Myers-Briggs SJ personality types who like systems and uphold traditional values).[9] More women fell into the categories of visionary (NT personality types, who are intellectual, creative and problem-solving) and catalyst leaders (NF personality types, typified by communicating, personal care and enthusiasm). Women are more collaborative and cooperative in working with people, and far less hierarchical or authoritarian than men.[10] Her most recent research, *Women with Attitude*, is a study of 19 business women.[11] She notes that women in male-dominated industries lead in ways which resemble their male colleagues' styles more than they differ from them. However, some of the most successful women leaders have resisted this trend. Among the common themes emerging from Vinnicombe's study were a transformational style of leading, openness, being a team player and care for staff and their development.

Another key book is *The Female Advantage: Women's Ways of Leading*,[12] by Sally Helgesen. This includes a study of Frances Hesselbein, whose role as leader of the US Girl Scouts is closer to that of women in church leadership than it is to that of women leaders in business. Helgesen has some interesting conclusions about how women lead: working at a steady pace, with breaks, rather than unrelentingly; viewing unscheduled tasks and encounters as opportunities not interruptions; keeping the long view in range rather than the day-to-day and sharing information rather than keeping it to themselves. These are all interesting observations in terms of church leadership.

The conclusion of all this new thinking on women as leaders is that women *do* lead differently. As we consider how to relate this to leadership in the Church, and the debates we are involved in, we need to look carefully at the 'small print' in these studies. Fisher is an anthropologist, and cites scientific studies which document biological and scientific differences between men and women. She and others note that there are many exceptions, however, and she sees all of us as a complex mixture of feminine and masculine traits. There is a continuum of hormone levels; and environmental forces also contribute to making us who we are.[13]

It is usually assumed that women's distinctive leadership style stems from a mixture of nature and nurture, and that what is developed can change, whether we are thinking of men or women. This raises interesting questions about the future of leadership; it has been suggested that as male and female spheres of responsibility become more blurred, the boundaries between masculine and feminine will blur also.[14]

Women leaders in the Church

Two research projects shed further light on women in the Church and their potential in leadership at a variety of levels. The first was in 1995, when I surveyed women who were leading church plants, most of them Anglican. At that time, some of them were exercising a level of leadership in church plants which would not have been possible in the parent churches, given that women could not be priests until 1994. In 2006 I asked similar questions about leadership styles of women participants in the Arrow Leadership Programme, women clergy in a couple of dioceses and women leaders in my organization (CPAS). My research on women church-planters[15] can be summarized as follows:

1. Roughly half the women surveyed thought there was no difference between male and female leadership styles: it was all down to personality.

2. The other half thought there were differences. They felt that women have a more inclusive and sharing leadership style, seeing themselves as enabling leaders, with gifts of team-building and encouraging. They thought women preferred to work incarnationally, starting with people and community, and gradually growing church. They also thought that women exhibit greater sensitivity to people.
3. The women surveyed were keen to find their own style and not just to copy men; however, they lacked role models.
4. Two male church-planting 'experts' observed that women had more of a servant mentality, were more patient and would persevere in the hard places, not feeling they had to be a success or make a name for themselves.

Analysing these responses, the 'differences' seem as much due to nurture, in terms of some women's different experience, as to any 'natural' explanation.

In my recent research on women who are mainly of incumbent status (vicars/rectors rather than curates) the dominant theme is again that different styles have more to do with personality than with gender. Most related these variations to types of personality, yet they also saw some aspects of style as being common to the majority of women. The differences they noted included women being more democratic, more collaborative and better at delegating and team-building. They thought themselves more concerned with pastoral issues and better at reading people. They felt they were less motivated by power, status and ambition than men, and were generally seen as more approachable. They said women tended to be less confident than men, and more concerned about issues of family and a balanced life.

It is hard to be sure whether this emphasis on personality reflects women's growing sense that they are called to do the same job in ministry as men do, and dislike past gender stereotypes either for themselves or for men. Alternatively, it could be that women prefer to attribute difference to personality rather than to gender because in the past these differences often had negative consequences for women. Some of the arguments for having women in ordained ministry used to assume that women would bring something 'different', but this has not been an obvious outcome in the Anglican Church or in other denominations. Research on gender seems to indicate that differences within the sexes are at least as great as those between them.

This suggests that women are needed in senior leadership not to bring some essence of 'femaleness' which is altogether lacking among male clergy or church leaders, but that their blend of life experience, personality and gendered talent would contribute things which are relatively lacking in current groups of senior church leaders, thus making their corporate leadership more effective.

Other research on women as leaders

Another source for women as leaders is Ian Jones's study *Women and Priesthood in the Church of England Ten Years on*, which has a short section on gender issues.[16] What the respondents noted was that different life experiences gave different insights which might be used in ministry. They too saw differences as being more about nurture (experience) than nature (anything to do with biology). One of the most interesting explorations of these issues is a 1999 paper by Anne Dyer in the journal *Anvil*.[17] She noted that the first women to be ordained priest had spent years as assistants, so it was not surprising that they had learnt the skills of collaborative ministry. Women are not necessarily more collaborative than men, and we needed to wait longer to see if women lost their ability to work in teams once they had moved into sole-responsibility posts. She also acknowledged that some women and men hold collaborative styles in high regard. I would concur that a more empowering and collaborative style is a continuing trend which women (and some men) are taking into parish ministry, even in the face of congregations who are used to a more traditional style.

Men and women in leadership together: the future of the Church?

Within five years or so half the clergy in the Church of England will be female, but the picture of women's deployment is not as healthy as that statistic might suggest in terms of leadership, both local and national. The majority of OLMs (ordained local ministers), of NSMs (nonstipendiary ministers) and a high proportion of those in sector ministry are women; so in 2004 only about 16 per cent of stipendiary clergy were women. In 2006 there were still no women bishops, and only 11 women archdeacons, two deans and 14 residentiary canons, plus 68 rural or area deans out of nearly 700. The Dean of Leicester, Vivienne Faull, has noted that 'women are particularly represented in roles which are local, flexible, family-friendly, voluntary, junior and of recent creation. Women are much *less* represented in stipendiary, senior roles or ancient institutions'.[18]

In the Episcopal Church in the USA, where women have been ordained for longer, there is still a stained-glass ceiling, and most ordained women are called to serve small, generally poor congregations, while rectors of large multi-staffed parishes are overwhelmingly male.[19] In other UK denominations the picture is mixed. There are significant numbers of women leading Methodist churches – but very few circuit superintendents. While women preached, taught and founded churches in the early days of the Baptist churches in the seventeenth century, in subsequent centuries their role was more restricted. Now, despite the fact that Baptists have officially affirmed the ordained ministry of women for 80 years, the proportion of women leading Baptist churches is very small. The Salvation Army has equality in its title deeds, but there are currently no women in the most senior posts. Married women can only effectively serve alongside their husbands, and cannot take a role more senior than theirs; the women who have held the most senior posts have been single. Thus even in a denomination with a long history of women in leadership, women do not necessarily rise to senior posts. In the new churches some networks, such as New Frontiers International, are more conservative than others.

Many people in the Anglican Church, both men and women, have looked forward to the changes which having women in leadership will bring, but some studies suggest that a critical mass of women in an institution is needed before norms change.[20] There is a need to see women leaders at all levels in the Church as a strategic (and biblical) necessity, not a reluctant concession to demands of justice.

In the Introduction to *Enlightened Power*, a collection of 40 articles on aspects of women's leadership, Linda Coughlin writes: 'Our resounding vision is one of organizations that invoke the full participation of men and women leaders ... we are changing the nature and use of power through our use of enlightened power – that which is manifest as we enact inclusive leadership that brings to bear the full and equal partnership of men and women leaders.'[21] It would have been wonderful had the Church, which after all is entrusted with perhaps the fullest vision of this equal partnership, been able to have shown the way. As it is, when we open up new possibilities for women in leadership in the Church we discover opportunities to learn from our sisters and brothers who have paved the way in other fields.

There are various ways in which the gifts of women might enhance the Church today, such as in relation to our changing culture. Church decline figures speak for themselves, and the Church is increasingly out of touch with society. Women appear to bring long-range and strategic thinking, which are needed to address the future. The presence of women in leadership also helps the Church to meet the challenges of finance and clergy deployment. Many dioceses have responded to these by a renewed emphasis on collaborative ministry, ministry leadership teams and the like, at which women appear to be gifted. It can also be argued that women enhance church unity in the face of division because they use more democratic, inclusive and unifying strategies. This could make them a key to unity rather than, as has so often been argued in the debate about women bishops, a source of *dis*unity.

Leadership is inevitably about power, but the 'enlightened power' which it is argued women bring to leadership is perhaps closer to Christian leadership than leadership thinking has ever been. Much past leadership thinking has been male, and has been challenged as women have contributed to the study of leadership. Reconnecting with the example of Jesus helps us to rediscover a different kind of power, that of serving rather than wanting to be served. Masculine power has too often been 'power over', whereas a better use of power is 'power to', a life-giving, enabling force; we may rightly aspire to a power that can be used to change things and empower others. Of course, women are as capable of bad leadership as men, but they have much to bring that is still denied.

Conclusion

The jury is still out on the question whether women lead differently. My own research seems to lead away from a theology of difference and arguments about this. If we accept the idea that women bring something different to leadership then this is good news for the Church, and we might echo Tom Peters in saying that the sooner they get into leadership roles, the better it will be for everyone. If, alternatively, women's leadership style is the product of personality rather than difference, there is still a need to see women take their place alongside men.

Alison White, in her contribution to *Jobs for the Boys*, wrote: 'I think one of the greatest gifts of ordained women is their innate sense of "we can do things better together".'[22] It is no glib generalization to say this thread runs through much of what has been written. One answer to the question as to whether women lead differently is that much is related to personality rather than gender, but that women tend to suggest collaboration more often.

This is what we should expect as Christians trying to define the essence of Christian leadership. There is something about the nature of God which is reflected in maleness and femaleness together, not in being a male or female separately, or being more male than female. If purposefulness is a male tendency and relational connection a female one, the Godhead is both purposeful and relational. It would be wrong to suggest that a tendency seen as linked with maleness is more like God than one linked to femaleness. Since God is in a Trinitarian relationship, to be truly human is to experience both male and female tendencies. In other words, humanness is the combination of maleness and femaleness. Thus the ideal for leadership is togetherness, fruit of the unique blend of experience and personality which women and men jointly offer the Church.

One way of seeing the Fall and the beginning of the gender war is in terms of precipitating for all of human history a tendency for men and women to move against each other rather than serve each other. When women and men find redemption in Christ then those tendencies should be channelled back into working with one another. The gender wars began in the Garden but should end at the Cross. Once women's and men's voices are heard and valued at all levels, we may get nearer to creating a Church and churches that are places of mutual trust, connected intimacy and shared power.

Bibliography

Ashley, R., 'Can a Woman have Authority over a Man? Some biblical questions and an evangelical response', in H. Harris and J. Shaw (eds), *The Call for Women Bishops* (London: SPCK, 2004), pp. 87–119.

Conn, J.W., *Spirituality and Personal Maturity* (New York: Paulist Press, 1989).

Coughlin, L., Wingard, E. and Hollihan, K. (eds), *Enlightened Power* (San Francisco, CA: Jossey-Bass, 2005).

Darling, P., *Reaching toward Wholeness II: Highlights of the 21st Century Survey* (Episcopal Church USA, Committee on the Status of Women: 2003), p.1.

Dyer, A., 'Reviewing the Reception', *Anvil*, 16.2 (1999), pp. 85–93.

Faull, V., 'A New Song in a Strange Land', 21st Eric Symes Abbott Memorial Lecture, King's College, London, 2006.

Fisher, H., *The First Sex: The Natural Talents of Women and how they are Changing the World* (New York: Ballantine Books, 1999).

Giles, K., *The Trinity and Subordinationism* (Downers Grove, IL: InterVarsity Press, 2002).

Grudem, W., *Evangelical Feminism and Biblical Truth* (Leicester: IVP, 2004).

Helgesen, S., *The Female Advantage* (New York: Doubleday, 1995).

——, 'The Sustainable Advantage', in L. Coughlin, E. Wingard and K. Hollihan (eds), *Enlightened Power* (San Francisco, CA: Jossey-Bass, 2005), pp. 37–8.

Hunt, S., 'Inclusive Transformation', in L. Coughlin, E. Wingard and K. Hollihan (eds) *Enlightened Power* (San Francisco, CA: Jossey-Bass, 2005), pp. 430–31.

Jones, I., *Women and Priesthood in the Church of England: Ten Years On* (London: Church House Publishing, 2004).

Morse, M.K., 'Gender Wars: Biology Offers Insights to a Biblical Problem' in *Priscilla Papers*, 20.1 (2006), pp. 3–7.

Nixson, R., *Liberating Women for the Gospel* (London: Hodder & Stoughton, 1987).

Peters, T., *Leadership* (London: Dorling Kindersley, 2005).

Rosener, J., 'Ways Women Lead', in *Harvard Business Review* (November–December 1990), pp. 119–25.

Saiving, V., 'The Human Situation: A Feminine View' in C. Christ and J. Plaskow (eds), *Womanspirit Rising* (San Francisco, CA: Harper & Row, 1979), pp. 25–42.

Vinnicombe, S., 'What Exactly are the Differences in Male and Female Working Styles?', in *Women in Management Review*, 3 (1987), pp. 1–10.

—— and Bank, J., *Women with Attitude* (London: Routledge, 2003).

White, A., 'The Art of Surprise', in L. and A. Barr (eds), *Jobs for the Boys* (London: Hodder & Stoughton, 2001), pp. 181–98.

Websites
www.cpas.org.uk/leadership
www.fulcrum-anglican.org.uk

Notes

1   A previous version of this was published in the *Church of England Newspaper* (August 2006). Used by permission.

2   The Arrow Leadership Programme equips Christian leaders to be led more by Jesus, to lead more like Jesus and to lead more to Jesus. Arrow began in the USA in 1992 and the CPAS-run UK programme, aimed mainly at Anglicans, is one of a number now run in seven countries worldwide. The definition of leadership is used in the UK Arrow, and the 'Growing Leaders' course (see www.cpas.org.uk/leadership).

3   W. Grudem, *Evangelical Feminism and Biblical Truth* (Leicester: IVP, 2004), Appendix 1, p. 538

4   See R. Ashley, 'Can a Woman have Authority over a Man? Some biblical questions and an evangelical response', in H. Harris and J. Shaw (eds), *The Call for Women Bishops* (London: SPCK, 2004), p. 119. For the debate about subordination in the Trinity, see K. Giles, *The Trinity and Subordinationism* (Downers Grove, IL: InterVarsity Press, 2002) and the conclusion of the General Synod July 2006 background article on the Fulcrum website www.fulcrum-anglican.org.uk. See also T. Wright and D. Stancliffe, 'Woman Bishops: A Response to Cardinal Kasper', (Fulcrum website) which concludes that 'those who support the ordination of women to priestly and episcopal ministry cannot be dismissed as treating scripture in a cavalier fashion'.

5   V. Saiving, 'The Human Situation: A Feminine View', in C. Christ and J. Plaskow (eds), *Womanspirit Rising* (San Francisco, CA: Harper & Row, 1979), pp. 25–42. See also J.W. Conn, *Spirituality and Personal Maturity* (New York: Paulist Press, 1989).

6   T. Peters, *Leadership* (London: Dorling Kindersley, 2005), p. 98.

7   J. Rosener, 'Ways Women Lead', in *Harvard Business Review* (November–December 1990), pp. 119–25.

8   H. Fisher, *The First Sex: The Natural Talents of Women and how they are Changing the World* (New York: Ballantine Books, 1999), p. 3.
9   The Myers-Briggs type indicator is a personality questionnaire designed to identify certain psychological differences, and uses four pairings, which are notated by their initial letters: Introversion–Extroversion; Sensing–Intuition; Thinking-Feeling; Judging–Perceiving.
10 S. Vinnicombe, 'What Exactly are the Differences in Male and Female Working Styles?', in *Women in Management Review*, 3 (1987), pp. 1–10 (1).
11 S. Vinnicombe and J. Bank, *Women with Attitude* (London: Routledge, 2003).
12 S. Helgesen, *The Female Advantage* (New York: Doubleday, 1995).
13 A recent article by Mary Kate Morse, 'Gender Wars: Biology Offers Insights to a Biblical Problem', in *Priscilla Papers*, 20.1 (2006), pp. 3–7, sheds further light on biological differences and their implications for behaviour. While scientists at present believe that there is a core of maleness and femaleness related to hormonal structure and brain structure, these are on a continuum in men and women and are not determinative for how all men and all women will act. Human beings are complex, and vary according to personality, home and national culture, as well as biological identity.
14 Helgesen, S., 'The Sustainable Advantage', in L. Coughlin, E. Wingard and K. Hollihan (eds), *Enlightened Power* (San Francisco, CA: Jossey-Bass, 2005), p. 377.
15 R. Nixson, *Liberating Women for the Gospel* (London: Hodder & Stoughton, 1987).
16 I. Jones, *Women and Priesthood in the Church of England: Ten Years On* (London: Church House Publishing, 2004), pp. 65–8.
17 A. Dyer, 'Reviewing the Reception', *Anvil*, 16.2 (1999), pp. 85–93.
18 V. Faull, 'A New Song in a Strange Land', 21st Eric Symes Abbott Memorial Lecture, King's College, London, 2006, p. 8.
19 P. Darling, *Reaching toward Wholeness II: Highlights of the 21st Century Survey*, Episcopal Church USA, Committee on the Status of Women, 2003, p. 1.
20 S. Hunt, 'Inclusive Transformation', in L. Coughlin, E. Wingard and K. Hollihan (eds), *Enlightened Power* (San Francisco, CA: Jossey-Bass, 2005), pp. 430–31.
21 L. Coughlin, 'Introduction: The Time is Now', in *Enlightened Power*, p. 2.
22 A. White, 'The Art of Surprise', in L. and A. Barr (eds), *Jobs for the Boys* (London: Hodder & Stoughton, 2001), pp. 181–98 (196).

Part 2

Historical Perspectives

6

Winifred Kiek: Migration and the Prophetic Role of Congregational Women Ministers in Australia, 1927–77[1]

Julia Pitman

It is not surprising that Manchester, a centre for Protestant nonconformity in the nineteenth and twentieth centuries, and the setting for the international conference that led to the publication of this collection of papers, is also the place where Winifred Kiek, the first woman ordained in a Christian denomination in Australia, was born and raised.[2] Born in 1884, Winifred was the second child of Robert and Margaret Jackson, a lower-middle-class Quaker family. They lived in Claremont Road, in the suburb of Moss Side, before moving to Urmston, and then to the countryside, when Winifred was 12. Her father was a socialist, a ventriloquist and a tea salesman, who worked on commission because he preferred to be self-employed. Her parents were total abstainers from alcohol and pacifists, and Margaret Jackson dressed her children in hand-made and hand-me-down clothes. The parents would go without food for the sake of the children, and when visitors were present they adhered to the code 'FHB' (family hold back), which is still used in Manchester today. The family followed the Friends' practice of home Sunday schooling, and later Winifred attended a Unitarian Sunday school. She signed the pledge at the age of 9. Winifred was educated at two elementary schools: the Dame's School and Raby Street, a Quaker school run by her Aunt Clara. She was admitted to Urmston British School in 1896 where she studied mathematics and science. At 16 she won a scholarship to study at Manchester Pupil Training Centre and worked as an apprentice teacher. She received her matriculation certificate in 1904 and entered Victoria University, Manchester. There, she was advised to give up science, as there were few opportunities for women, and pursued an arts course instead, majoring in Latin and French. She graduated in 1907, and was appointed to Manley Park School as a teacher. As a Sunday school teacher and a leader of Band of Hope meetings, she witnessed first-hand the effects of alcohol abuse on families and the gulf between her values of thrift, sobriety and punctuality, and those of the working class.

Winifred Kiek would eventually migrate to Australia and become the first woman ordained in a dominion of the British Empire. Her story illustrates key themes in the history of the ordination of women within the Commonwealth, particularly the role of migration in influencing the timing and extent of women's ordination as well as the transmission of ideas within the Commonwealth. This chapter explores the main elements of Kiek's path toward ordination and her subsequent ministry, and sets this story within the wider context of the history of women's ordination internationally.

Despite the growth of women's history over the past 40 years, the history of women's ordination in Congregationalism in England and Wales, and in Australia, has only recently attracted sustained academic interest.[3] This stands in contrast to the literature for the American context, where interest in Puritan and evangelical origins has been evident in both mainstream historical research and women's history.[4] For example, the biography of Antoinette Brown Blackwell, the first woman to be ordained in America in 1853, was published over 20 years ago.[5] In England, the dominance of the Church of England in narratives of church history has meant that the story of nonconformity has remained comparatively unexplored, and, within that field, women's history has also been neglected. While a biography of Maude Royden was published in 1989, which includes details of her campaign for women's ordination in the Church of England from the First World War to the 1950s, it would be another 15 years before a significant study of women in nonconformity appeared.[6]

For the Australian context, historians of religion have sought to establish how, from 1788, Australia was not 'the most godless place under heaven',[7] but that Church and community leaders were relatively successful in making Australia a Christian country.[8] However, research into the experience of Australian Christian women, who form at least half of this story, is still in its infancy. The first major academic study of Australian women church workers was released in 2005.[9] While feminist historians have shown how women played a role in the emerging nation,[10] recent revisions of feminist narratives and close studies of particular individuals have found that women were motivated not just by class, race or gender, but also by religion.[11]

A brief analysis of the life and thought of Winifred Kiek will demonstrate that the migration of church leaders was the catalyst in a range of factors that influenced the timing of women's ordination both in Australia and also in other settler societies such as South Africa and New Zealand. Christian women migrating from the United Kingdom to settler societies found greater opportunities in their new country to respond to their sense of religious duty than they would have found at home. Migration also played a role in the transmission of ideas within the Commonwealth. Like their sisters in the United Kingdom, women ministers in settler societies adopted a prophetic role informed by feminism to influence the theology, practice of ministry and public role of their denomination, but their perspective was also influenced by local conditions. However, their conception of the prophetic role could also serve to reinforce as much as challenge British notions of class, race, gender, religion and nationalism.

Before considering these arguments in detail, the ordination of Winifred Kiek should be understood in the context of her marriage to a Congregational minister and his subsequent career. While holidaying in Switzerland in the summer of 1909, Winifred met her future husband, Edward Sidney Kiek, a student for the Congregational ministry at Mansfield College, Oxford, who was staying in the same chalet. She had requested her friends and relatives address her letters without her BA after her name, but they either forgot or ignored this request. When collecting his mail, Edward noticed one of her letters and eventually met and became captivated by this young scholar, with her attractive curls, her modest demeanour and her fierce intellect. Edward, a southerner and Londoner, was an energetic preacher, lover of sport and good fellowship, and had already been ordained in the Congregational Church at Newcastle-On-Tyne when he passed his final examinations for his BD. He proposed marriage within a fortnight of their first meeting, but Winifred insisted on a long engagement, and they were married on 28 August 1911 in Chorlton Road Congregational church, with a breakfast at Mount Street Friends' Institute. Edward convinced Winifred that of all Christian denominations Congregationalism was the most closely related to the Quakers. A month after her marriage, Winifred became a Congregationalist.

Over the next ten years, Edward Kiek served as a Congregational minister in England. The family settled in Newcastle at first, but before long Edward accepted a call to Square Church, Halifax, in Yorkshire. Winifred, with the aid of domestic servants, conducted the usual duties of a minister's wife. She provided pastoral care to the congregation, led the Square Church Sisterhood, and, during the First World War, used her French to assist Belgian refugees.

In 1920 the Kieks migrated to Australia. Edward had responded to an advertisement in the *Christian World* for the position of Principal of Parkin College, Hackney, which was the Congregational theological college in Adelaide, South Australia, established in 1910. Over a period of almost 40 years, 'Prin Kiek', as he became known, emerged as one of the most respected church leaders in South Australia.[12] A committed but cautious ecumenist, Kiek was an important player in the agreement between the Congregational, Presbyterian and Baptist churches in South Australia to engage in joint theological education from 1921. In church union debates he worked to ensure that Congregationalism did not sacrifice its principles, and he was a leading commentator on social questions, as a spokesperson both for his denomination and for the wider ecumenical movement.

Winifred Kiek maintained her involvement in church and community organizations while she raised a young family. She brought out with her to Australia a nurse and a housekeeper to help her manage Parkin College. Her new home was probably unlike anything she had experienced in England: it had plenty of rooms, not only for her growing family but also for guests, two studies, balconies, verandahs, large windows and doors opening onto grounds with fruit trees and a tennis court. Winifred joined women's temperance and citizenship organizations such as the Woman's Christian Temperance Union, the National Council of Women, and the Woman's Non-Party Association (later renamed the League of Women Voters). She also maintained set times after school for playing games, reading and praying with her young family. In 1923 she was the first woman awarded the degree of Bachelor of Divinity from the Melbourne College of Divinity. The shortage of ministers in Congregationalism meant that before long she would be called upon to assist a congregation in its ministry. In 1926 the Congregational Church in the new suburb of Colonel Light Gardens asked her to be their pastor. The previous year the family had bought a motor car, and this was to be most useful for commuting between home and church. So impressed was the congregation with Winifred that it sought to ordain her immediately, but she insisted on the concurrence of the Congregational Union of South Australia. On 13 June 1927, aged 43 and with her youngest child not yet 10 years old, Winifred Kiek was ordained to the Christian ministry, 'the first woman minister in the Commonwealth'.[13]

Winifred Kiek exercised her ministry at Colonel Light Gardens Congregational Church until 1933, and then at Knoxville from 1939 to 1946, before working as the Australian liaison officer for the women's programme of the World Council of Churches. Women's ordination was a live issue in Australian Congregationalism in the 1920s, but the churches had not yet ordained a woman. During the nineteenth century, Unitarians and Methodists had fostered a number of female lay preachers,[14] and Australian churches welcomed female itinerant evangelists from overseas.[15]

The migration of the Kieks to Australia made women's ordination possible earlier than it might otherwise have been. Australian Congregationalism shared all the features that had allowed women's ordination in Congregationalism in America from 1853 and Britain from 1917. The denomination had no formal barrier to women's leadership. It also experienced cultural pressure from similar denominations that had ordained women overseas (in this instance, the Congregational Union of England and Wales). The theology of its ministers was generally liberal, its polity was decentralized, the women's guild system was autonomous, and there was no sacerdotalism, or expectation that the administration of the sacraments had to reflect literally the image of Christ at the Last Supper.[16] As a Reformed church, Congregationalism viewed the ministry as the priesthood of all believers and used the call system, in which ordination followed the call of a congregation to a minister.[17]

Australian Congregational churches continued to rely on ministers from Britain until the mid-twentieth century. Lack of emerging leadership was a function of the fact that, while Congregationalists had hoped that their church system would flourish in the colonies, it did not respond well to the low population density found in Australia, and the large distances to be travelled both across the colonies and within them. Congregationalists often attended the nearest Protestant church, which was more likely to be Methodist or Presbyterian than Congregational. Australian Congregationalism was much smaller as a percentage of the population than it was in England, numbering only 3 per-cent of the population in South Australia according to the census in 1921. Support from Britain for colonial missions was weak.[18] The identification of Australian Congregational churches with English Congregational polity meant that expansion was not encouraged and ministers were shared. The churches refused state aid, had few wealthy benefactors, and were weak in country areas as their itinerant ministry had not been as effective as that of Methodists.[19] By the late nineteenth century, Congregationalists found it hard to attract men to attend the meetings of the state-based Congregational Unions and began to admit women as members. From the 1920s, women were preaching in congregations and occupying the lay pastorate.

Migration was also an important factor more generally in the ordination of women in Congregationalism in the British dominions. The first woman ordained in the Congregational Union of South Africa, for example, Mrs Euphemia W. Macintosh, who was ordained in 1929, migrated to South Africa from Scotland with her parents during her childhood. She returned to Scotland for her education and graduated from Glasgow University with honours in classics and a teaching diploma. After a career as a teacher and as secretary to the British and Foreign Bible Society and the South African Temperance Alliance, she worked from 1926 as a supply minister. She shared a pastorate with her husband at the Central Congregational Church, Johannesburg, and was ordained after three years' probation.[20] While in the same year in New Zealand, Unitarians appointed Wilna Constable, also from Scotland and a former Congregational minister, to the ministry of Auckland Unitarian Church with her husband,[21] there was no woman minister in New Zealand Congregationalism until the 1950s. The Revd Nancie Ward, who was born in Manchester and educated at Lancashire Independent College, migrated from Scotland to New Zealand in 1951, and became minister of Miller Memorial Church, Napier.[22]

Continued migration to Australia helped to ensure that 15 women were ordained in Australian Congregationalism gradually over a period of 50 years. A third of these women had migrated from England, or had either settled in Australia after missionary service in Africa, Asia or the Pacific, or had parents who had settled in Australia following missionary service. Lack of continued migration to South Africa and New Zealand may explain the small numbers of ordained women in South African and New Zealand Congregationalism. In New Zealand there were no ordinations of women before church union with the Presbyterians in 1969.[23] In South Africa, the second ordination of a woman did not occur until 1934 and only 12 women would be ordained by the early 1990s.[24] In Britain and America by the 1920s, women ministers were comparatively numerous and had formed voluntary professional associations. By contrast, ordained women ministers in Commonwealth countries suffered isolation from one another and depended for support on the international networks of women ministers based in America and Britain.

Migration provided Congregational ministers with greater opportunities for service in Church and community than they would have had in England. Edward Kiek may have had significant pastorates in England, but probably would never have become principal of a theological college. Similarly, had Winifred Kiek pursued ordination in England, the timing of her ordination would not have been

particularly significant and she probably would have worked as an assistant
minister rather than as a minister of her own congregation.

The second half of this chapter considers Winifred Kiek's ministry in
Australia. Like female candidates for ministry in America and Britain before
her, Winifred Kiek needed to justify women's ordination. In 1921, less than
a year after she arrived in Australia, Kiek published an article in the
newsletter of the Australian Student Christian Movement, the *Australasian
Intercollegian*. Her arguments were informed by theology, and by the
women's movement as it had been expressed in Australia. First, she argued
that women should be ordained on the basis of the Church's own distinctive
rationale. This was a relatively conservative theological standpoint – she did
not believe that the Church should merely accommodate modern thought.
For Kiek, gender equality, as a theme of Christianity, justified women's
ordination, for it recognized 'men and women as standing on exactly the
same plane of need, responsibility, privilege and opportunity'.[25] Kiek argued
that the refusal of the Church to ordain women was a poor reflection on
itself, for it lowered ministerial standards by 'arbitrarily restricting the area
of selection', which may have been a 'sin against the Holy Spirit'.[26]

Second, Kiek used the 'additional argument'[27] that women would bring
a feminine perspective to the theology and practice of ministry of the Church
because of the Victorian notion of the superiority of womanhood. She
thought it ironic that women, the majority of church members, who were
often considered more religious than men, were excluded from the Christian
ministry by tradition. Her apologetic was also couched within the context
of the women's suffrage movement, which had achieved votes for women in
South Australia from 1894. The debate on women's ordination in Australia
followed the success of the women's suffrage movement, which stood in
contrast to America, where the first ordination of a woman (1853) had
preceded women's suffrage (1920) by almost 70 years. There, the first
women ordinands started in parish ministry, but then worked within the
women's suffrage movement as an extension of their Christian ministry.[28]
Moreover, in Britain and South Africa, the achievement of women's
ordination and women's suffrage was virtually simultaneous (1917, 1918
and 1929, 1930). Against the background of the women's movement in
Australia, Kiek used the Victorian idea of the Church as the emancipator of
women to argue that the Church now 'lags behind secular societies in the
application of its own professed ideals'.[29] Against the argument used by
opponents of women's ordination that women would not be able to manage
the responsibilities of motherhood and ministry, Kiek argued that women
could manage both home and a career. She also maintained, however, that
proponents for women's ordination should distance themselves from the
crusading style of the women's movement. Kiek did not see the Christian
ministry as simply 'an ordinary profession, nor women's admission to it
merely as the conquest of another masculine stronghold'.[30]

   The additional argument for women's ordination based on the different
experience of women from men was often reinforced by involvement in the

women's movement. After the First World War, the international women's movement sought to make public life a partnership between men and women so that the interests of women and children were represented in national and international relations and that peace was preserved. However, the argument of the special ministry of women based on their experience as wives and mothers carried a different meaning in the dominions than it did in Britain. Australian Christian women reflected the 'oppositional stance' found within Australian nationalism, and saw themselves as 'both leaven and critic'.[31] Winifred Kiek, for example, referred to the relationship of women to men in the Church as 'leaven'.[32] She believed that Australian Christian women were 'creatures of the pioneer spirit', 'heirs of the brave and strong founders of a new feminism'.[33]

Australian Congregational women ministers sought ordination to extend to a wider audience a prophetic role that had been developed in the women's guild system. There, lay Congregational women had begun to develop a feminist interpretation of scripture and social policy as it affected women and children. They considered Christian discipleship from the perspective of women, assuming that women would need to give account of their use of their talents on the Day of Judgement. They also assumed that women had experiences and responsibilities as wives and mothers that were different from those of men. They believed that in pastoral care situations, lay people may prefer to seek a female minister as they may prefer to seek a female doctor. They focused on examples of Jesus's ministry to women and the experience of women disciples in the Bible that had been neglected by male interpreters. Their social critique was influenced by the temperance, missionary, citizenship and peace movements, and they believed that the prophetic role of the Church should include this critique. At a meeting of the Congregational Church Women's Society in New South Wales in 1934, for example, one speaker argued that to 'make the world safe for our children, we must exercise a ministry that will make war impossible'.[34] The ministry of Winifred Kiek in particular was marked by this theme.

To some extent, Kiek extended the prophetic role of Congregational women to their own denomination. In 1939 she offered a speech to the Assembly of the Congregational Union of Australia and New Zealand, held in Brisbane. She argued that the Church should combat the militarism of nation-states that was driven by business interests and had adverse effects on the health of women and children. As mothers who risked their lives in childbirth and sacrificed them in childrearing, a 'woman's whole existence is a protest' against war, and therefore: 'The maintenance of family life in strength and purity is the great demand woman must always make of social organization and the state'.[35]

In its response to war, however, Australian Congregationalism did not appropriate Winifred Kiek's perspective, and she had better success as an advocate for women's ordination in the women's movement and in the ecumenical movement. Kiek acted as a female minister within the women's movement, preaching in civic services and advocating women's ordination at conferences such as the British Commonwealth League.[36] One of the first acts of the ecumenical organization Australian Church Women (established in 1963) was to set up the Winifred Kiek Scholarship, which provided women from Asia, Australasia and the Pacific with opportunities for further education in ministry. The Revd Violet Sampa, for example, the first woman ordained in Zambia, had been the Winifred Kiek Scholar for 1971.

In the women's movement, Winifred Kiek expressed a distinctively nationalist and denominational perspective on the role she hoped Australia would play in the international movement for women's ordination. Kiek hoped that the circumstances of the constitution of Christian denominations in Australia, founded as free churches in a nation without an established church, would influence their approach to women's ordination positively. She believed that the 'idea that a woman is unfit to speak in church because it is a consecrated building cannot be held in this land of freedom today'.[37] She underestimated, however, the strength of Anglican doctrinal opposition, both Evangelical and Anglo-Catholic, to the ordination of women. Women's ordination in the Anglican Church was not achieved until 1992 – two years before the Church of England – and continues to be opposed in some dioceses such as Sydney in New South Wales (evangelical) and the Murray in South Australia (Anglo-Catholic).

Problems with the conception of the prophetic role meant that it could also reflect, as much as challenge, traditional notions of class, race, gender and nationalism. The prophetic role could reinforce the assumption that only middle-class values of thrift, sobriety and sexual purity were legitimate. Secondly, with the notion that women could manage both home and a career, Congregational women ministers contributed to the expectation that women should assume a double burden of domestic and professional work. Thirdly, Congregational women ministers could reinforce the assumption found in the missionary movement that it was appropriate for Christian women to justify religious and public work by adopting the role of the 'selfless helping the helpless'.[38] Winifred Kiek's ministry among ecumenical groups of women, for example, formed to celebrate the Centenary of the State of South Australia in 1936, reinforced the identity of Christian women as the descendants of pioneers with a special responsibility toward missions in Africa, Asia, the Pacific and among Indigenous people.[39] Ironically, the access of white women to public speaking was predicated on the assumption that they would speak on behalf of their Indigenous sisters and women of other nations who, they assumed, were unable to speak for themselves.

As women's ordination became accepted after the Second World War, however, the distinctive arguments that Congregational women ministers had used to gain access to the ordained ministry declined. The next generation of women ministers would not be as concerned as the first generation had been to extend a special female message to a wider sphere. Similarly, concepts of national identity and the relationship of white women to Indigenous women were changing. Congregational women ministers would support the struggle of Indigenous people for land rights, and eventually the first Indigenous woman would be ordained in Australia in September 1991, the

Revd Liyapidiny Marika, in the Northern Synod of the Uniting Church in Australia.[40]

When the Uniting Church in Australia, a union of Presbyterian, Methodist and Congregational churches, was inaugurated in 1977, it accepted women's ordination as part of its *Basis of Union*. In church union negotiations in the 1950s, Congregationalists had forced the issue of women's ordination in the union church as eight women had already been ordained in Congregationalism.[41] The expectation that women would be ordained in the Uniting Church influenced the sense of identity of that church, and also helped lay people to accept women ministers.[42] It is now possible to see men and women ministers working together in the church in partnership, and to hear male ministers preaching sermons informed by feminist theology.

The migration of the Kieks from England to South Australia made the ordination of women possible in Australian Congregationalism before other settler societies. Continued migration played a significant role in the ordination of 15 women in Australian Congregationalism over 50 years. While Winifred Kiek sought to extend the prophetic role, which had been developed in the women's guild system, to a wider audience, her arguments could serve not only to challenge but also to reinforce denominational perspectives and assumptions of class, race, gender and nationalism. Her advocacy of women's ordination in other denominations, for example, did not account for doctrinal conservatism. Her class assumptions could alienate women who were not middle-class and her consideration of the role of women 'pioneers' in Australian history could reinforce Australian nationalism. Furthermore, her argument about women's special contribution to the Church could serve to limit as much as to extend the roles of Congregational women ministers, with implications for the experience of later generations of women clergy. Winifred Kiek could probably have never imagined how, partly as a result of her achievements, women ministers in the Uniting Church would resent the expectation that they should argue for women's rights within the Church.[43] This assumption remains a legacy of the history of women's ordination from which we are not yet entirely free.

Bibliography

Manuscripts
Winifred Kiek papers, PRG [Private Records Group] 225, State Library of South Australia, Adelaide.

Books, articles and thesis
Australian Dictionary of Biography, Vol. 9, p. 588.
Bollen, J.D., 'English Christianity and the Australian Colonies', *Journal of Ecclesiastical History*, 28.1 (1977), pp. 361–85.
Breward, I., *Australia: 'The Most Godless Place under Heaven'?* (Melbourne: Beacon Hill Books, 1988).
——, *A History of the Australian Churches* (Sydney: Allen & Unwin, 1993).

——, *A History of the Churches in Australasia* (Oxford: Oxford University Press, 2001).

Byrnes, J.S., 'A Descriptive and Hermeneutical Consideration of the Experiences of Ordained Women in Parish Ministry' (unpublished masters dissertation, La Trobe University, 1992).

Carey, H.M., Breward, I., Doumanis, N., Frappell, R., Hilliard, D., Massam, K., O'Brien, A. and Thompson, R., 'Australian Religion Review, 1980–2000, part 2: Christian Denominations', *Journal of Religious History*, 25.1 (2001), pp. 56–82.

Cazden, E., *Antoinette Brown Blackwell: A Biography* (Old Westbury, NY: Feminist Press, 1983).

Chambers, J.B., *A Peculiar People: Congregationalism in New Zealand, 1840–1984* (Levin, NZ: Congregational Union of New Zealand, 1984).

Chaves, M., *Ordaining Women: Culture and Conflict in Religious Organisations* (Cambridge, MA: Harvard University Press, 1997).

Congregational Union of New Zealand, *Yearbooks* (Wellington, New Zealand: Congregational Union of New Zealand, 1951–69).

Dutney, A., *Where Did the Joy Come From: Revisiting the Basis of Union* (Melbourne: Uniting Church Press, 2001).

Fletcher, S., *Maude Royden: A Life* (Oxford: Basil Blackwell, 1989).

Huxtable, J., 'Ordination: Aspects of a Tradition', *Journal of the United Reformed Church History Society*, 2.4 (1979), pp. 94–107.

Jackson, H.R., 'Moving House and Changing Churches: The Cases of the Melbourne Congregationalists', *Historical Studies* 19.74 (1980), pp. 74–85.

Kaye, E., Lees, J. and Thorpe, K., *Daughters of Dissent* (London: United Reformed Church, 2004).

Knauerhase, M., *Winifred: The Story of Winifred Kiek, the First Woman to be Ordained to the Christian ministry in Australia, 1884–1975* (Adelaide: Lutheran Publishing House, 1978).

Lake, M., *Getting Equal: The History of Australian Feminism* (St Leonards, NSW: Allen & Unwin, 1999).

Lehman, E.C., *Women in Ministry: Receptivity and Resistance* (Melbourne: Joint Board of Christian Education, 1994).

Lockley, G.L., *Congregationalism in Australia*, ed. B. Upham Melbourne: Uniting Church Press, 2001).

Magarey, S., *Unbridling the Tongues of Women: A Biography of Catherine Helen Spence* (Sydney: Hale & Iremonger, 1985).

Manley, K.R., *From Woolloomooloo to 'Eternity': A History of Australian Baptists, Vol. I: Growing an Australian Church, 1831–1914* (Milton Keynes: Paternoster Press, 2006).

McHarg, T., 'The Bible Christians – A New Standard for Women in Leadership?', *Proceedings of the Uniting Church Historical Society of Victoria*, 12.2 (2005), pp. 18–43.

McNaughton, W.D., *The Scottish Congregational Ministry, 1794–1993* (Glasgow: Congregational Union of Scotland, 1993).

Munster, P., 'Notes on Aspects of Research into the History of Australian Congregationalism', *Proceedings of the Victorian Congregational Historical Society* 1.7 (1965).

Northcroft, D.M., *Women Free Church Ministers* (London: E.G. Dunstan, 1929).

O'Brien, A., *God's Willing Workers: Women and Religion in Australia* (Sydney: UNSW Press, 2005).

Phillips, W., *Edward Sidney Kiek: His Life and Thought* (Adelaide: Uniting Church Historical Society, 1981).

Pitman, J., 'Prophets and Priests: Congregational Women in Australia, 1919–1977', unpublished doctoral dissertation, University of Adelaide, 2005.

Smart, J., 'Modernity and Mother-Heartedness: Spirituality and Religious Meaning in

Australian Women's Suffrage and Citizenship Movements, 1890s–1920s', in I.C. Fletcher, L.E.N. Mayhall and P. Levine (eds), *Women's Suffrage in the British Empire: Citizenship, Nation and Race* (London and New York: Routledge, 2001), pp. 51–67.

Swain, S., 'In these Days of Female Evangelists and Hallelujah Lasses: Women Preachers and the Redefinition of Gender Roles in the Churches in Late Nineteenth-Century Australia', *Journal of Religious History*, 26.1 (2002): pp. 65–77.

Taylor, J.H., 'Ordination among Us', *Transactions of the Congregational Historical Society*, 20.7 (1968), pp. 210–22.

Thompson, R.C., *Religion in Australia: A History* (Melbourne: Oxford University Press, 1994).

Thorpe, K.E., 'Gender and Ministry: The Experience of Early Women Congregational Ministers', unpublished doctoral dissertation, University of Manchester, 2005.

Van der Linde, H.W.D., 'The Admission of Women to Ecclesiastical Offices in the Congregational Church: A Study of the Ministry of the Congregational Church of Southern Africa up to the Uniting Assembly of 1967', unpublished masters dissertation, University of South Africa, 1998.

Welter, B., 'The Cult of True Womanhood, 1820–1860', *American Quarterly*, 18.2, Part 1 (1966).

Wilkinson, P., 'The Selfless and the Helpless: Maternalist Origins of the US Welfare State', *Feminist Studies*, 25.3 (1999), pp. 571–97.

Zink-Sawyer, B.A., *From Preachers to Suffragists: Woman's Rights and Religious Conviction in the Lives of Three Nineteenth-Century American Clergywomen* (Louisville, KY and London: Westminster John Knox Press, 2003).

Newspapers and journals
Australasian Intercollegian, 1 October 1921.
Australian Christian World, 28 July 1939.
Church and Nation, 6 November 1991.
Congregationalist [New South Wales], 8 November 1934.
SA Congregationalist, 1920–48.
Vote (organ of the Woman's Freedom League [London]), 1926–31.
White Ribbon Signal, 1 May 1933.

Notes

1 This chapter has been peer-reviewed and is deemed to meet the definition of original research required of scholars by the Department of Education, Science and Training of the Australian Federal Government.

2 M. Knauerhase, *Winifred: The Story of Winifred Kiek, the First Woman to be Ordained to the Christian Ministry in Australia, 1884–1975* (Adelaide: Lutheran Publishing House, 1978); *Australian Dictionary of Biography*, vol. 9, p. 588.

3 K.E. Thorpe, 'Gender and Ministry: The Experience of Early Women Congregational Ministers', unpublished doctoral dissertation, University of Manchester, 2005; J. Pitman, 'Prophets and Priests: Congregational Women in Australia, 1919–1977', unpublished doctoral dissertation, University of Adelaide, 2005.

4 B. Welter, 'The Cult of True Womanhood, 1820–1860', *American Quarterly* 18.2, part 1 (1966), pp. 151–74.

5 E. Cazden, *Antoinette Brown Blackwell: A Biography* (Old Westbury, NY: Feminist Press, 1983).

6 S. Fletcher, *Maude Royden: A Life* (Oxford: Basil Blackwell, 1989); E. Kaye, J. Lees and K. Thorpe, *Daughters of Dissent* (London: United Reformed Church, 2004).

7 I. Breward, *Australia: 'The Most Godless Place under Heaven'?* (Melbourne: Beacon Hill Books, 1988).

8   I. Breward, *A History of the Australian Churches* (Sydney: Allen & Unwin, 1993); I. Breward, *A History of the Churches in Australasia* (Oxford: Oxford University Press, 2001); R.C. Thompson, *Religion in Australia: A History* (Melbourne: Oxford University Press, 1994).

9   A. O'Brien, *God's Willing Workers: Women and Religion in Australia* (Sydney: UNSW Press, 2005).

10 M. Lake, *Getting Equal: The History of Australian Feminism* (St Leonards, NSW: Allen & Unwin, 1999).

11 H.M. Carey, I. Breward, N. Doumanis, R. Frappell, D. Hilliard, K. Massam, A. O'Brien and R. Thompson, 'Australian Religion Review, 1980–2000, Part 2: Christian Denominations', *Journal of Religious History*, 25.1 (2001), pp. 56–82; J. Smart, 'Modernity and Mother-heartedness: Spirituality and Religious Meaning in Australian Women's Suffrage and Citizenship Movements, 1890s–1920s', in I.C. Fletcher, L.E. N. Mayhall and P. Levine (eds), *Women's Suffrage in the British Empire: Citizenship, Nation and Race* (London and New York: Routledge, 2001), pp. 51–67.

12 W. Phillips, *Edward Sidney Kiek: His Life and Thought* (Adelaide: Uniting Church Historical Society, 1981).

13 *Vote*, 17 June 1927, p. 186.

14 S. Magarey, *Unbridling the Tongues of Women: A Biography of Catherine Helen Spence* (Sydney: Hale & Iremonger, 1985); T. McHarg, 'The Bible Christians – A New Standard for Women in Leadership?', *Proceedings of the Uniting Church Historical Society of Victoria*, 12.2 (2005), pp. 18–43.

15 S. Swain, 'In these Days of Female Evangelists and Hallelujah Lasses: Women Preachers and the Redefinition of Gender Roles in the Churches in late Nineteenth-Century Australia', *Journal of Religious History*, 26.1 (2002), pp. 65–77; K.R. Manley, *From Woolloomooloo to 'Eternity': A History of Australian Baptists, vol. I: Growing an Australian Church, 1831–1914* (Milton Keynes: Paternoster Press, 2006), pp. 211–16, 304.

16 M. Chaves, *Ordaining Women: Culture and Conflict in Religious Organisations* (Cambridge, MA: Harvard University Press, 1997).

17 J.H. Taylor, 'Ordination among Us', *Transactions of the Congregational Historical Society*, 20.7 (1968), pp. 210–22; J. Huxtable, 'Ordination: Aspects of a Tradition', *Journal of the United Reformed Church History Society*, 2.4 (1979), pp. 94–107.

18 J.D. Bollen, 'English Christianity and the Australian Colonies', *Journal of Ecclesiastical History*, 28.1 (1977), pp. 361–85.

19 G.L. Lockley, *Congregationalism in Australia*, ed. B. Upham (Melbourne: Uniting Church Press, 2001); P. Munster, 'Notes on Aspects of Research into the History of Australian Congregationalism', *Proceedings of the Victorian Congregational Historical Society*, 1.7 (1965).

20 D.M. Northcroft, *Women Free Church Ministers* (London: E.G. Dunstan, 1929), p. 17.

21 Northcroft, *Women Free Church Ministers*, p. 5.

22 J.B. Chambers, *A Peculiar People: Congregationalism in New Zealand, 1840–1984* (Levin, NZ: Congregational Union of New Zealand, 1984), pp. 73–6, 156, 375; W.D. McNaughton, *The Scottish Congregational Ministry, 1794–1993* (Glasgow: Congregational Union of Scotland, 1993), p. 274.

23 Congregational Union of New Zealand, *Yearbooks* (1951–69).

24 H.W.D. Van der Linde, 'The Admission of Women to Ecclesiastical Offices in the Congregational Church: A Study of the Ministry of the Congregational Church of Southern Africa up to the Uniting Assembly of 1967', unpublished masters dissertation, University of South Africa, 1998, pp. 1–2, 14, 30, 33.

25 *Australasian Intercollegian* (1921), pp. 190–91.

26 *Australasian Intercollegian* (1921), p. 191.

27 *Australasian Intercollegian* (1921), pp. 190–91.

28 B.A. Zink-Sawyer, *From Preachers to Suffragists: Woman's Rights and Religious Conviction in the Lives of Three Nineteenth-Century American Clergywomen* (Louisville, KY and London: Westminster John Knox Press, 2003).

29 *Australasian Intercollegian* (1921), p. 190.

30 Kiek to Bedome, 11 March 1927, W. Kiek Papers, PRG 225/2, State Library of South Australia, Adelaide.

31 O'Brien, *God's Willing Workers*, pp. 11–2.

32 T.H. Coates, 'The Formation of Australian Church Women', 28 June 1963, Kiek Papers, PRG 225/9.

33 *SA Congregationalist*, January/February 1948, p. 203.

34 *Congregationalist* (New South Wales), 8 November 1934, p. 18.

35 *Australian Christian World*, 28 July 1939, p. 6; Kiek Papers, PRG 225/15.

36 *Vote*, 3 July 1931, pp. 213, 215.

37 *White Ribbon Signal*, 1 May 1933, p. 92.

38 P. Wilkinson, 'The Selfless and the Helpless: Maternalist Origins of the US Welfare State', *Feminist Studies*, 25.3 (1999), pp. 571–97.

39 Kiek Papers, Women Pioneers' Address (11 November 1936), PRG 225/14; *SA Congregationalist* (September 1936), p. 188.

40 *Church and Nation*, 6 November 1991, pp. 7, 9.

41 A. Dutney, *Where did the Joy Come from: Revisiting the Basis of Union* (Melbourne: Uniting Church Press, 2001), pp. 3–4.

42 E.C. Lehman, *Women in Ministry: Receptivity and Resistance* (Melbourne: Joint Board of Christian Education, 1994), p. 120.

43 J.S. Byrnes, 'A Descriptive and Hermeneutical Consideration of the Experiences of Ordained Women in Parish Ministry', unpublished masters dissertation, La Trobe University, 1992, pp. 235–41.

7

Women and Ministry within the British Unitarian Movement

Ann Peart

In 2004 British Unitarians celebrated the centenary of the recognition of the first woman to acquire full status as a Unitarian minister in England. This essay considers some of the conditions within the Unitarian movement that led up to this, both those which were helpful and those which hindered the recognition, and briefly reviews the numbers of women ministers in the following century. Although the histories of British Unitarianism still largely ignore women,[1] articles about particular women have appeared in the *Transactions of the Unitarian Historical Society*[2] and several events were held to mark the centenary of the induction of Gertrude von Petzold as the first fully recognized minister in 1904.[3] Kathryn Gleadle has written on radical women who left the Unitarian movement, while Ruth Watts has written extensively on Unitarian women and education,[4] and I have written a general article on women within Unitarianism.[5] Other twentieth-century biographies of Unitarian women have concentrated on their achievements outside the movement, and have had little to contribute on the role of women within Unitarianism.[6] Apart from the work on von Petzold and some references in *Growing Together*, a Unitarian feminist theology report,[7] very little has been written directly on Unitarian women and ministerial recognition.

The position of Unitarianism on the liberal end of the Christian spectrum is significant for its attitude to women. Although the oldest congregations now calling themselves Unitarian date back to the seventeenth century, most of them did not claim the Unitarian title until after theological debates in the eighteenth century had led to the rejection of the doctrine of the Trinity as unbiblical, and passing of the Trinity Act in 1813, which extended the protection of the Toleration Act to Unitarians. During the nineteenth century the traditional emphasis on enlightened reason was joined by recognition of the authority of conscience rather than external teaching, and an appreciation of the developing biblical criticism.

Unitarians' emphasis on the importance of education is of great significance for women. The tradition of rationality in matters of belief led to the need to cultivate the rational mind of both men and women. Joseph Priestley, a prominent Unitarian minister, wrote in 1790, '[Women should be given] the highest [education] of which they were capable ... the learned and the modern languages ... mathematics and philosophy. Certainly the minds of women are capable of the same improvement and the same furniture as those of men'.[8] Though, as Harriet Martineau noted 30 years later, as long as girls and boys were educated in the same way, their achievements were similar; however, the opportunities open to women were not the same as those for men.[9] Many Unitarian ministers taught both boys and girls, and gave lectures to both women and men, but the dissenting academies, which provided higher and professional education for men, were not open to women. Although a Unitarian woman was the main founder of Bedford College in London in 1849, it was many years before it could offer the same education that men received.

One of the main conflicts in Unitarian practice has been between the valorization of rationality, freedom and theoretical equality and the less noble desire for acceptance within English society in general and the Christian community in particular. Thus civil and religious liberty was a toast proposed at all convivial Unitarian occasions; however, this liberty was often restricted by social conventions and the need to appear 'respectable'. This burden was applied particularly to middle-class women, who were expected to conform to what became Victorian standards of propriety. Ruth Watts commented, 'because of their anxious quest for "respectability" in a world which anathematized their religious beliefs, they tended to mind the proprieties which restricted the lives of middle-class women'.[10]

Middle-class women were expected to be well enough educated to discuss serious matters, and to bring up children and run households, but they were not expected to be able to earn their living. So when the Martineau family lost their money when their textile firm failed, Harriet, whose deafness prevented her from becoming a governess or opening a school, as many of her Unitarian acquaintances did, started to sew a variety of clothing items to sell in order to make money. It was only when her brother suggested that she could earn more money by writing than she could by sewing that she concentrated on her career as a journalist and writer. If the opportunity had been open to her, she might have considered being a Unitarian minister like her brother. However, in the 1830s, it was still unusual for middle-class women to speak on public platforms, and Unitarians would not wish to be associated with the lower-class evangelical women preachers of the Methodists, as described by Chilcote and Field-Bibb.[11] This particularly concerned women who felt they had a gift for public ministry, because public speaking by women was associated with lower classes and dangerously 'enthusiastic' sects. So although in theory Unitarians identified themselves with equal rights, their nineteenth-century practices often restricted this for women, and so limited women's participation in ministry.

How did women come to gain recognition as ministers? One battle, that for higher theological education, was fought in part by a woman who had converted to Unitarianism from her evangelical Anglican roots in Ireland: Francis Power Cobbe.[12] She was a devotee of James Martineau, a prominent

Unitarian minister, who in the 1830s in Liverpool had given lectures on philo-
sophical and theological subjects to both women and men. In the 1870s,
when Manchester College, where many Unitarian ministers and lay men were
educated, was in London and James Martineau was principal, Cobbe
petitioned him to allow women to attend lectures at the college. He replied
sympathetically, but went on to state two difficulties: firstly the fact that the
college building was owned by University Hall, whose permission would be
necessary, and whose (male) students, 'think the place their own for romps
and fun'. Secondly, the small number of male Unitarian students, and the
informality of the teaching, would mean that the presence of ladies would
inhibit the 'poor shy youth'. Nevertheless, he offered to put the matter to the
college committee.[13]

Cobbe did not take no for an answer. There is an undated manuscript, in
handwriting similar to James Martineau's, headed 'list of occasional
students'; and under 'Ethics' there are seventeen names, 15 of which are
women, many recognizably Unitarian, including Miss Cobbe, Miss Lloyd
and Mrs A. Swanwick.[14] According to one college history:

> The controversy over the admission of women to the college was settled
> in London, after a resolute little company headed by Frances Power
> Cobbe and Anna Swanwick had made their way into Martineau's
> lecture-room. The debate was prolonged over two years, ending with the
> vote for admission at an adjourned meeting of the Trustees in February
> 1876.[15]

Cobbe went on to preach and conduct worship in Unitarian churches and
chapels in the London area.[16] She also wrote on the role of women in the
Church. 'Women's Work in the Church', is mainly concerned with the
Church of England and was published in *The Theological Review* in 1865.
In this Cobbe dismissed the idea of separate women's organizations and
attacked institutional religion.[17]

A second, longer, article is 'The Fitness of Women for the Ministry', first
published in *The Theological Review* in 1876 and reprinted in the collection
entitled *The Peak in Darien* in 1882. In this article, Cobbe rehearsed various
reasons why women should not be ministers, ranging from lack of education,
brains or strong voices to the fact that 'women are (thanks to all sorts of
causes, historical, political, personal with which we need not concern
ourselves) actually much *deconsidered* by men'. Would not their deconsid-
eration be reflected on Religion itself if they were to become authorized
ministers? she asked.[18] She went on to note that, 'the Broad Church school
has been trying to efface the stamp of effeminacy from their order, to
cultivate "Muscular Christianity", and make lay men of the order of the
author of *Sword and Gown* remember that a priest is not necessarily on old
woman'.[19] Cobbe recognized that many of these problems could be
overcome: only particularly able women would get through the selection and
training at places like Manchester New College, and some women had
some advantages over many men. Thus she considered that women could be

better at expressing ideas and oratory, and that their ready sympathy and 'special facilities' would give them an advantage in pastoral matters.[20] Women she thought were also better at practical acts of religious duty and living by their conscience.[21] The last section introduced what would now be called feminist theology, seeing female qualities in both Jesus Christ and God. Cobbe ended her article with a plea both for women ministers and for the expression of more motherly aspects of God.

While twenty-first-century feminists would want to take issue with Cobbe's assumptions about the nature of gender differences, and about qualities of motherhood, most would also recognize that her writing was considerably in advance of most people's thought:

> If there be, then, as I humbly believe and trust, in the nature of our great Parent above, certain characters of tenderness and sympathy with His creatures which are more perfectly shadowed, more vividly reflected, in the love of human mothers for their children than by aught else on earth, if there be, in short, a real meaning to the old lesson that God created Woman as well as Man in His own image, – the image being only complete in the complete Humanity, – then I think it follows that there is urgent need that woman's idea of God should have its place in all our teachings of religion.[22]

Unitarians continued to wrestle with almost identical ideas a hundred years later.[23] In the second part of the nineteenth century Cobbe's advocacy of opening the ministry to women was undoubtedly influential, especially amongst Unitarians.

Cobbe was not the only woman to preach in Unitarian churches and chapels, and to act unofficially as minister. British Unitarians learned of women ministers in America, including Antoinette Brown, who was ordained by the Congregationalists in 1853, though she became Unitarian after a few years;[24] Lydia Ann Jenkins who was officially sanctioned by the Universalist Church in 1858;[25] and Olympia Brown, who knew and was inspired by Antoinette Brown (no relation) entered the Universalist ministry in 1863, and is widely acclaimed as the first woman ordained by full denominational authority rather than by a local congregation or district.[26] By 1870 five women had been accepted by the Unitarians and Universalists; in the next 20 years this grew to 70 women ordained, but not all had paid pastorates. There was a concentration of women ministers in the small congregations of Iowa, where there was a shortage of ministers, and very few women ministered in the more comfortable and popular East Coast.[27] Meanwhile, in Australia in 1873 Martha Turner became minister of the Melbourne Unitarian Church. Turner came to Britain ten years later, and preached in many English and Scottish congregations.

The Scottish connection was significant, in that there was already one woman Universalist minister in Scotland: Caroline Soule. Caroline Soule was an American by birth, the widow of a Universalist minister. She organized the first national women's group within the Universalists, the Women's Centenary Aid Association, which raised funds and did practical work. The experience of public speaking that this involved led her to start preaching. In 1875 she travelled in England and Scotland, where she helped to organize the Universalist Convention and returned as a missionary for the Women's Centenary Association. She became minister of the Universalist Church in Glasgow, where she was ordained in March 1880 at the age of 56.[28] This was possibly the first formal ordination of a woman minister in Britain. Soule ministered until her retirement in 1892, and for a time had pastoral oversight of the Dundee Unitarian Church while its minister was away.[29]

Therefore, while there were no fully recognized women ministers in England, women's ministry was still not completely unknown. Added to this were the numerous occasions, mainly unrecorded, when women did the minister's job, not just visiting and so on, but also preaching. When Lucretia Mott, the American Quaker anti-slavery campaigner came to England on a speaking tour in 1840, she spoke from several Unitarian pulpits.[30] Later women on rare occasions conducted worship and preached (the example of Frances Power Cobbe has already been cited). Mrs R. J. Jones, still spoken of with respect in Aberdare, South Wales, was active in educational, philanthropic and political spheres and also, according to her 1899 obituary, 'When her husband was prevented from preaching, she often occupied the pulpit for him.'[31] Women's speaking in church was not restricted to the middle classes. For instance, George Fox, minister from 1857 to 1865 of the working-class Methodist Unitarian congregation in Mossley, Lancashire, wrote that 'From their connection with Methodism, quite a number of people, both men and women, could pray and speak at meetings.'[32]

But speaking at meeting, or even preaching, is of course by no means the same as being recognized as a minister. Unitarians had prided themselves on having a learned ministry, and for this a formal higher education was seen to be required. The opening of Manchester College to women occasional students in 1876 has already been noted. In 1892 the college formally accepted two of the American women ministers for a year's study and was even prepared to grant them a certificate. This was one of the factors that encouraged Gertrude von Petzold to apply for ministerial training in 1897. It is no coincidence that the first woman to go through the long formal training for full ministerial recognition was a foreigner. She had left behind the constraints of her own family and society, and was less bound by British conventions than were native women.

Gertrude von Petzold was born in what was then Thorn in east Prussia in 1876. She came to Britain in 1894 as a newly qualified teacher in order to gain a higher education. She was interested in matters of faith and theology, and felt a call to the ministry, though she seems to have had no experience of a Unitarian congregation. She embarked on an arts degree at St Andrews University, Scotland, and then applied for entry as a ministry student to Manchester College, in Oxford. She was awarded a bursary and then went on to read moral philosophy at St Andrews and later to do an MA in classical languages at Edinburgh University, all the while receiving grants from Manchester College. After the acceptance of von Petzold as an external exhibitioner in 1897, the various committees and subcommittees of the college had struggled to decide on a policy about accepting women students for the ministry. They came eventually to the conclusion that each case should be judged on its merits, but considered that only exceptional women would warrant full theological training.[33]

In 1901 von Petzold finally took her place in Oxford as a regular student for the ministry. She was the only one who was not in residence in college, but there was another woman, Harriet Johnson, who was admitted to classes, though not apparently for ministerial training. The college appeared to be gracious in its welcome, with the President, William Colfox, stating 'She is cordially welcomed to the class-rooms of the college, and the committee hope that her career within its walls may lead to successful work in a ministry in which there is room for the high religious influence of cultured womanhood.'[34] However, she received a very mixed reception. Some of the male students refused to let her sit at the same table in the dining hall, but she did not let incidents like this deter her. During her training she was already in demand as a guest preacher, so fears that she would have difficulty finding a ministerial appointment were unfounded. Out of a field of nine candidates she was chosen unanimously as minister of the Narborough Road Church in Leicester in 1904. Here she ministered successfully for four years, before spending two years in America. She returned to minister in Birmingham, until at the outbreak of the First World War, when she was deported, since she had not completed naturalization papers. During the years up to 1914 she preached and spoke at meetings and churches throughout Britain, in Germany and in America.

Meanwhile, other women had been accepted as lay pastors, and were doing the work of ministry. One woman, Rosalind Lee, started with a lay charge, and became district minister in South Wales in 1932 – probably the first woman to attain a senior position. Margaret Crook was the second woman to go through the full training at Oxford, from 1915 to 1918, but only ministered for two years before emigrating to America for family reasons. Between 1920 and 1927, six women ministers were trained at Oxford, and most had long and successful ministries. At this point the college council decided that it was 'too difficult to have a small group of women in a community of men', and suspended the acceptance of women students until they could make better provision for them, the next woman being accepted in 1936. Meanwhile, at Unitarian College in Manchester four women were trained between 1928 and 1936.[35] The principal was not enthusiastic. He felt that he ought to admit women students on the grounds of natural justice; however, he was wary of having too many, as he was afraid that congregations would be unwilling to appoint them.

How much congregational polity was an excuse rather than a reason I have yet to discover. Chaves has commented on the freedom that congregational polity gave for individual congregations to appoint ministers in America.[36] Unitarian ambivalence to women ministers is partly explained by Chaves' concept of loose coupling: i.e. a dissonance between formal rules and actual practice. The movement wanted to appear progressive and enlightened, and to support women's rights, and so was proud to appear to promote women as ministers, but the less articulated social pressures to conform to norms of middle-class respectability acted as a significant restraining influence.

When looking at figures it is important to bear in mind how small the Unitarian movement is: there are currently fewer than 200 congregations in the UK, and fewer than 150 ministers (including those retired). The actual number of women ministers appointed to congregations increased from three in 1920 to eight in 1933 (when there was a total of 20 churches with a woman minister in the UK) to 15 during the Second World War, when there was probably a shortage of men. After the war the backlash against women in work affected ministers. One woman was trained during the war, and only one in the 1950s. Six were recognized in the 1960s and five in the 1970s. By the time I trained in the 1980s about one-eighth of Unitarian ministers were women; now the proportion is about a third. The big change over the last 20 years has been the impact of second-wave feminism, with its influence on both thought and practice. Since the 1980s there has been an agreed policy that our ministry is open to people regardless of sex, race, or sexual orientation, but while the power to appoint its minister rests with each congregation, individual pockets of discrimination can still occur.

This broad picture seems to have commonalities with other nonconformist denominations; notably the Baptists, with their similar congregational ecclesiology, and where less emphasis on civil rights is balanced by less need to conform to middle-class respectability.[37] The significance of the centralized organization of the Methodists and the Church of England together with different notions of 'priesthood' are discussed in Field-Bibb and Gill, and the Congregationalist story has been well documented and discussed by Kaye et al.[38] The Unitarians' earlier formal recognition of women's ministry has much to do with the enlightenment legacy of prioritizing rationality, education and equality, and Victorian ideas of progress; but equally Victorian ideas of middle-class propriety and emphasis on an educated ministry rather than one empowered by the spirit disadvantaged Unitarian women compared with Baptists and Congregationalists.[39] Nevertheless, the past 102 years, since the recognition of Gertrude von Petzold, have seen the broad acceptance of women ministers within Unitarianism, and though I am the first woman to be principal of one of our theological colleges, I don't expect to be the last.

Bibliography

Manuscripts
Harris Manchester College, Oxford
    J. Martineau 15
    MNC Misc. 12, 85
    MNC Minute Books, N, O.
Huntington Library, San Marino, CA, Frances Power Cobbe collection.

Books and articles

Bolam, C.G, Goring, Jeremy, Short, H.L. and Thomas, R., *The English Presbyterians: From Elizabethan Puritanism to Modern Unitarianism* (London: George Allen & Unwin, 1968).

Chaves, M., *Ordaining Women: Culture and Conflict in Religious Organizations* (Cambridge, MA: Harvard University Press, 1997).

Chilcote, P.W., *She Offered them Christ: The Legacy of Women Preachers in Early Methodism* (Nashville, TN: Abingdon Press, 1993).

Cobbe, F.P., 'The Fitness of Women for the Ministry of Religion', in *The Peak in Darien, with Some other Inquiries Touching Concerns of the Soul and the Body* (London: Williams & Norgate, 1882), pp. 199–262.

——, *Life of Frances Power Cobbe by Herself*, 2 vols (London: Richard Bentley, 1894).

——, *The Kingdom of God: A Sermon* (privately printed for Frances Power Cobbe, 1901).

Croft, J. (ed.), *Growing Together: The Report of the Unitarian Working Party on Feminist Theology* (London: General Assembly of Unitarian and Free Christian Churches, 1984).

Davis, V.D., *A History of Manchester College from its Foundation in Manchester to its Establishment in Oxford* (London: George Allen & Unwin, 1932).

Field-Bibb, J., *Women towards Priesthood: Ministerial Politics and Feminist Praxis.* (Cambridge: Cambridge University Press, 1991).

Gill, S., *Women and the Church of England: From the Eighteenth Century to the Present* (London: SPCK, 1994).

Gilley, K., 'Gertrude von Petzold – the Pioneer Woman Minister', *Transactions of the Unitarian Historical Society*, 21.3 (1997), pp. 157–72.

——, *Gertrude von Petzold* (London: General Assembly of Unitarian and Free Christian Churches, 2004).

Gleadle, K., *The Early Feminists: Radical Unitarians and the Emergence of the Women's Rights Movement 1831–1851* (London: Macmillan, 1995).

Gouldbourne, R.M.B., *Reinventing the Wheel: Women and Ministry in English Baptist Life* (Oxford: Whitley, 1997).

Harris, M.W., *Historical Dictionary of Unitarian Universalism* (Lanham, MD, and Oxford: Scarecrow Press, 2004).

Hitchings, C.F., *Universalist and Unitarian Women Ministers*, 2nd edn (Boston, MA: Unitarian Universalist Historical Society, 1985).

Kaye, E., Lees, J. and Thorpe, K., *Daughters of Dissent* (London: United Reformed Church, 2004).

Manton, J., *Mary Carpenter and the Children of the Streets* (London: Heinemann, 1976).

Martineau, H. (under the pen-name Discipulus), 'Female Writers on Practical Divinity', *The Monthly Repository*, 17 (1882), pp. 593–7, 746–50.

McCarthy, W. and E. Kraft (eds), *The Poems of Anna Letitia Barbauld* (Athens, GA: University of Georgia Press, 1994).

—— (eds), *Anna Letitia Barbauld: Selected Poetry and Prose* (Ontario: Broadview Press, 2002).

Mitchell, S., *Frances Power Cobbe: Victorian Feminist, Journalist, Reformer* (Charlottesville, VA: University of Virginia Press, 2004).

Peacock, S.J., *The Theological and Ethical Writings of Frances Power Cobbe, 1822–1904,* (Lampeter: Edwin Mellen Press, 2002).

Peart, A., 'Forgotten Prophets: Unitarian Women and Religion', in George D. Chryssides (ed.), *Unitarian Perspectives on Contemporary Religious Thought* (London: Lindsey Press, 1999), pp. 61–76.

——, 'Gertrude von Petzold 1876–1952', keynote address at conference celebrating women and ministry 2 October 2004, organized by the Ecumenical Network for Women in Ministry.

Rodgers, B., *Georgian Chronicle: Mrs Barbauld and her Family* (London: Methuen, 1958).

Ruston, A., 'Clementia Taylor (1819–1908)', *Transactions of the Unitarian Historical Society*, 20.1 (1991), pp. 121–42.

Smith, L., *The Unitarians: A Short History* (Arnside: Lensden, 2006).

Stinchcombe, O., 'Elizabeth Malleson (1828–1916) and Unitarianism', *Transactions of the Unitarian Historical Society*, 20.1 (1991), pp. 56–61.

Tolles, F.B. (ed.), *Slavery and 'The Woman Question': Lucretia Mott's Diary of her Visit to Great Britain to Attend the World's Anti-Slavery Convention of 1840* (London: Friends' Historical Society, 1952).

Tucker, C.G., *Prophetic Sisterhood: Liberal Women Ministers of the Frontier, 1880–1930* (Boston, MA: Beacon Press, 1990).

Unitarian Renewal Group, *Viewsletter* (spring, 2005).

Unitarian Universalist Women's Heritage Society, *Notable Universalist and Unitarian Women* (Medford, MA: Unitarian Universalist Women's Heritage Society, 1997).

Wakefield, D., *Anna Laetitia Barbauld* (London: Centaur Press, 2001).

Watts, R., 'The Unitarian Contribution to the Development of Female Education 1790–1850', *History of Education*, 9 (1980), pp. 273–86.

——, 'Rational Dissent and the Emancipation of Women, 1780–1860', *Faith and Freedom*, 9.113 (summer 1985), pp. 71–82.

——, 'Knowledge is Power – Unitarians, Gender and Education in the Eighteenth and Early Nineteenth Centuries', *Gender and Education*, 1 (1989), pp. 35–50.

——, 'Education and Cultural Transfer: The Case of Unitarian Women from the Late Eighteenth Century to 1869', *History of Education Society Bulletin*, 55 (1995), pp. 11–19.

——, *Gender, Power and the Unitarians in England 1760–1860* (London: Longman, 1998).

——, 'Mary Carpenter: Educator of the Children of the "Perishing and Dangerous Classes"', in Mary Hilton and Pam Hirsh (eds), *Practical Visionaries: Women, Education and Social Progress 1790–1930*, (London: Longman/Pearson Education, 2000), pp. 39–51.

——, 'Rational Religion and Feminism: The Challenge of Unitarianism in the Nineteenth Century', in Sue Morgan (ed.), *Women, Religion and Feminism in Britain, 1750–1900* (Basingstoke: Palgrave Macmillan, 2002), pp. 39–52.

Wilbur, E.M., *A History of Unitarianism in Transylvania, England, and America*, 2nd edn, 2 vols (Boston, MA: Beacon Press, 1969).

Newspapers
The Inquirer, obituary of Mrs R.J. Jones (18 March, 1899), p. 167.

Notes

1   Charles G. Bolam, Jeremy Goring, Harry L. Short and Roger Thomas, *The English Presbyterians: From Elizabethan Puritanism to Modern Unitarianism* (London: George Allen & Unwin, 1968); Earl M. Wilbur, *A History of Unitarianism in Transylvania, England, and America*, 2 vols, 2nd edn (Boston, MA: Beacon Press, 1969); L. Smith, *The Unitarians: A Short History* (Arnside: Lensden, 2006).

2   O. Stinchcombe, 'Elizabeth Malleson (1828–1916) and Unitarianism', *Transactions of the Unitarian Historical Society*, 20.1 (1991), pp. 56–61; A. Ruston, 'Clementia Taylor (1819–1908)', *Transactions of the Unitarian Historical Society*, 20.1 (1991), pp. 121–42; K. Gilley, 'Gertrude von Petzold – the Pioneer Woman Minister', *Transactions of the Unitarian Historical Society*, 21.3 (1997), pp. 157–72.

3   Gilley, 'Gertrude von Petzold'; Ann Peart, 'Gertrude von Petzold 1876–1952', keynote

address at conference celebrating women and ministry, 2 October organized by the Ecumenical Network for Women in Ministry; Unitarian Renewal Group, *Viewsletter* (spring, 2005).

4   Kathryn Gleadle, *The Early Feminists: Radical Unitarians and the Emergence of the Women's Rights Movement 1831–1851* (London: Macmillan, 1995); R. Watts, 'The Unitarian Contribution to the Development of Female Education 1790–1850', *History of Education*, 9 (1980), pp. 273–86; Ruth Watts, 'Rational Dissent and the Emancipation of Women, 1780–1860', *Faith and Freedom*, 9.113 (summer 1985), pp. 71–82; Ruth Watts, 'Knowledge is Power – Unitarians, Gender and Education in the Eighteenth and Early Nineteenth Centuries', *Gender and Education*, 1 (1989), pp. 35–50; Ruth Watts, 'Education and Cultural Transfer: The Case of Unitarian Women from the Late Eighteenth Century to 1869', *History of Education Society Bulletin*, 55 (1995), pp. 11–19; Ruth Watts, *Gender, Power and the Unitarians in England 1760–1860* (Harlow: Longman, 1998); Ruth Watts, 'Mary Carpenter: Educator of the Children of the "Perishing and Dangerous Classes"', in Mary Hilton and Pam Hirsh (eds), *Practical Visionaries: Women, Education and Social Progress 1790–1930*, (Harlow: Longman/Pearson Education, 2000), pp. 39–51; Ruth Watts, 'Rational Religion and Feminism: The Challenge of Unitarianism in the Nineteenth Century', in Sue Morgan (ed.), *Women, Religion and Feminism in Britain, 1750–1900* (Basingstoke: Palgrave Macmillan, 2002), pp. 39–52.

5   Ann Peart, 'Forgotten Prophets: Unitarian Women and Religion', in George D. Chryssides (ed.), *Unitarian Perspectives on Contemporary Religious Thought* (London: Lindsey Press, 1999), pp. 61–76.

6   Jo Manton, *Mary Carpenter and the Children of the Streets* (London: Heinemann, 1976); William McCarthy and Elizabeth Kraft (eds), *The Poems of Anna Letitia Barbauld* (Athens, GA: University of Georgia Press, 1994); Betsy Rodgers, *Georgian Chronicle: Mrs Barbauld and her Family* (London: Methuen, 1958); Dick Wakefield, *Anna Laetitia Barbauld* (London: Centaur Press, 2001).

7   J. Croft (ed.), *Growing Together: The Report of the Unitarian Working Party on Feminist Theology* (London: General Assembly of Unitarian and Free Christian Churches, 1984).

8   Watts, *Gender, Power and the Unitarians in England*, p. 13.

9   Harriet Martineau (under the pen name Discipulus), 'Female Writers on Practical Divinity', *The Monthly Repository*, 17 (1882), pp. 593–7, 746–50.

10 Watts, 'Rational Religion and Feminism', p. 41.

11 Paul W. Chilcote, *She Offered them Christ: The Legacy of Women Preachers in Early Methodism* (Nashville, TN: Abingdon Press, 1993); Jacqueline Field-Bibb, *Women Towards Priesthood: Ministerial Politics and Feminist Praxis* (Cambridge: Cambridge University Press, 1991).

12 Frances Power Cobbe, *Life of Frances Power Cobbe by Herself*, 2 vols (London: Richard Bentley, 1894).

13 Huntington Library, CB 600, James Martineau to Frances Power Cobbe (1 June 1873).

14 Harris Manchester College, Oxford (HMCO), MS James Martineau, 15, viii.

15 V.D. Davis, *A History of Manchester College from its Foundation in Manchester to its Establishment in Oxford* (London: George Allen & Unwin, 1932), p. 194.

16 Frances Power Cobbe, *The Kingdom of God: A Sermon* (privately printed for Frances Power Cobbe, 1901); Manton, *Mary Carpenter*, p. 152; Sally Mitchell, *Frances Power Cobbe: Victorian Feminist, Journalist, Reformer* (Charlottesville, VA: University of Virginia Press, 2004), pp. 213, 265; A. Ruston, conversation on 28 June 2005 about Frances Power Cobbe's Unitarian preaching and other involvement.

17 Sandra J. Peacock, *The Theological and Ethical Writings of Frances Power Cobbe, 1822–1904*, (Lampeter: Edwin Mellen Press, 2002), pp. 99–101; Mitchell, *Frances Power Cobbe*, p. 415.

18 Cobbe, 'The Fitness of Women for the Ministry of Religion', p. 219.
19 Cobbe, 'The Fitness of Women for the Ministry of Religion', p. 219.
20 Cobbe, 'The Fitness of Women for the Ministry of Religion', pp. 233–40.
21 Cobbe, 'The Fitness of Women for the Ministry of Religion', pp. 243-9.
22 Cobbe, 'The Fitness of Women for the Ministry of Religion', pp. 261–2.
23 Croft (ed.), *Growing Together*.
24 Unitarian Universalist Women's Heritage Society, *Notable Universalist and Unitarian Women* (Medford, MA: Unitarian Universalist Women's Heritage Society, 1997), p. 7.
25 Unitarian Universalist Women's Heritage Society, *Notable Universalist and Unitarian Women*, p. 9.
26 Unitarian Universalist Women's Heritage Society, *Notable Universalist and Unitarian Women*, p. 9; C.F. Hitchings, *Universalist and Unitarian Women Ministers*, 2nd edn (Boston, MA: Unitarian Universalist Historical Society, 1985), p. 31.
27 Cynthia G. Tucker, *Prophetic Sisterhood: Liberal Women Ministers of the Frontier, 1880–1930* (Boston, MA: Beacon Press, 1990), pp. 3-4.
28 Mark W. Harris, *Historical Dictionary of Unitarian Universalism* (Lanham, MD and Oxford: Scarecrow Press, 2004), pp. 438–9; Hitchings, *Universalist and Unitarian Women Ministers*, pp. 134–5.
29 K. Gilley, *Gertrude von Petzold* (London: General Assembly of Unitarian and Free Christian Churches, 2004), p. 2.
30 Frederick B. Tolles (ed.), *Slavery and 'The Woman Question': Lucretia Mott's Diary of her Visit to Great Britain to Attend the World's Anti-Slavery Convention of 1840* (London: Friends' Historical Society, 1952).
31 Obituary of Mrs R.J. Jones, *The Inquirer*, 18 March 1899, p. 167.
32 Peart, 'Forgotten Prophets', p. 70.
33 Minutes of Meeting of General Committee, Monday, 21 November 1898.
34 HMCO 1902 annual report.
35 Croft (ed.), *Growing Together*.
36 Mark Chaves, *Ordaining Women: Culture and Conflict in Religious Organizations* (Cambridge, MA: Harvard University Press, 1997), p. 140.
37 Ruth M. B. Gouldbourne, *Reinventing the Wheel: Women and Ministry in English Baptist Life* (Oxford: Whitley Publications, 1997).
38 Elaine Kaye, Janet Lees and Kirsty Thorpe, *Daughters of Dissent* (London: United Reformed Church, 2004).
39 Field-Bibb, *Women towards Priesthood*; S. Gill, *Women and the Church of England: From the Eighteenth Century to the Present* (London: SPCK, 1994); Kaye *et al.*, *Daughters of Dissent*, pp. 191–3.

8

The Ordination and Consecration of Women in the Church of Sweden

Christina Odenberg

Prior to the inauguration of the World Council of Churches at the worldwide church assembly in Amsterdam in 1948, a survey was sent to member churches asking (amongst other things) about the role of women within the churches. The question of women in the Church was clearly timely, since the response was overwhelming. The results were reported in a book, edited by Kathleen Bliss, entitled *The Service and Status of Women within the Churches*.[1] At the opening of the Amsterdam Assembly itself, groups from the participating nations were introduced. When it came to the turn of the Swedish delegation (and its one and only woman), the introduction spoke volumes about the position of women in its churches: 'Margit Sahlin from the Church of Sweden – the worst in the world'. From this unpromising start, how did the Church of Sweden progress towards having women as both priests and bishops? This essay offers a brief outline of the history, albeit from my own perspective as someone who has been intimately involved in that story throughout my ministry.

The Church of Sweden is an Evangelical Lutheran Church, a member of the Lutheran World Federation and (until 1 January 2000) the established state church in Sweden. Surveys regularly suggest that Sweden is amongst the most secular countries in the world (in 1990 only 15 per cent of the adult population professed belief in a personal God, and only 4 per cent attended church weekly). Nevertheless, church membership remains high (80 per cent of the population) – partly because, until 1996, membership was automatically conferred at birth (unless both parents were non-members).[2] Being the established state church for much of its history meant that until recently, church law was made jointly by the government, the Riksdag (the Swedish parliament) and the Church Assembly (although the latter took responsibility for internal church affairs and retained a veto over laws concerning the Church). Until the Church gained greater independence from the state in 1983, the power to convene a general meeting of the Church Assembly also resided solely with the Minister for Church Affairs. Constitutionally, this was to take place at least every sixth year, but also as frequently as desired. Far from being incidental, these constitutional arrangements exerted significant influence on the Church of Sweden's journey to

women's ordination as priests and bishops, since it was unable to act without
state approval. Having said that, it is wrong to suppose that the eventual
decision to ordain women as priests in 1958 came about solely through
government intervention. Sometimes, those who have objected to this reform
have spoken as though the Church of Sweden was taken totally by surprise,
its wishes overrun by the Riksdag and the government; a poor little church
with no opportunity to discuss the matter in peace and quiet. As this chapter
will show, this was not actually the case.

*   *   *

The issue of women priests was raised in Sweden for the first time in the
1860s. At that time, of course, the prospect was unrealistic: women had
neither the vote nor access to higher education. However, consideration of
women's ordination began to gather pace during the early twentieth century.
In 1916 an article entitled 'Kvinnan och prästbristen' [Woman and the
Shortage of Priests] was published. Three years later a motion on women's
access to priestly service came before the Riksdag for the first time. In the
same year, 1919, the question was considered again as a result of a state
investigation into 'Behörighetslagen' (the 'law of competence'), which
considered women's access to various occupational positions within the
state sector. The investigation committee published its report in 1921,
arguing in favour of a change in the law that would give women the right
to employment as priests. The proposal was circulated for debate. At the
University of Lund, the Faculty of Theology was unanimously in favour,
expressing its conviction of the value of developing the role of women in the
church. It also stated that there was no reason for hindering women's
admission to the priesthood in principle, although some practical issues
required further investigation.

There now followed a series of shortlived attempts to advance the
prospects of women's ordination. In 1923 a further official report was
published, signed by one of my predecessors as Bishop of Lund, which
unanimously endorsed women's competence for priestly office, though with
some reservations: first, it suggested that women priests should only work
in parishes where an ordained male colleague was also present and where
the parochial church council (PCC) was in favour.[3] However, no measures
were taken. In 1938 six of the major women's organizations in Sweden wrote
to the government requesting an enquiry into access to the priesthood for
women. Again, no measures were taken. At the Church Assembly of 1938,
a committee considering a motion written by rector Manfred Björkquist
about 'Ny kvinnlig tjänst i kyrkan' ('a new female ministry in the Church')
again found no reason why women should not be admitted to the priesthood,
but favoured (for reasons of suitability) a proposal to create a separate
'order' of ministry for women. Following a long and lively debate, the
Church Assembly decided to ask the government to establish an enquiry into
the need for, and inauguration of, a new, specifically female, ministry in the
Church. No measures were taken. At the 1941 meeting of the Church

Assembly, Bishops Rodhe and Aulén submitted a further motion requesting the establishment of several 'travelling secretary' posts in the church at national level. The Church Assembly passed the motion, and recorded:

> it is inevitable that qualified female workers must to a larger extent than at present be made available to the church ... This demand is not founded on any claims by women to formal equality with men with regard to the church, but is based on urgent needs for extended and deeper female contributions to the work of the church.

The Church Assembly requested an investigation, but no measures were taken. The lack of women's positions in our Church up to the end of the Second World War was exemplified by the events of a Women's Assembly meeting held in Stockholm in April 1945. In preparation for the peace treaty that would end six years of war, the Assembly's discussions centred around the subject 'As the New World of Peace is planned'. Significantly, the Church was not invited to the conference, did not feature in any discussion and no church representatives were present.

Though progress had been slow to this point, however, events were about to change. In 1945 the Riksdag passed a new Equal Rights Law, which amongst other things provided for women's equal access to state employment. Though church posts were explicitly excluded from the legislation, it gave new impetus to discussions about women's ordination. The same year, a female theologian, Margit Sahlin (who later became together with two others our first ordained woman priest), was employed for the first time at a senior level in the church at Diakonistyrelsen as a travelling secretary for women and youth work. Significantly, the post was financed by the Church's women's sewing clubs, to whom an appeal for support had been made. In 1946, church leaders and theologians were invited to a meeting on the subject of 'the Church and the Ministry'. At that meeting, it was stated that

> with regard to the opening of the historically given priesthood to women it is, although there is no hindrance of either an exegetical or a dogmatic nature, necessary with regard to the tradition from the Early Church and for ecumenical reasons, that this question, following a thorough investigation, should be submitted to an ecumenical meeting.

Furthermore,

> the position of the Church of Sweden in the contemporary period strongly underlines the need for an immediate establishment of a full time ministry for women within the church, confirmed by ordination by a bishop and with the purpose of preaching and pastoral care, but without the ministry of the sacraments.

This final clause was a concession made not on theological grounds but out of regard for those who could not accept women performing a full priestly ministry. At the Church Assembly the same year, a new motion was submitted, calling for the opening-up of the priesthood to women or the establishment of a new church ministry for women. As a result, a committee of 15, chaired by a bishop, was set up to consider the way forward. In 1950 that committee published its report, with ten of the members favouring the admission of women to the priesthood and four preferring the establishment of a separate ministry for women. The report provoked extensive discussion. Amongst university teachers of New Testament exegesis at Uppsala and Lund, all except one took a stand against the opening of the priesthood to women, whilst the theological faculties as a whole were in favour.[4] (And guess what happened – no measures were taken!)

Here we return to my starting-point: the Church of Sweden as 'the worst in the world' regarding women's ministry. At the same time as this debate, women in other countries and other churches were already working as *Gemeindehelferinn, Vikarinnen, assistantes de paroisses, auxiliatrices de l'évêque*, layworkers licensed by the bishop and ordained deaconesses. By contrast, just one single woman with a theological education was employed by the Church of Sweden. The church had deaconesses, but theirs was an entirely pastoral ministry. There were female missionaries, but they were a safe distance away in foreign countries. There were temporary youth workers in the parishes, but only one post for a female theologian. Women were often to be found in unpaid posts, as Sunday School teachers, members of sewing clubs and of choirs. However, there were virtually no female lay representatives on PCCs. In the Church Assembly of 1948 there were no women at all; whereas in society at large, women were to be found as ministers of state, judges and leaders of industry. 'The worst in the world' – it is a strange expression for a people who have considered (and still consider) themselves as future-orientated and egalitarian. Year by year, attempts were made to advance the cause of women's ordination as priests, but each time, 'no measures were taken'. Even so, this catalogue of failed resolutions and reports makes it difficult to believe that the 1958 vote in favour of women priests – when it came – should have been surprising or found the Church unprepared.

The events immediately preceding that vote took place as follows. At the Church Assembly of 1957, the Minister for Church Affairs submitted a proposal for legislation opening the priesthood to women. In the debate that followed, it was unanimously agreed that 'the Bible should be our guiding principle' – but at this point, agreement ended. Immediately, interpretational differences emerged concerning what was central, and what peripheral, in scripture; and concerning what was the 'letter' of the text, and what was the 'spirit'. Similar differences of interpretation also arose in conversation about the normative power of tradition and normativity in the writings of the reformers. Differences also emerged in discussions about equality: for some, equality before God was one thing, but equality in society was another. The idea of representation was also differently interpreted, some seeing the representation of Christ as demanding physical likeness, thus precluding the possibility of a woman at the altar. Others saw representation as relating primarily to the mission to hand on the gospel to other people on behalf of Christ. The debate was only partly about theology, with social, political and cultural considerations also discussed. In the event, the Church Assembly voted no.[5]

At this point, the Minister for Church Affairs took the unusual step of calling the Church Assembly to meet again the following year, to settle the question once and for all. At that meeting, the treatment of the issue was very different, and with a large majority, the Church Assembly decided that women, as from 1 January 1959, could be ordained priests in the Church of Sweden. The factors behind the apparently sudden reversal have been hotly debated ever since: opponents of women's priesting attribute the swing to external pressure by government and press following the 'no' vote of 1957 and to 'single-issue' voting in elections to the new Church Assembly the following year. Supporters of women's ordination note how the 1958 Assembly was in fact no less political than its 1957 predecessor, the crucial difference being a sudden upsurge in awareness and debate about women's ordination amongst the Swedish laity.[6] A further significant factor was that in order to make it easier for those who believed that the church had taken the wrong decision, an introduction was added to the law, discussing women's competence for priesthood. That clause underlined that no bishop would have to ordain a woman against his own will, that no priest would be forced into service that would offend his conscience and that those who were against female priests would nevertheless continue to be eligible for ordination. However, the opponents made the conscience clause into a law, and used it as a weapon in the fight against women priests and their ministry.

My own view is that, instead of helping to resolve a difficult situation, the conscience clause became the way for a minority to exert its power and to avoid engaging in a continued dialogue. On 10 April 1960, the first three women – Margit Sahlin, Elisabeth Djurle and Ingrid Persson – were ordained as priests in the Church of Sweden. Immediately, opponents of women's priesting formed the 'Coordination Council for the Church Consolidating around Bible and Confession' [Kyrklig Samling Kring Bibel och Bekännelse], publishing a manifesto known as 'The 17 Points'.[7] This document contained advice on how priests and lay people should relate to women priests, given that their ordination was against the word of God and scripture. Additionally, it stated that objecting clergy should refuse to serve alongside a woman priest, to participate in services, or do any other work with them. Organists, it continued, should refuse to play, and lay people should not attend services led by a woman. In short, they proposed a boycott.

The next significant step in the journey came in 1979, when a new Church Assembly convened, with the conscience clause as its main item of business. A working group appointed by Archbishop Olof Sundby proposed that the conscience clause should be replaced by Regulations for Cooperation in the Church of Sweden between those who hold different opinions concerning the right of women to ordination.[8] Basically, these proposed that a male priest would not be permitted to hinder the ministry of a female colleague, although he did not have to participate himself. This was the so-called 'right to make way'. As the first woman priest elected into the Church Assembly, I myself participated a great deal in this debate, joining a minority fighting for a proposal to abolish the conscience clause altogether and impose a duty to follow the law as it was in force – that is, to accept women priests without reservation. This proposal also contained a time delay, affecting only those clergy ordained from 1983 onwards, so as not to prohibit ordination for those opposed who had already begun their studies. This proposal was voted down. The reality was that the Church created a divided priesthood, one half of which was accepted by everyone, and the other half considered by certain groups to be invalid and objectionable. Since the ministerial actions carried out by women priests could also be called into question, and priests could not meet at the eucharistic table, a fragmented church became the reality. Significantly, the solution was unsustainable, again partly due to a widespread public outcry against the treatment of women in the Church. Already by 1981, a review of the conscience clause had been produced.[9] In 1982 the Church Assembly voted to abolish the conscience clause, and the general law of equality dating from 1945 at last applied to the employees of the Church of Sweden. With the Church now forced to handle its own tensions, there was increased talk of coexistence and collaboration.

Since 1983 the Church of Sweden has its own governing body and a Church Assembly that meets each year. At every meeting, questions about women priests have appeared on the agenda. The resultant fatigue from these annual conflicts has become ever more obvious. When the decision to ordain women was taken in 1958, it was obviously believed that there would be few women priests, and that any disagreements could therefore be easily handled. However, that has not been the case. Today more than 40 per cent of priests in the Church of Sweden are women. Indeed, since 1994, the Church Assembly and the College of Bishops have taken a further step towards establishing the priestly ministry of women and men on the same level:

According to the confession and teaching of the Church of Sweden, it is a mark of the Church of Sweden that there is one ministry. The shape of the ministry can however vary and in that sense it is an issue of practical ordering. But behind the decision that women also may be ordained as priests in the Church of Sweden was a decision with regard to the confession and the teaching of the church, namely that it is accordant with the Evangelical-Lutheran confession to introduce such a church order. From a theological and pastoral point of view, it is basic that women and men are ordained and serve as ministers.

Different views about the shape of the ministry find room in the church of Sweden. At the same time, it is clear that our church has only one applicable order. The ordination promise implies a promise to follow this order.

The issue of orders becomes an issue of confession if the validity of the ordination is called into question and if the administration of the sacraments is made dependent on the person of the priest. With regard to the issue of validity, the Church of Sweden does not accept two views as accordant with its confession. It is therefore correct from a doctrinal perspective that only those who accept the validity of the ordination of both men and women, and their administration of the sacraments, may be ordained to the priesthood. This means that a candidate for priestly ordination must be prepared to collaborate fully with other priests in services and in other aspects of ministry.

For the sake of the unity of the church it is important that all ordained ministers should be able to collaborate together in the service and in that way manifest their common confession. The individual minister is not free to choose for him- or herself the consequences of his or her view with regard to the exercise of a mission in the church. The common order of the church is superior to the minister.

In 1997 the Church of Sweden received its first female bishop when I was elected bishop of the diocese of Lund. The news brought great joy across the country – the decision affirmed the position of women in the Church, and their entry into its highest office. Of the 800 or so letters I received about my election, only two were negative. The following year, the diocese of Stockholm also received a woman bishop. With the opening of the priesthood to women, it was only a matter of time before the Church also had women bishops. The view of the Church of Sweden is that the ministry is one, and by being ordained to the priesthood one becomes a potential candidate for the episcopate. In my conversations with women before their ordination to priesthood, it has never been a question of differentiating the ministry of a bishop as something special. No new problems arose within the Church of Sweden itself over the advent of a woman bishop (although of course those who are opposed to women priests are also opposed to women bishops – though they do loyally consider us as diocesan managers). Rather, the biggest issues arise in relation to wider ecumenical contact: having women bishops does, for example, affect relations with the Church of England. Currently there are no women bishops in the Church of England, and the priests I have ordained are not permitted to serve in England in spite of the Porvoo Agreement.[10] This is a problem, for which we in Sweden pray that a solution will be found.

*   *   *

In conclusion, let me offer a few reflections on why it has been important, despite the problems along the way, that the Church of Sweden has opened its priesthood to women. Many people have considered the Church of Sweden one of the most clericalized and male-dominated churches in the world. When discussions about opening up the priesthood to women became increasingly intense, it was not only its view of priesthood which was at stake, but something larger: the church's view of humanity, the basis for relationships between men and women, questions about women's subordination and about the Church and society.

First, here was a choice between a static or dynamic view of the Bible, about tradition and renewal. A static view of the Bible implies security. The Word of God stands clear and firm for all times with the same requirements of obedience. You know what to keep to. But it is so easy to forget that the Bible has always been interpreted. It is not verbally inspired. Somewhere we will always run into conflict with a locked and fundamentalist view of the Bible and the world in which we live and in which we are to be stewards of our vocation as disciples. By contrast, a dynamic view of the Bible implies faith that the stories of the Bible must be translated anew in every generation in order to meet people where they are. God creates continuously, and into that change people must be prepared to find new ways to live out their vocation as disciples. You cannot be locked into old patterns and stand there with ready-made answers. The opening of the priesthood to women is precisely an example of this. Sometimes those who objected to the reform describe themselves as 'we who stand for the traditional Christian faith'. It is certainly traditional that there have never before been any women priests. However, if you look back into history, the arguments against have altered all the time. The basis on which 'traditional Christian faith' has been determined has therefore been defined through a variety of different arguments.

Second, one of the main objections to women as priests centres on arguments about the subordination of women. However, this objection chimes poorly with the view of Genesis 1 that 'God created man in his image, male and female he created them'. Here, there is not even the slightest hint of subordination. Rather, this is an expression of complementarity. Man and woman were together an image of God's own being. Here is no thought of the super- or sub-ordination of one or the other. To claim today that men and women are theologically but not socially equal is therefore deeply problematic. Equality is, as I see it, a deeply theological issue. It is about liberation on all levels, and it is part of the Church's calling to realize this, since it has been given to us already in creation itself. The entire discussion about the priesthood has forced new thinking about the relationships between women and men. For women, it is about discovering that the Church stands for, and accords them, full and equal value as human beings.

Third, the ordination of women signalled a changed relationship between Church and society. What happened in our country when the decision was taken was like extracting a cork from a bottle. So much joy was released, and there was renewed hope for the Church. Suddenly, further opportunities were opened up for women in the church. Women became elected lay representatives, members of PCCs and members of the Church Assembly. Today it is taken for granted that women serve on staff teams and take responsibility at all levels and in all areas of church life. Women priests have also by their very existence forced some quite new thinking about inclusive language. Today the Church is much more careful about how to express things. This is evident not least in recent hymnals, service-books and prayer-books, and this important work is still ongoing. Male colleagues ordained with me in 1967 have since said that their priestly role was also changed by women becoming priests: a staid image was dissolved, and men too have experienced this as liberation.

Much prejudice against the clergy was also shattered with the advent of women priests. To take one example from my own experience, a woman from my parish once rang me to ask me to take her mother's funeral. The date she suggested was impossible for me, but she still wished me to take the funeral. We agreed an alternative date and I asked her to tell her father that I would come to see him the next day. 'No, that is impossible', the woman said, 'you must not go and visit my father – he will not let you in.' It turned out that the father hated priests because once, when very young, he had been badly treated by a priest. Since then he had refused to attend his children's baptisms, confirmations or weddings and only the mother had come. She was now about to have a Christian funeral, and her children of course wished for their father to attend. However, now that the parish had a female priest, the daughter began to get the idea that it might be possible to get her father to come. I said, 'tell your father I will come and see him tomorrow'. So the next day, I dressed up in full clerical attire, went to the house and rang on the doorbell. As the door began to open I quickly put my foot inside and began to pull the door further. 'How do you do? My name is Christina Odenberg and I am a priest', I said. With gaping mouth, the father backed off down the hallway, into the living room and onto the sofa – where he could go no further. All this had happened without him uttering a single word or sound. I sat down in a chair opposite and said nothing. The ensuing silence felt like hours but was probably only half a minute. Then, suddenly, he stretched out his hand across the table and introduced himself as Knutte. Faced with this young woman sitting in front of him, all his ingrained prejudice had fallen away. We became the best of friends, Knutte and I. That which is different, which is unexpected, can mean a new beginning.

With women priests, something new had arrived after almost 2,000 years. It is obvious that such a fundamental change could not take place without causing anxiety and difficulty. The assumption that priests are male has been so deeply ingrained and has obviously meant a great deal to many people. Theological differences persist, and we must continue to engage in dialogue about these. In thinking about women priests, it is also important that we recognize our sometimes very ordinary feelings. We are governed not only by our intellect but also by our emotions. Many people who were previously against the opening of the priesthood to women have since changed their minds and done so saying 'this felt wrong'. It is important to give one another time to reflect upon this aspect of our humanity, and upon the attitudes of which our emotional life is an expression. I am convinced that, for many people who have experienced diffi-culties accepting women as priests, their reservations have not primarily been on grounds of theology, but because they have simply not been able to conceive of a woman as a priest. As a 6-year-old girl said after the ordination of the first woman priest in Sweden in 1960, 'I met a priest. She was a lady and she wore a green cardigan. But it was OK.'[11]

Yes, it is 'OK' with women priests. Men and women in the ministry of the Church and at the altar express an image of God and a theology which I believe is entirely necessary in people's search for God. It speaks of a Christian view of humanity and human value, regardless of gender. It is true that the Church of Christ here on earth should not live *by* the world's values. But it is equally true that the Church must live *in* the world, and in the midst of a rapidly and continuously changing society, in which the gospel must be handed on to new generations. In this sense, the Church is continually facing new challenges to live in context. The opening of the priesthood to women is only one expression of this necessary work: it should be in the Church's very nature to be the place where the Spirit of God may soar freely and find new ways to reach people by God's call.

Bibliography

Bliss, K., *The Service and Status of Women within the Churches* (London: SPCK, 1952).
Hamburg, E. M., 'Christendom in Decline: the Swedish Case', in H. McLeod and W. Ustorf (eds), *The Decline of Christendom in Western Europe* (Cambridge: Cambridge University Press, 2003), pp. 47–62.
Sahlin, M., *Man and Woman in the Church of Christ* (Stockholm: Svenska Kyrkans, 1950).
Stendahl, B., *The Force of Tradition: A Case Study of Women Priests in Sweden* (Philadelphia, PA: Fortress Press, 1985).

Notes

1 K. Bliss, *The Service and Status of Women in the Churches* (London: SPCK, 1952).
2 Figures taken from E.M. Hamburg, 'Christendom in Decline: The Swedish Case', in H. McLeod and W. Ustorf (eds), *The Decline of Christendom in Western Europe* (Cambridge: Cambridge University Press, 2003), pp. 47–62 (pp. 47, 49).
3 Brita Stendahl, *The Force of Tradition: A Case Study of Women Priests in Sweden* (Philadelphia, PA: Fortress Press, 1985), p. 69.
4 Stendahl, *The Force of Tradition*, p. 69.
5 A fuller account of the 1957–58 debate is given in Stendahl, *The Force of Tradition*, pp. 65–79.
6 See, for example, the reminiscences of Bishop Bo Giertz and the journalist Ingmar Ström in Stendahl, *The Force of Tradition*, pp. 9–22.
7 Reproduced in abridged form in Stendahl, *The Force of Tradition*, pp. 89–92.
8 Reproduced in abridged form in Stendahl, *The Force of Tradition*, pp. 93–5.
9 The review, E. Palm, *Reconsideration of the Conscience Clause: Men and Women as Priests in the Church of Sweden* (Stockholm: Statens Offentliga Utredningar [SOU]: Swedish Government Official Report, 1981), is discussed in Stendahl, *The Force of Tradition*, pp. 96–7.
10 An ecumenical agreement between the Scandinavian Lutheran churches and the Anglican churches of the British Isles, signed in 1996, establishing intercommunion and a degree of mutual recognition of ministerial orders.
11 This anecdote is related by Margaret Sahlin, the priest in question.

9

The Ordination of Women in Africa: An Historical Perspective

Esther Mombo

The ordination of women is important for the full integration of women in the Church, affirmation of women's equality and empowerment of women's ministry in the face of the interlinked problems of gender inequality, poverty, violence and HIV/AIDS. Ordination provides a space for women to contribute to the well-being of the people in a given society. Like other continents, Africa has had ordained women for three decades or more, as deacons, priests and ministers in various denominations. It is better to qualify what one means by Africa, however, for it is not a homogenous cultural set and its inhabitants are not members of a homogenous cultural system.

Africa is the second largest continent on earth, measuring about 5,000 miles from north to south and about 4,600 miles from east to west. With a population slightly less than 14 per cent of the world total the reality of Africa and African goes far beyond the continent and the people who live there. There is great ethnic, linguistic and cultural diversity among Africans. To the untrained eye, all Africans might look alike, but a judicious anthropologist could make out the tell-tale physical features that belong to various African tribes. This essay presents a general picture of the ordination of women within the spectrum of contemporary challenges that Africa is facing.

Ordination of women: the diversity

Before looking at the diversity in the ordination of women, it is proper to point out the overwhelming presence of African women in the churches, attesting to the fact that the Church is sustained by their unceasing devotion. Nevertheless, men take up the paid and officially recognized leadership positions. Even if they are in the majority in their churches, women continue to be subjected to a subordinate role, with their presence and their needs not fully recognized. Through the ordination debate women have begun questioning their positions and some of them have been ordained and appointed to key positions in their churches.

The ordination of women is not a new phenomenon in the continent. There have been women ordained in the mainline churches since the late 1970s, although there is no uniformity. One denomination ordains women in one part and does not do so in another part. In the Anglican tradition, some provinces have ordained women while others have not done so. Within a province, some dioceses will have ordained women while others will not. The same diversity of practice is present among member denominations of the World Alliance of Reformed Churches.

In Kenya, for example, the Presbyterian Church of East Africa has ordained women since 1980, but the Reformed Church of East Africa has not done so yet, and looks as if it will take a while to do so. The Lutheran tradition is similarly diverse, and while Lutherans have women ministers in most parts of Africa, in some parts of Kenya they do not. The Moravian Church has women ministers in some provinces but not in others. The ordination of women is as complex as the denominations themselves. Its existence in a given denomination largely depends on the history of that tradition, the local context and the leadership of the immediate context.

This survey is divided into three parts. First, it considers the period of the Church's missionary expansion and its effects in relation to women's ordination. Second, it looks at what has happened in the period since political independence. Third, it looks at ordination in the Anglican tradition and some wider issues associated with the ordination of women in the continent.

Phase 1: the missionary phase

Modern Christianity came to Africa via a detour from North Africa to Europe and America. It then returned to Africa from Europe and America through the missionary activities of the seventeenth, eighteenth and nineteenth centuries. Missionary Christianity was fourfold in its scope, including evangelism, education, health and industrial training. Work among women was undertaken within these areas.

Missionary work among women was seen as an integral part of mission for two reasons. First, it was one way of liberating women from what the missionaries saw as their oppression. Labode Modupe notes that for the mission agencies during this period, women were viewed as victims of traditional practices: of food taboos, initiation, marriage and funeral rites.[1] Most missionary societies that worked in Africa adopted an evangelical theology of mission, which was consonant with the ideology of domesticity. This ideology defined woman as complementary to man, physically inferior but morally superior.[2] Women were supposed to be more affectionate, selfless, dependent and devout by nature. The woman's sphere was the home, which was a refuge from the public realm, in which men competed for money and power.

Since most mission agencies had adopted this ideology, they saw women as very significant in the creation of Christian families. Mission work among and for women was therefore influenced by the ideology of separate spheres and it defined the notions of 'space, work, gender and power'.[3] Missionary wives disseminated the ideology of separate spheres through home visitations, sewing lessons, childcare, cookery and prayer meetings. Ideas of domesticity were also carried into the formal education of girls, the aim of which was to make them good Christian mothers, and enable them to enter professions such as teaching if circumstances allowed. The methods and philosophy of missionary education were influenced by the ideologies of separate spheres for men and women, which were prevalent in the USA and Europe at the turn of the nineteenth century.[4]

When mission agencies thought about education for women they started from a fixed image of the degraded African woman. Given this presumed idea of female degradation, it is not surprising that the reasons given by mission-aries for taking women into their care and giving them simple literacy skills were couched in the language of moral rescue.

The other aim of mission work was to prepare Christian wives for Christian men, thus creating Christian families. To this end, women's education included childcare and hygiene. In childcare, women were given instruction on nutrition and different feeding methods. This culminated in the preparation of Christian homes, which were seen as being important places for moral and spiritual training. MacDannell has observed that: 'a home symbolised fundamental values of the Victorians – Christianity, civilisation, morality, aesthetics, stability, sentiment – one was not building a shelter, but a sanctuary'.[5]

With the whole notion of the ideology of domesticity, there was a strong link between the home and the morality of the people. Mission work with and for women was designed in such a way that women should become wives, mothers and guardians of the family and the home. All this was based on the notion that maternal influence was of social value to society at large and the kingdom of God.

Missionary work among women was influenced by the position of women in the missionary agencies who, according to Robert Strayer, remained in distinctly subordinate positions. This fact had no small effect on missionary efforts among the African female population.[6] Women's work was not mission as such but merely an appendage to it. It produced what are today very strong women's organizations in most mainline churches.[7] These are the backbone of the denominations and some have been instrumental in the ordination of women to the ministry. Others are portrayed as against the ordination of women.

For instance, in the Presbyterian Church of East Africa women won the vote to become elders in 1964. Although the request took over a decade to be granted, the women had persistently raised the issue and supported the debate until it was agreed.[8] The first woman minister, Revd Nyambura Njoroge, was ordained in 1980, and today there are 38 women ministers.

In some churches the women's organizations have been cited as being more opposed to the ordination of women than are men. Where this happens, the women's organizations have fitted very well into the patriarchal structures of the church and have been used to divide the women in these same churches. This raises questions as to what ordination is for and whether it makes women into pseudo-men. Such issues, which have implications for both men and women, will not be dealt with here.

Phase 2: post-independence, 1970–85

With the post-independence period in Africa, educated women began to take their rightful place in business, government, education and the professions. In most churches, however, the status quo remained and women were often kept in their subordinate status. They were marginalized and isolated in separate and unequal women's organizations. Because many churches would not ordain women they served in different capacities.

The reasons against women's ordination have varied from one denomination to another and relate to how each denomination had been started and was structured. Common arguments put forward against women's ordination have included the notion that a priest is the icon of Christ and therefore should be male. Another argument was that Jesus appointed 12 male apostles (assumed to be leaders of the church later) and therefore ordination is only for men. Some evangelical Protestant denominations have resisted the ordination of women on the grounds of 'headship' based on the practice of the late first-century Church described in some of the pastoral letters which deal with household codes of the time (for instance Eph. 5.21-30; Col. 3.18-25; 1 Tim. 2.11-16; 3.1-7; 6.1-2). As well as these, individuals have advanced arguments based on traditional African culture, which varied from one ethnic community to another, in regard to women's participation in religious ceremonies. In some ethnic communities, women served as leaders of religious ceremonies, whereas in others that practice was unacceptable.

All these arguments have been open to question, and during the post-independence period it was within the ecumenical organizations that the debate on the ordination of women began, before it was taken on by the different denominations.

It is the ecumenical initiatives that created the space for questioning the positions of the churches on the ordination of women. Issues of ordination have been easier to discuss in forums outside denominational settings rather than within them. One such place was in the All Africa Conference of Churches (AACC), a continental organization which was inaugurated in 1958, just after Ghana became the first country in Africa to gain independence from British colonial rule.

In 1963 the AACC held its first assembly held in Kampala, Uganda, and discussed the place of women in the Church, including their ordination. The question that the ordination of women raised was how women should be integrated into the life of the Church, including its sacramental life, rather then being excluded on the basis of gender.[9]

Meanwhile, the World Council of Churches (WCC) began to consider these issues and in 1970 held a consultation on the ordination of women, reported under the title *What is Ordination Coming to*. The conference noted that the low status of women in historic mainline churches had more to do with imported Western assumptions about women's place than with their actual place in African traditional culture. In some traditional societies women had participated fully as prophets, healers and diviners. In some of the

African instituted churches women held key positions, even if they were not founders themselves. In many communities, even within the mainline churches, it was the women who were running the churches. Brigalia Bam noted the following in a study conducted by the WCC:

> In my view the instances cited above from both African traditional life and the prophet movements suggest that the question of the inferiority of African women in African thought and life is much exaggerated. For instance, we have discovered that in practically all-African societies women can be religious leaders (and) discharge the duties of ritual or sacred specialists. They may even rank higher in importance than their male counterparts.[10]

In the third AACC assembly, held at Lusaka in 1974, the voices of women were also heard urging the Church to include them in areas such as theological education, which was exclusively male. Even those women who accompanied their husbands in their studies were never taught. After deliberation, the assembly in Lusaka decided that there was a need for:

> an advisory committee of men and women to draw up programmes for the advancement of women in all spheres of church and society. A need for churches to open doors of theological training centres to women, and the inclusion of regular courses at theological colleges for wives of pastors, lay women and students.[11]

In 1980 a conference was held in Ibadan, Nigeria, under the title 'African Women in Church and Theology'. This conference discussed various aspects of this topic and passed several resolutions including that 'a call for equal rights and opportunities for service in the Church as laity and ordained ministers with full pastoral responsibilities in parishes and administrative areas be assured to women'.[12]

By this time some women had studied theology, and those like Mercy Amba Oduyoye, who had a role in ecumenical forums, had begun linking up the few women in seminaries and departments of religious studies as a way of creating solidarity, and encouraging others in the same area.[13] These women were few, but their presence made the churches realize that they were not going to keep quiet about women in ministry, nor were women going to remain in the area of women's groups such as the Mothers' Union and Women's Guild. Within ecumenical organizations, women were able to raise all aspects of ordination and ministry, challenging cultures and readings of the biblical texts.[14]

Ecumenical organizations continued to play a big role in the quest for the ordination of women in various denominations, particularly through two pieces of work that began towards the end of the twentieth century. The first of these was the Ecumenical Decade of Churches in Solidarity with Women (1988–98), set up by the WCC to continue its study of issues surrounding women in the churches, and to raise awareness of this beyond the Church as well. The decade's aims have been summarized in these terms:

> In 1988 the Ecumenical Decade of Churches in Solidarity with
> Women was launched. It was aimed at empowering women to
> challenge oppressive structures in the global community, their
> churches and communities. To affirm – through shared leadership and
> decision-making, theology and spirituality – the decisive contributions
> of women in churches and communities; to give visibility to women's
> perspective and actions in the work and struggle for justice, peace and
> integrity of creation. To encourage the churches to take actions in
> solidarity with women.[15]

In Africa, national and regional gatherings launched the decade in more than a dozen countries. Some were women's events; others were mixed and included processions, seminars and workshops. Heads of churches and even heads of states participated in many of these events, which received considerable media coverage. This was the time when many denominations agreed to talk about ordination or began ordaining women. The number of women ordained was small compared to the number of men ordained during the same period, but the fact that discussions were held and some women ordained was in itself commendable.

A second significant ecumenical movement is the Circle of Concerned African Women Theologians, which was launched in Trinity College, Legon, near Accra, Ghana, in 1989, a year after the Ecumenical Decade of Churches in Solidarity with Women. It is an ecumenical and interfaith body of African women theologians, tracing its background from such organizations as the Ecumenical Association of Third World Theologians (EATWOT), the Ecumenical Association of African Theologians (EAAT), and the Conference of African Theological Institutions (CATI). The Circle is different from the other ecumenical bodies whose membership is predominantly Christian, however, as its members also include Muslim women and those from indigenous African religions.

The Circle aims to empower lay and ordained women to study and write theology which will impact on the churches. Since 1989 members have discussed various theological themes and published over a dozen books.[16] The themes addressed include the Bible, an objective critique of African culture, violence against women and interfaith issues. This way of doing theology deals with issues from the experience of women, who are often in the majority in faith groups, and who have as yet not been taken seriously.

These two movements outside the Church have produced results, as seen in the increasing numbers of women studying theology for ordination or as lay women. A number of women have obtained Bachelors, Masters and doctoral degrees. One of the mainline denominations in Kenya, which does not ordain women, has seen ten women gaining Bachelors degrees in only five years, a situation which some of the men in senior leadership do not have.

Without these two movements, most women now offering leadership in the churches of Africa would not have seen the door of a theological college. The issue the Church faces now is to talk about and with these women. There is pressure from women inside the Church, and such pressure cannot continue unanswered for long. Those women who have obtained degrees in theology are influencing the Church in various sectors. Across Africa today there are ordained women in most traditions of the Church, usually serving largely in the lower echelons of church life.

Phase 3: an overview of the ordination of women in the Anglican provinces of Africa

Events before 1978

Anglican women's ordination in Africa can be divided into two phases, with the first phase covering the period from independence (1960s) to the Lambeth Conference of 1978. Although the Anglican Communion worldwide is a loose federation of Anglican provinces, it meets once every ten years in a Lambeth Conference. The conference is one of the four instruments of unity, the others being the Archbishop of Canterbury, the Primates' meeting and the Anglican Consultative Council. When the Bishops of the Anglican Communion meet every ten years they deliberate over current issues and their implications for the Church. Issues of women within family and in society have been raised in several Lambeth Conferences. When this happens, and resolutions are passed, it is up to each province to deliberate on their implementation. The resolutions are not binding as the Lambeth Conference is not a decision-making body and each province is an autonomous organization.

During the period after independence and before the 1978 Lambeth Conference, some of the African provinces began to discuss the ordination of women in their synods, led by what could be called forward-looking bishops. Some of them had allowed women to go to theological colleges or Bible schools. In 1976, for example, the then province of Kenya (now the Anglican Church of Kenya) found the matter of the ordination of women being raised in a provincial synod led by the late Rt Revd Henry Okullu, whose diocese was the first to ordain women to the priesthood.

After deliberation, the provincial synod agreed in principle that women could be ordained but at an appropriate time. Before a diocese ordained a woman, the bishop of the diocese should examine the candidate thoroughly. Furthermore, the candidate should have undergone training in a theological college in readiness for ordination. Once the candidate had completed her training the bishop should further consult the House of Bishops before ordaining her. Following this discussion, some bishops began sending women to prepare for priesthood by studying theology, while others waited to see what the overall outcome would be. The Rt Revd Henry Okullu put this synod discussion into action by sending the late Lucia Okuthe to study theology at St Philip's Theological College,

Maseno. He later made her a deaconess in the diocese and she continued to serve under the male clergy.

Similarly, the Church of Uganda also deliberated on the issue of the ordination of women in the 1975 synod led by the late Rt Revd Festo Kivengere. During the debate some bishops argued that the Church of Uganda should wait for the Church of England's decision on the same issue. The late Bishop Kivengere did not agree with this suggestion and said:

> 'If you wait for the Church of England you wait until doomsday.' A bishop replied, 'Well, okay, let us write a paper on the subject.' Festo snorted in derision. 'If you write a paper on it, you'll produce something for the archives which will gather dust for ever.' In the end, it was sixteen three against ordaining women immediately. So the matter was referred for debate to the diocesan synods and the provincial assembly, several years later.[17]

The period of the late 1970s was a difficult one in Uganda because it was when Archbishop Luwum was assassinated, under the reign of then President Idi Amin, and Bishop Kivengere was exiled from 1976 to 1979. While in exile, the Bishop attended the 1978 Lambeth Conference. Returning home in 1979 he ordained several women as deacons, three of them later being ordained as priests by him in 1983. This act caused an outcry from bishops who said the time was not yet right. The then Archbishop Silvanus Wani was one such opponent, to whom Bishop Kivengere wrote saying:

> In vain I have been waiting to hear from my fellow Bishops who said they were going to take up the issue with their synods. I feel the delay is unfair on my lady deacons and no reason whatever has been given to me to stop this next step. My synod is fully in agreement with priesting those lady deacons who deserve to be priested.[18]

As well as writing to the Archbishop, the Bishop wrote to other bishops of his intention to ordain women in his diocese. On 11 December 1983 Bishop Kivengere ordained Margaret Byekwaso, Grace Ndyabahika and Debora Micungwe. Grace Ndyabahika (as she is now) is chaplain at the school of business in Makerere University today, but the whereabouts of the other two are not known.

While these events were going on in Uganda the debate in Kenya was hotting up. In 1980 Bishop Okullu made Deaconess Lucia Okuthe a deacon, and the battle between the bishops began. The other bishops led by the then Archbishop, the Rt Revd Mannasses Kuria, challenged Bishop Okullu on his move. In his response, Bishop Okullu defended it by saying that the office of deaconess had been discontinued by the Anglican Consultative Council, so he had gone ahead and made her a deacon. The Lambeth Conference of 1978 had passed a resolution on not admitting women to a separate order of deaconesses.[19]

According to Bishop Okullu, the ordination of women to the diaconate was not a controversial issue, but the ordination of women to the priesthood was. The view of the then Archbishop of Kenya was that it was wrong to ordain women, even as deacons, before the Church of England had done so. Bishop Okullu was not popular in the House of Bishops, and some of the bishops contemplated him being disciplined or sent out of the House of Bishops, but no one had the courage to do so. Looking back, it can be seen that there were other issues than the ordination of women involved in events, including ethnicity and the fear of a vocal and controversial bishop.

No other diocese in Kenya took on the issue of the ordination of women until after 1985, when several women had completed their theological training and some had been made deaconesses, even though this office had been abolished. Each diocese followed its own procedures and ordained women when it could. From 1988 even those synods that had been adamantly opposed to it at the beginning had begun ordaining women.

What emerges from this period, and especially from experiences in Kenya and Uganda, is that the debate on the ordination of women was dependent largely upon the bishops. The declared position of some bishops was that they wanted to wait for the Church of England to lead in the ordination of women. This may have been one way of delaying events, in the hope that the issue of ordination would disappear because of the patriarchal nature of their societies and the inherited tradition of the Church. It was those bishops who understood both the autonomy of the provinces and the dioceses who took a lead in the ordination of women. They were ready to confront the issues within their own localities, as they understood them within the context of the wider society. Apart from the Church of Uganda and the then province of Kenya, the ordination of women seems not to have been an issue in other provinces in Africa during this period.

From Lambeth 1978 to 2008

The Anglican Church in Africa has a number of different provinces, which are grouped together and known as the Conference of Anglican Provinces in Africa. Since 1978 there have been many changes in the worldwide Anglican Communion, including the holding of Lambeth Conferences in 1988 and 1998, and the creation of many new dioceses. The situation regarding the ordination of women differs from one province and diocese to another, as the following brief survey shows.

The Anglican Church of Burundi Research has indicated that there are four women priests. The reason for such a small number compared to the men priests is lack of adequate education, especially theological education. This is not to say that men who are priests are any better at theological study, but it is harder for women to attain basic education, let alone theological education.

The Church of the Province of Central Africa The church of the Province of Central Africa covers Botswana, Zimbabwe, Zambia and Malawi, and is among the three provinces in Africa that still do not ordain women. In 1988 Bishop Ralph Hatendi of Zimbabwe said a woman could be a queen, a judge or a prime minister but never a bishop. He argued that in his culture a woman would not qualify to offer the sacraments to church congregations. Should a woman be ordained in his diocese of Harare, the membership would drop because the men would walk out in protest.[20] The issue here could be cultural, but in the same region studies have shown that women were active in traditional religion, so it is possible that the issue is the Anglican high church tradition, which is prevalent in the area.

The Church of the Province of the Congo (Zaire) This province has over eight dioceses and has not yet ordained women. The situation of war and terror has meant that the church is more in exile than within Congo.

The Anglican Church of Kenya The Anglican Church of Kenya now has 29 dioceses, with a total of 125 women priests, a development which has happened since the 1988 Lambeth Conference. It took up to 20 years of bitter debate on the ordination of women before some dioceses agreed to this.[21] Some dioceses did not debate the ordination of women because they had been created by dividing an earlier diocese that did ordain women, and so inherited this practice.

Most of the first generation of women priests had to work hard to prove themselves, even though they worked in institutions and not in full-time parish ministry. As their numbers have increased, and parishes have become more receptive towards women priests, more women have taken parish jobs and some are now rural deans and archdeacons. The education levels of the women also differ widely; some have doctoral degrees, while others have been ordained after little or no formal theological education.

The church of Nigeria (Anglican Communion) The Anglican Church of Nigeria, with ten provinces, maintains the following position on the ordination of women: 'The church does not approve of the ordination of its women to the priesthood for now. However, the church approves the commencement of the permanent/vocational Diaconate Ministry and women are included in it.'[22] Meanwhile, other denominations in Nigeria have ordained women, including some of the African-instituted churches, Presbyterians, Methodists and Reformed.

The Episcopal Church of Rwanda There are nine dioceses in the Episcopal Church of Rwanda. It agreed to ordain women in the 1990s and the first women were ordained in 1996. Of the nine dioceses only two do not ordain women and there are currently 19 ordained women serving the Church. The only other church that has ordained women is the Presbyterian Church of Rwanda, which has had women ministers since 1980.[23]

The Anglican Church of Southern Africa This province covers the whole of South Africa, Lesotho, Namibia, Mozambique, Swaziland and Angola. South Africa has a number of dioceses within it, whereas other dioceses cover an entire country. Discussion on the ordination of women began in 1960 but the motion to ordain women was not passed until 1992.[24] Since then, three dioceses have not ordained women, those of Lebombo, Niassa and the island of St Helena. The highest post a woman has held is to be a cathedral dean, and the Very Revd Nangula E. Kathindi now serves at St George's Cathedral in Windhoek.[25]

The Episcopal Church of the Sudan The situation in Sudan is complex because of the continuing war in that country. While the Episcopal Church of Sudan has 27 dioceses, some of these have operated outside Sudan. The Church agreed to the ordination of women at a synod meeting in Limuru, Kenya, in 2002, after which the diocese of Bor went ahead with this. However, before that meeting, Bishop Rorik (a government officer) had ordained his wife as a deacon and priest. Since the motion to ordain women was passed not all dioceses have done this, but the diocese of Bor currently has six ordained women.[26] Because of the war, it is impossible to impose the rules and regulations of ordination as they work in other provinces, and correct procedures are a low priority. Those women who have been ordained in the church are illiterate or semi-literate. Women outnumber men because most men have fled or died during the war, and it is these women who have kept the church alive.

The Anglican Church of Tanzania The province, which has 17 dioceses, approved the ordination of women after the Lambeth Conference of 1988. So far the diocese of Central Tanganyika has ordained women, and currently in Tanzania there are five women, one of whom is in the diocese of Mount Kilimanjaro.

The Church of the Province of Uganda The church of Uganda has 28 dioceses, and has had ordained women since 1983 when the first ordinations were done by the late Bishop Kivengere. Other ordinations have taken place since the 1988 Lambeth Conference. Accurate numbers are not easy to obtain, though it is safe to assume that ordained women remain few in number by comparison with men.

The Church of the Province of West Africa Covering the Gambia, Ghana, Guinea, Liberia and Sierra Leone, this province permitted each diocese to ordain women from 1987. Liberia began ordaining women the same year, followed by Sierra Leone and later the Gambia. The number of ordained women is now nine, five of them in Liberia, two in the Gambia and two in Sierra Leone. To date the dioceses in Ghana and Guinea have not started to ordain women. As in Nigeria, other churches including Presbyterian, Methodists and some African-instituted denominations have ordained women.

What difference has it made to have ordained women?
From the above survey it is clear that women can be seen and heard in Africa. The numbers are still small compared to those for men. Some churches are better at this than others, and it will take a while before some even consider

the ordination of women. The major reasons why there are to be so few women within the church structures are the lack of theological education and the context in which most women work.

For a long time, availability of theological education for women has been linked to their ordination. As in other forms of education, churches have invested in men rather than women. For men it has been automatic that they would be seconded to study, because they would return to serve the Church; whereas for women it has depended on whether the diocese concerned ordained women or not. Dioceses have feared sending single women to theological college because they could get married to men from other dioceses or denominations, which would be seen by the sending diocese as a loss. In the case of married women, the worry has been for her husband, or who would take care of the family when she is studying. These reasons still persist, so that it is twice as difficult for women as for men to find their way to theological college and gain the education which will enhance their chances of working in the Church as lay or ordained people.

Theological education is gendered both in content and perspective, which raises questions as to what ordination is for. Very few colleges have managed to offer theological education in such a way that it is for the whole people of God rather than for an exclusive group of men. In addition, it should be noted that African forms of Christianity are still interpreted through the eyes of traditional African cultures, as illustrated by the following episode:

> Ndonga was serving as a priest in a local parish which was well mixed, men and women, professional and laity. Her first children were triplets and she had them when serving in another parish. The new parish knew her as a mother of triplets, and the boys were a joy for the congregation. Ndonga became pregnant again and gave birth to a baby girl. As usual she was entitled to a maternity leave of 60 working days. The parish council did what was needful to allow Ndonga to rest after delivery. When the maternity days were over Ndonga reported back to work and there was panic in the church. Both men and women asked if she did not need more time to be away. On the surface it would appear the members wanted Ndonga to rest, but underneath it was the belief that she was not yet out of the state of having a baby to take her role as a priest. This was communicated to Ndonga in a language that made her know the reason why the members were not yet ready for her.[27]

One is left wondering whether the attitudes illustrated in this story are from traditional culture or from the reading of scripture, especially the Old Testament, or even from an amalgamation of both. The story indicates that both traditional culture and readings of the Old Testament are used still to deny women entry to priesthood. I have written elsewhere on the wait for women bishops in Africa, citing the traditional reasons given as to why women are not bishops and why it will take a while before they become so.[28] This is not the whole picture, however, because researches that have been done on culture show that women in some African cultures served as priests, and it was only after the arrival of Christianity that their roles changed. [29]

In the light of this, African women, both lay and ordained, have embraced culture critically, appropriating and reviving some cultural practices and values that are life-giving and affirming. At the same time they have challenged those practices and values that are not life-affirming, as in the case of Ndonga and her parish. The presence of women of childbearing age in the parishes provides opportunities for them to pass on positive practices and values while discarding those attitudes that hamper women's humanity and their full participation in all spheres of life. A critical analysis of some of these negative practices points to patriarchy as the source of these evils. Even if there are instances where some negative practices have been discarded, others that relate to women are still kept. The inconsistency in this area shows that it is the dominant groups in society which decide what is valuable in the community. A patriarchal mindset always holds the existence of cultural practices that involve the domination of others as the natural norm.

Lack of theological education and cultural norms are among the evident reasons that inhibit women from either seeking ordination or fully partici-pating in the ministries of the Church. These are on the surface, but the fundamental problem is one of inequality in power relations between women and men. This existed in traditional societies, but was reinforced by colonialism and justified by the theological positions and teaching of the churches.

As this is the context in which the ordained women work, their role therefore is to challenge the systems which deny them full participation in the churches. They are doing this in several ways, including engendering theological education and theologizing on issues of life.

Engendering theological education
In writing about theology in Africa, Mercy Oduyoye has talked of a two-winged theology, for a bird with one wing cannot fly.[30] The Ecumenical Decade of Churches in Solidarity with Women helped to create critical awareness of women's theological concerns, both in the churches and in theological institutions. These issues include HIV/AIDS, violence against women, sex and stigma. The task of engendering theological education is about creating a curriculum that will take seriously the issues that are facing the churches, especially the women within them.

The process of engendering theological education is primarily to encourage women to study theology, which has been a preserve of men for two reasons. Firstly, this has resulted from the way scripture has been interpreted and some forms of traditional African cultures have been used. Secondly, it has been because theological education was for those who were going into the ordained ministry of the Church. For these reasons, women remained on the periphery of church ministry, engaged in service rather than in leadership roles. With the reinterpretation of scripture, however, and the detaching of theological education from ordination, women who would not previously have had a chance to study and serve in the church are now able to do so.

Before this it was difficult for female candidates to face training committees and defend their call to ministry, as they were judged in accordance with their social location and their marital status. This affected women across the board in different ways.

Those who were married had to justify their calling with regard to the position of their husbands, and whether they had approval to study theology for the purpose of ordination. Women who were single were equally disadvantaged because the boards feared they would get married during their training, thus depriving the Church or the diocese. Potential candidates who were single mothers did not have a chance, because of the social stigma they encountered from society in general, and especially in the Church. The factor underlying all this was the fear of female sexuality within patriarchal society, where women are seen as morally weak, and as being those who wield the power to lure men into sin. Bringing them to 'holy ground', in terms of the male space in which the study of theology takes place, would be to contaminate the space.

In order to deal with the above it was important to unlink theological education from ordination. The fruits of this have been witnessed by the increase in the number of women choosing to study theology. An analysis of six years in one institution showed the number of women students rose from ten to a hundred.[31] The women come from different backgrounds and marital status. Some are married, others separated or divorced, and some are single mothers. The challenge for these women has largely been to get funding for their studies. While some of the churches have not objected to their training, most have not funded the women. Once they have completed their studies, most of the women have been absorbed into the churches in various capacities. A survey of women graduates showed they had entered a variety of ministries, including ordination. In the Anglican Church some dioceses had appointed these women to various positions, including senior diocesan roles such as that of an archdeacon. While the churches may not have invested in the theological education of these women they are willing to use them after training.

The above analysis shows how engendering theological education has served to increase the number of women doing theological education. As for the second aspect of engendering theological education, this has to do with opening up the curriculum of theological study in terms of structure and content, so that it prepares men and women for ministry in Church and society. This process has encouraged the development of a gender-sensitive curriculum in all areas of teaching: one that takes note of the presence of women as a majority in many churches.

While adding new units onto the existing curriculum, the project also advocates seeing issues of women in Church and society as mainstream concerns within the curriculum. In order to do this, the production of literature has been one key area for most theological subjects. Engendering theological education also means ensuring that the delivery of theological information acknowledges the presence of women not only as objects of study but as participants in the study. Courses such as masculinity, gender and theology and women's theologies are part of the theological curriculum. The end-product of this kind of theological education is to prepare women and men who are sensitive to the needs within society.

HIV/AIDS and related issues

As well as engendering theological education, those women who have studied theology, whether lay or ordained, are theologizing life in the face of death. This is because of the daunting challenges facing Africa. The continent is said to have the highest proportion of people in the world living in situations of extreme poverty, war, political instability, social disintegration and economic stagnation. This is reflected in devastating diseases like malaria, which has grown more deadly and resistant to drugs. HIV/AIDS is decimating communities and undermining growth, particularly in the socioeconomic sector, and adversely affecting human resources. The statistics of UNAIDS, the United Nations organization involved in the HIV/AIDS epidemic, state:

> In 2005 there were world wide over 40 million people living with HIV/AIDS. Of these, 25.8 million lived in sub-Sahara Africa.[32] Although Africa houses only 10 per cent of the world population, it contains 64 per cent of the HIV-infections. UNAIDS research shows that out of 23.7 million HIV-infected adults in sub-Sahara Africa 13.5 million are women. The women's share in Africa is 57 per cent while worldwide this is 46 per cent.[33]

Many would ask why this is the case, when other researches show that education about HIV/AIDS is no longer the issue in most settings. The reason why women in Africa are suffering disproportionately from HIV/AIDS is due partly to biological differences between men and women but in particular to gender differences. Reports of organizations such as UNAIDS and the World Health Organization refer to the social and cultural constructions of being male and being female in Africa, which are strengthening the vulnerability of women to HIV-infection.[34] Part of these constructions are the social, economic and power relations between women and men, and cultural practices such as bride price and widow inheritance.

The process of engendering theological education has meant teaching theology in the light of the issues facing society, especially those emanating from HIV/AIDS. Even if both women and men are educated in the same way on issues of HIV/AIDS, the women have taken a lead in seeking ways of dealing with the issues in a wider context. Through the Circle of Concerned African Women Theologians, the lay and ordained women of the Church are busy dealing with issues emanating from HIV/AIDS in terms of prevention and care for the dying. They are doing this in workshops, preaching, conferences and in writing books that can be used to sensitize communities of learning. For instance, in 2002 a continental conference was held in Addis Ababa, Ethiopia with the theme 'Sex, stigma and HIV/AIDS: African women challenging religion, culture and social practices'. In 2007 another conference was held on a similar theme.

The Circle of Concerned African Women Theologians gives a gender-based response to this call, since African women are hit most because of the unequal power relations between men and women. For women theologians the gender factor is one of the social structures that makes HIV/AIDS an issue of justice. According to the Circle, 'if we do not deal with gender and HIV, the world will not make a difference in combating the virus'.[35]

Meanwhile, four Circle books on HIV/AIDS have been published.[36] As well as naming and critiquing the cultural and social issues that strengthen the vulnerability of women to HIV/AIDS, the writings provide an alternative way of reading the scriptures in the context of HIV/AIDS. They are read from the perspective of justice and of God being on the side of the exploited, marginalized and discriminated against, namely those who are powerless. The book *Grant me Justice* is an example of this kind of reading of the scriptures.[37] The aim of the Circle is to establish a society with just relations, where service has been moved away from the hierarchical power of dominance.

Challenging power issues in the church

Whether it is in combating HIV/AIDS by raising gender issues, or engendering theological education, or challenging violence against women in all its forms, the fundamental problem is one of inequality in power relations between women and men, which exists even within the life of churches. This is too often reinforced by the theological positions and teaching of the churches themselves.

Lay and ordained women are calling on the churches to look inward and question the years when scripture has been misused and patriarchal structures uncritically accepted within culture and history. All of this made the Church an accomplice and sometimes a major player in terms of inequality between women and men. Women are often denied full participation in all aspects of the life of the Church, even in cases where they have experienced God's call to service. Instead of a holistic approach to human beings, the Church has often resorted to an empty dualism, in which it has focused on spiritual needs and ignored the needs of the body.

Because of its influential role in terms of formal and informal education, the Church can provide leadership in changing societal attitudes and has definitely been an instrument of change in many aspects of life. Considering that the majority of its members are women, it should not be difficult to pass on the message of change in relation to their status. What appears to be the problem, however, is that in some ways the Church has not wanted this to happen. Perhaps because of its predominantly patriarchal nature it has thus far not allowed or encouraged change in terms of attitudes towards women.[38]

As a result of this, those organizations in the churches which are predominantly women-led have remained a source of survival for most women, providing them with spiritual and moral support. In many cases women find in these groups a way to exercise their freedom to minister to one another, to explore scriptures together, to speak of their family lives and their lives as a whole. Organizations such as the Mothers' Union (Anglican), Women's Guild (Presbyterian), United Society of Friends' Women (Quakers) and others within the various denominations remain a source of strength for many in these churches, though they are limited in their hermeneutical critique of patriarchy. The need therefore is for women to stand together with each other and refuse to be divided by being lay or ordained, theologically trained or not. This is what projects like engendering theological education are meant to do for all women.

As noted above, the real issue of women in the Church lies in the inequality of power relations between men and women. In this case, ecclesiastical and clerical powers need to be transformed in such a way that opportunities for their misuse are eliminated. Ecclesiastical power must become a shared power of caring, community building, just relations and service, moving away from the hierarchical power of dominance.

Conclusion

This essay has considered the ordination of women in Africa in broad terms and the impact that ordained women have had in the churches. It has shown that each denomination has a different history even if within mission work all women were originally treated the same. The survey of women's ordination in the Anglican provinces of Africa has shown that there is no uniformity of practice for this matter in the continent, even within one denomination. The argument presented has been that ordained women still live and work in the shadow of African traditional culture, which is part of the problem-riddled context of the church in modern Africa. As this paper has shown, some women have chosen to deal with that context differently, by engendering theological education and placing within the mainstream issues of gender and power relations within theological education.

Bibliography

Ackermann, D., Draper, J. and Mashinini, E. (eds), *Women Hold up Half the Sky: Women in the Church in Southern Africa* (Pietermaritzburg: Cluster, 1991).

'African Women in Church and Theology', *AACC Bulletin*, 11.2 (1980), pp. 32–3.

Akintunde, D.O., Amoah, E. and Akoto, D.B.E.A. (eds), *Cultural Practices and HIV/AIDS: African Women's Voices* (Accra: Sam-Woode, 2005).

Amoah, E. (ed.), *Where God Reigns: Reflections on Women in God's World* (Accra: Sam-Woode, 1996).

Living No Longer for Ourselves but for Christ: The Struggle Continues (Lusaka: AACC, 1974).

Bam, B., *What is Ordination coming to?* (Geneva: WCC, 1971).

Bowie, F., Kirkwood, D. and Ardener, S., *Women and Missions: Past and Present Anthropological and Historical Perceptions* (Oxford: Berg, 1993).

Burman, S. (ed.), *Fit Work for Women* (London: Oxford Women Studies, 1979).

Coomes, A., *The Authorised Biography of Festo Kivengere* (Eastbourne: Monarch, 1990).

Cott, N.F., *The Bonds of Womanhood: Woman's Sphere in New England* (New Haven,

140 ESTHER MOMBO

CT: Yale University Press, 1977).
Epstein, B., *The Politics of Domesticity: Women, Evangelism, and Temperance in Nineteenth-Century America* (Middletown: Wesleyan University Press, 1981).
Davidoff, L. and Hall, C., *Family Fortunes: Men and Women of the English Middle Class, 1780–1850* (London: Routledge, 1992).
Dube, M. (ed.), *Other Ways of Reading: African Women and the Bible* (Geneva: WCC, 2001).
Dube, M. and Kanyoro, M. (eds), *Grant me Justice! HIV/AIDS and Gender Readings of the Bible* (Pietermaritzburg: Cluster, 2004).
Facing the Challenges of HIV/AIDS/STDs: A Gender-Based Response (Amsterdam, Harare, Geneva: KIT/SAfAIDS/WHO, 1995).
Gender and HIV/AIDS: UNAIDS technical update (Geneva: UNAIDS, 1998).
Getui, M., *Violence against Women* (Nairobi: Acton, 1996).
Getui, M., and Obeng, E.A. (eds), *Theology of Reconstruction: Exploratory Essays* (Nairobi: Acton, 1999).
Harris, H., and Shaw, J. (eds), *The Call for Women Bishops* (London: SPCK, 2004).
Hinga, T., Kubai, A. and Mwaura, P. (eds), *HIV/AIDS, Women and Religion in Africa* (Pietermaritzburg: Cluster, 2005).
De Jong, M., 'Protestantism and its Discontents in the Eighteenth and Nineteenth Centuries', in *Women Studies*, 19 (1991), pp. 260–69
Kanyoro, M. and Njoroge, N. (eds), *Groaning in Faith: African Women in the Household of God* (Nairobi: Acton, 1996).
Living Letters: A Report of Visits to the Churches during the Ecumenical Decade of the Churches in Solidarity with Women (Geneva: WCC, 1997).
MacDannell, C., *The Christian Home in Victorian America 1840–1900* (Bloomington, IN: Indiana University Press, 1986).
Miller, C., *Missions and Missionaries in the Pacific* (New York: Edwin Mellen Press, 1986).
Moore, H.L., *Space, Text and Gender: An Anthropological Study of the Marakwet of Kenya* (Cambridge: Cambridge University Press, 1996).
Njoroge, N., *Kiama Kia Ngo: An African Christian Feminist Ethic of Resistance and Transformation* (Ghana: Legon Theological Studies series, 2000).
Njoroge, N. and Musa, D. (eds), *Talitha Cum: Theologies of African Women* (Pietermaritzburg: Cluster, 2001).
Oduyoye, M., *Daughters of Anowa, African Women and Patriarchy* (New York: Orbis, 1995).
——, (ed.), *Transforming Power: Women in the Household of God. Proceedings of the Pan-African Conference of the Circle of Concerned African Women Theologians* (Accra: Sam-Woode, 1997).
Oduyoye, M. and Kanyoro, M. (eds), *Talitha Qumi, Proceedings of the Convocation of African Women Theologians 1989* (Ibadan: Daystar Press, 1990).
——, (eds), *The Will to Arise: Women, Tradition, and the Church in Africa* (New York: Orbis, 1995).
Phiri, I.A., *Women, Presbyterianism and Patriarchy: Religious Experience of Chewa women in Central Malawi* (Blantyre: Kachere, 1997).
Phiri, I.A., Govinden, D.B. and Nadar, S. (eds), *Her Stories: Hidden Histories of Women of Faith in Africa* (Pietermaritzburg: Cluster, 2002).
Phiri, I.A., Haddad, B. and Masenya, M. (eds), *African Women, HIV/AIDS and Faith Communities* (Pietermaritzburg: Cluster, 2003).
Pobee, J.S. and Von Wartenberg-Potter, B., *New Eyes of Reading: Biblical Reflections from the Third World* (Geneva: WCC, 1986).
Strayer, R., *The Making of Mission Communities in East Africa* (Nairobi: Heinemann, 1978).
UNAIDS, *AIDS Epidemic Update* (Geneva: World Health Organization, December 2007), p. 15 (http://www.unaids.org/epi/2005/doc/report_pdf.asp).

Welter, B., 'The Cult of True Womanhood, 1820–1860', in *American Quarterly*, 18.2 (summer 1966), pp. 151–74.

Whelan, D., *Gender and HIV/AIDS: Taking Stock of Research and Programmes* (Geneva: UNAIDS, 1999).

Notes

1   M. Labode, 'From Heathen Kraal to Christian Home: Anglican Mission Education and African Christian Girls, 1850–1900', in F. Bowie, D. Kirkwood and S. Ardener (eds), *Women and Missions: Past and Present Anthropological and Historical Perceptions* (Oxford: Berg, 1993), pp. 126–42.

2   M. de Jong, 'Protestant and its Discontents in the Eighteenth and Nineteenth Centuries', in *Women Studies*, 19 (1991), p. 260.

3   H.L. Moore, *Space, Text and Gender: An Anthropological Study of the Marakwet of Kenya* (Cambridge: Cambridge University Press, 1996), pp. 147–52.

4   B. Epstein, *The Politics of Domesticity: Women, Evangelism, and Temperance in Nineteenth-Century America* (Middletown, CT: Wesleyan University Press, 1981); B. Welter, 'The Cult of True Womanhood, 1820–1860' in *American Quarterly*, 18.2 (summer 1966), pp. 151–74; C. Miller, *Missions and Missionaries in the Pacific* (New York: Edwin Mellen Press, 1986); C. Hall, 'The Early Formation of Victorian Domestic Ideology', in S. Burman (ed.), *Fit Work for Women* (London: Croom Helm, 1979), pp. 15–31; L. Davidoff and C. Hall, *Family Fortunes: Men and Women of the English Middle Class, 1780–1850* (London: Routledge, 1992).

5   C. MacDannell, *The Christian Home in Victorian America 1840–1900* (Bloomington, IN: Indiana University Press, 1986), p. 50. Similar views have been expressed by N.F. Colt in *The Bonds of Womanhood: 'Woman's sphere'* (New Haven, CT: Yale University Press, 1977), p. 64.

6   R. Strayer, *The Making of Mission Communities in East Africa* (Nairobi: Heinemann, 1978), p. 6.

7   The Women's Guild (Presbyterian), Mothers' Union (Anglican) Methodist Women's Group (Methodist), United Society of Friends' Women (Quakers) and Dorcas Group (Seventh Day Adventist).

8   N. Njoroge, *Kiama Kia Ngo: An African Christian Feminist Ethic of Resistance and Transformation* (Ghana: Legon Theological Studies Series, 2000), pp. 63–9.

9   'Christian Women of Africa Share in Responsibility: Consultation on the Responsibility of Christian Women in Africa', *AACC Bulletin*, 1.3. (Nairobi: 1963), p. 32.

10 B. Bam, *What is Ordination Coming to* (Geneva: WCC, 1971), pp. 9–10.

11 'Living no Longer for Ourselves but for Christ. The Struggle Continues', *AACC Bulletin*, 11.2 (1974), pp. 25–6.

12 'African Women in Church and Theology', *AACC Bulletin*, 11.2 (1980) p. 33.

13 J. Scott and B.Y. Wood (eds), *We Listened Long before we Spoke: A Report of the Consultation of Women Theological Students, Cartigny, Switzerland, July 1978* (Geneva: WCC, 1979).

14 M. Oduyoye, 'Church Women and the Church's Mission' and R.M. Edet, 'Woman and Ministry in Africa', in J.S. Pobee and B. Von Wartenberg-Potter (eds), *New Eyes for Reading: Biblical and Theological Reflections by Women from the Third World* (Geneva: WCC, 1986), pp. 90–92, 68–80.

15 *Living Letters: A Report of Visits to the Churches during the Ecumenical Decade of the Churches in Solidarity with Women* (Geneva: WCC, 1997), p. 13.

16 I.A. Phiri, *Women, Presbyterianism and Patriarchy: Religious Experience of Chewa women in Central Malawi* (Blantyre: Kachere, 1997); M. Getui, *Violence Against Women* (Nairobi: Acton, 1996); M. Oduyoye and M. Kanyoro (eds), *The Will to*

Arise: Women, Tradition, and the Church in Africa (New York: Orbis, 1995); M. Kanyoro and N. Njoroge (eds), *Groaning in Faith: African Women in the Household of God* (Nairobi: Acton, 1996); M. Dube (ed.), *Other Ways of Reading: African Women and the Bible* (Geneva: WCC, 2001); E. Amoah (ed.), *Where God Reigns: Reflections on Women in God's World* (Accra: Sam-Woode, 1996); I.A. Phiri, D.B Govinden and S. Nadar (eds), *Her Stories: Hidden Histories of Women of Faith in Africa* (Pietermaritzburg: Cluster, 2002); N. Njoroge and M. Dube (eds), *Talitha Cum: Theologies of African Women* (Pietermaritzburg: Cluster, 2001); M. Oduyoye (ed.), *Transforming Power: Women in the Household of God, Proceedings of the Pan-African Conference of the Circle of Concerned African Women Theologians* (Accra: Sam-Woode, 1997).

17 A. Coomes, *The Authorised Biography of Festo Kivengere* (Eastbourne: Monarch, 1990), p. 347.

18 Coomes, *Festo Kivengere*, p. 427.

19 Resolution 20, Women in the Diaconate: 'The Conference recommends, in accordance with Resolution 32(c) of the Lambeth Conference of 1968, those member Churches which do not at present ordain women as deacons now to consider making the necessary legal and liturgical changes to enable them to do so, instead of admitting them to a separate order of deaconesses.'

20 'Women Bishops: "It's satanic" says male bishop', *Viva*, 4 (August/September 1988), p. 10.

21 For example in the diocese of Eldoret, in the Anglican Church of Kenya, the first motion on this was brought to Synod in 1985 but the first ordination of women only took place in 2002.

22 George Njoku, Clerical Secretary and Director of Theological Education and Doctrinal Matters of the Church of Nigeria, email (30 May 2006).

23 Emmanuel Ngendahayo, Diocesan Secretary of Byumba Diocese, Episcopal Church of Rwanda, email interview (June 2006).

24 P. Swart-Russell and J. Draper, 'A Brief History of the Movement for the Ordination of Women in the Church of the Province of Southern Africa (CPSA)', in D. Ackermann, J. Draper and E. Mashinini (eds), *Women Hold Up Half the Sky: Women in the Church in Southern Africa* (Pietermaritzburg: Cluster, 1991), pp. 220–37.

25 www.virtueonline.org

26 Interview with Mary Achong Deng, Archdeacon of Duk Panyan, diocese of Bor, 8 May 2006.

27 Ndonga, oral interview, Kabuku, Kenya (April 2006).

28 E. Mombo, 'Why Women Bishops are Still on the Waiting-list in Africa', in H. Harris and J. Shaw (eds), *The Call for Women Bishops* (London: SPCK, 2004), pp. 163–7.

29 Phiri, *Women, Presbyterianism and Patriarchy*, pp. 21–42 and M. Oduyoye, *Daughters of Anowa, African Women and Patriarchy* (Maryknoll, NY: Orbis, 1995).

30 M. Oduyoye and M. Kanyoro, *Talitha Qumi, Proceedings of the Convocation of African Women Theologians 1989* (Ibadan: Daystar Press, 1990), p. 31.

31 St Paul's United Theological College, Limuru, Kenya (registrar's records, 2007).

32 UNAIDS, *AIDS Epidemic Update* (Geneva: World Health Organization, December 2007), p. 15 (http://www.unaids.org/epi/2005/doc/report_pdf.asp).

33 UNAIDS, *AIDS Epidemic Update* (December 2005), pp. 1, 4.

34 D. Whelan, *Gender and HIV/AIDS: Taking Stock of Research and Programmes* (Geneva: UNAIDS, 1999); *Gender and HIV/AIDS: UNAIDS Technical Update* (Geneva: UNAIDS, 1998); *Facing the Challenges of HIV/AIDS/STDs: A Gender-based Response* (Amsterdam, Harare, Geneva: KIT/SAfAIDS/WHO,1995).

35 I.A. Phiri, 'African Women of Faith Speak Out in an HIV/AIDS Era', in I.A. Phiri, B. Haddad and M. Masenya (eds), *African Women, HIV/AIDS and Faith Communities* (Pietermaritzburg: Cluster, 2003), p. 8.

36 Phiri, Haddad and Masenya, *African Women, HIV/AIDS*; M.W. Dube and M.

Kanyoro (eds), *Grant me Justice! HIV/AIDS and Gender Readings of the Bible* (Pietermaritzburg: Cluster, 2004); T. Hinga, A. Kubai and P. Mwaura (eds), *HIV/AIDS, Women and Religion in Africa* (Pietermaritzburg: Cluster, 2005; D.O. Akintunde, E. Amoah and D.B.E.A. Akoto (eds), *Cultural Practices and HIV/AIDS: African Women's Voices* (Accra: Sam-Woode, 2005).

37 Dube and Kanyoro, *Grant me Justice*, p. 19.

38 H. Ayanga, 'Liberation of the African woman', in M.N. Getui and E.A. Obeng (eds), *Theology of Reconstruction: Exploratory Essays* (Nairobi: Acton, 1999), p. 101.

10

Women's Ordination in the Old Catholic Churches of the Union of Utrecht[1]

Angela Berlis

On Whit Monday 1996, the first two women were ordained to the priesthood in the Old Catholic Church of Germany. This ordination of Catholic women was a great spiritual feast, marking the end of long years of heated discussion for members of the Old Catholic Churches. To many, it signified acceptance of the religious authority of women. This was also expressed in the way women's names were included in the litany at the ordination in the Christuskirche, Constance.[2] The ordination also had effects outside the Old Catholic Church, causing quite a stir in the press and in the ecumenical movement. Many saw it as a sign of hope that a church in the Catholic tradition had taken this step.

This essay will start with an overview of discussion and decision-making about this question within the Old Catholic churches. It will then describe four dimensions of the question of the ordination of women which were quite important during the process of decision-making. Finally it will consider the conflicts which arose within the Old Catholic Communion and suggest that such conflicts have the creative potential to deepen our understanding of who we are.

Three phases of the discussion about the ordination of women

The Old Catholic churches are Catholic churches with a synodical–episcopal structure. Every diocese is led by a bishop, with responsibility shared by clergy and lay people. All those who take leadership functions are officially elected. The churches are united in the Union of Utrecht,[3] and their bishops regularly meet at the International Bishops' Conference (IBC). The Old Catholic Churches of the Union of Utrecht have been in full communion with the Anglican Communion since 1931. The ministries of the Old Catholic churches are viewed by the Roman Catholic Church as valid but illegitimate, inasmuch as they are not in communion with Rome.

Discussion about the ordination of women, and the importance of the argument, developed steadily at different levels in the Old Catholic churches.

Opinions were formed in the various dioceses and gave rise to synodical recommendations or resolutions to the bishops. The IBC deliberated on the subject extensively and issued a number of statements. Resolutions from the International Old Catholic Congress and the International Old Catholic Theologians Conference, as well as from women, also played a role. This essay will focus on the actions and responses of the various Old Catholic churches and the IBC, which can be seen in three phases.

The first phase began in the 1960s, when this matter was initially taken up by the Old Catholic Bishops' Conference because the Anglican Communion was also dealing with it. In the 1970s it became a topic of discussion mainly among bishops and male theologians, culminating in a 1976 statement that the IBC:

> in accordance with the ancient undivided Church, does not agree with a sacramental ordination of women to the catholic apostolic ministry of a deacon, presbyter, and bishop. The Lord of the Church, Jesus Christ, through the Holy Spirit has called twelve men to be his Apostles, in order to perpetuate his work of the salvation of mankind.[4]

This statement was not the result of a unanimous decision; it provoked critical reactions in several Old Catholic churches, mainly concerning its treatment of the question of women and the diaconate.[5]

The second phase began in 1981, when the synods of the Swiss and German Old Catholic churches declared their support for the ordination of women as deacons because 'the early church also had women deacons'. Meanwhile the IBC declared 'that a permanent diaconate of men and women is fundamentally possible and is desired in many places'.[6] The IBC offered individual Old Catholic churches the option of introducing this diaconate and ordered the Old Catholic Liturgical Commission (IALK) to draw up a service of ordination which was approved in 1985. In 1987 the Swiss Old Catholic Church ordained its first woman deacon, and the Old Catholic churches of Germany (1988), Austria (1991), the Netherlands (1996) and the Czech Republic (2003) soon followed suit.

The third phase started in the mid-1980s. In 1989, 1991 and 1994 three diocesan synods of the Catholic diocese of the Old Catholic Church in Germany passed resolutions concerning the ordination of women. The 1994 synod decided there would be no more restrictions on the ordination of women into the apostolic ministry of the Church, that is to the threefold ministry of the diaconate, presbyterate and episcopate.[7] Two years later the first ordination of two women to the priesthood, of whom I was one, took place.[8]

Following the German synod's decision in 1994, the IBC suspended the German bishop's membership of the Bishops' Conference, arguing that the ordination of women was premature because it had taken place before the IBC arrived at a joint decision. The German synod appealed against this decision as a misinterpretation of the 'Agreement between the Old Catholic Bishops United in the Union of Utrecht' (1974).[9]

To understand this it is necessary to look at developments across the Union of Utrecht. In 1991 there was an IBC meeting in Wislikofen, Switzerland, on the ordination of women to the priesthood. At this conference the churches had not reached consensus; Germany and Switzerland had already dealt with the issue at a synodical level while Poland and the Czech Republic had not even started discussions. Indeed, in the late 1970s the Polish National Catholic Church in the USA (PNCC) had unilaterally withdrawn from full communion with the Episcopal Church in the USA after that church had begun ordaining women to the priesthood. The 1991 IBC meeting decided to begin a study process on the ordination of women to the priesthood and each Old Catholic Church was asked to convene a consultation. The IBC also decided that there should be a dialogue with other churches about this question, in particular with those churches with which the Old Catholic Church 'shares the ordained ministry in apostolic succession'. The aim was to 'reach a conclusion to which it could stand'.[10] The lack of consistency in the process, together with the contradictory positions which were beginning to make themselves clear, were to cause enormous tensions between the churches of the Union of Utrecht in the years after 1991.

In 1997, the IBC initiated a second conference on the ordination of women and at this meeting the vote of the German bishop was reinstated. This conference established that although the Polish National Catholic Church in the USA wished to stand by the IBC's statement of 1976, that statement had not been unanimous and was not accepted by the Old Catholic churches of Germany, Switzerland and the Netherlands. At the conclusion of the 1997 conference the IBC stated:

some Old Catholic churches deem the ordination of women necessary for the sake of the credibility of their mission, which is why they want to implement it as soon as possible. Other churches are convinced that they cannot ordain women, because their internal and external credibility would be damaged. Faced with this situation, the Bishops' Conference states that a provision of the Agreement of the Union of Utrecht, which is one of the fundamental documents of the churches united in the Union of Utrecht, can no longer be fully implemented. According to this provision, the Old Catholic churches are in full communion with each other. Since some churches cannot, for the sake of their convictions, recognize the ordination of women, this communion is no longer fully shared.[11]

The IBC then declared by majority vote that the introduction of the ordination of women to the priestly ministry 'lies in the responsibility of each local or national Old Catholic church'.[12] Although this declaration lacks unanimity and does not have the status of an official IBC statement it has found widespread application in practice.

Since 1998 women have been ordained to the priesthood in the Old Catholic churches of Austria, the Netherlands and Switzerland in addition to those in Germany. The Polish National Catholic Church in the USA responded by severing communion with all those Old Catholic churches that ordain women. That created a problem, for according to the statutes of the IBC all bishops and their churches are in full communion with the other churches of the Union of Utrecht.[13] This impaired communion led the IBC in 1997 to declare a six-year moratorium on discussion of membership, in order to investigate healing the divide.[14] This proved impossible and in 2003 the PNCC left the Union of Utrecht.

The dimensions of the problem

Four dimensions that have played a role in the discussion in the Old Catholic Church will now be considered. First, there was the theological question of whether women could be admitted to the threefold ministry, in which the interpretation of scripture and tradition played a major role. Secondly, the question of identity became very important. Was the introduction of the ordination of women consistent with the basic theological principles of the Old Catholic Church? The main consideration was whether a decision to ordain women would be true to the original 'mission statement' of Old Catholicism. References to the Early Church were important here, for the famous maxim of Vincent of Lerins ('We hold fast to what has been believed always, by all and in all places: for that is truly catholic')[15] and the engagement to reform the Church without any innovations are essential to the Old Catholic programme. Another factor was the need to avoid any action which would deepen the chasm between Christian churches.

Therefore, the third dimension is the overall effect of such a decision on ecumenical relationships. During discussions at synods, parish meetings and the consultations at diocesan or provincial level, one question kept being asked: what will this decision mean for our relationships with other churches, in particular those with whom we have had cordial relations for some time, and to whom we are related or feel related? With respect to the diaconate, the answers to these questions about the theological dimension, about identity and the ecumenical dimension, were relatively easy to find. It was concluded that there are indications that women in special offices are part of the divine plan for salvation, and there is clear evidence for women deacons in the New Testament and the Early Church.

On the question of identity, it was noted that the introduction of the ministry of women deacons was not an innovation but the reintroduction of a ministry that had existed earlier before being abandoned. The diaconate for women had never officially been abolished by an ecumenical council. It was realized, however, that this reintroduction would have to take account of contemporary demands and expectations in its form and design. For example, issues of modesty in the Early Church meant that female deacons assisted the bishop only in the baptism of women, but a modern woman deacon need not limit herself in this respect. Regarding the ecumenical dimension, it should be remarked that since the diaconate of women has its origins in tradition, many ecumenical partners would approve of it.

The questions were much more complex with respect to priestly ministry. To begin with, it was necessary to consider whether the traditional theological arguments against the ordination of women to the priesthood were still valid. The problem was compounded by the limited evidence for the existence of women priests in the Early Church and the long tradition of a priestly ministry which excluded women. Secondly, how could this innovation be justified? If the Old Catholic Church decided to ordain women, would this mean a violation of its constitution or its basic theological principles?[16]

Finally, who has the authority to decide these matters? Ideally such a question should be decided by a general, ecumenical council, like those of the first millennium, but the divided state of Christianity makes this impossible. During the 1990s the Roman Catholic Church and the Anglican churches had moved in different directions over the ordination of women, with the papal encyclical *Ordinatio sacerdotalis* and the first ordinations of women priests in the Church of England both in 1994. The consultation with other churches envisioned by the IBC was consequently less open than had been intended, not least because more and more Old Catholic churches already had taken a stance.

However, consultations with other churches should not be interpreted as a sign that the Old Catholic Church was not prepared to take responsibility for its own decisions. Instead, the idea was to take a responsible decision, even though it was clear not all of Christ's Church would follow. It was felt that even a small church, or communion of churches, should be able to make such a move while expressing its readiness to have its practice over this issue considered by a general ecumenical council.[17]

As the discussion progressed, it became clear that besides the three factors discussed above, a fourth dimension of social and cultural issues played an important role. Its effects would be much more dramatic for the question of the ordination of women to the priesthood than to the diaconate. In particular, the changing roles of women in society from the 1960s onward had important consequences for their image and roles within the Church. The growing self-consciousness of women and their organizations were influential in the debate.[18]

A survey of church attitudes toward the ordination of women in the USA by American sociologist Mark Chaves has shown that a decision to ordain (or not ordain) women is seen as 'signifying the identity' of a church and determining its position in modern culture. Determining factors in making this decision are pressure from outside the churches, public opinion and alliances with other churches.[19] However, Chaves's sociological insights must be complemented by a more profound theological perspective. Conflicts about the ordination of women are also conflicts about the religious authority of women, and this is a very old question.[20]

After a long process of consultation and discussion, the IBC left the decision to admit women to the diaconate (1982) or the presbyterate (1997) to individual Old Catholic churches.[21] This showed the independence of the local churches and also allowed for the different contexts in which the churches found themselves, as a church in strongly Roman Catholic Poland has a different scope for action to one in the Netherlands.

Conflict and reception

The ordination of women not only causes conflict but also demonstrates the creative potential of such conflict. This will now be considered on the basis of a series of theses.

(a) Discussion of the ordination of women has revealed differences between individual Old Catholic Churches, or within the Union of Utrecht, that probably existed before but were never clearly visible. These concern not only theological questions such as the interpretation of the Bible and tradition, but also the differing social and cultural contexts of the individual churches. The debate has been a catalyst in the articulation of such differences.

(b) The discussion about the ordination of women can be seen as a theological learning process or process of clarification. This applies not just to ideas about women and relations between the sexes but also to a better understanding of revelation through Christ and soteriology. Those on both sides of the debate have experienced this learning process. The dialogue has never been purely internal but ecumenically fed by exegetical and theological insights from male and female theologians in other churches. Similar exchanges of arguments and insights can also be seen in other churches debating the ordination of women. They show that questions of such importance can never be answered by individual churches or church communions alone but need to be part of an ecumenical learning process.

(c) This debate relates to the ecclesiological foundations of the Old Catholic churches of the Union of Utrecht and has caused people 'to rethink the relation between the IBC and the autonomy of the member churches'.[22] Those who expected a conclusive verdict from the IBC either way were disappointed. Instead, this decision had to be taken at the local level and not from the top down. Thus, the discussion of the ordination of women has contributed to a growth in the self-awareness of the Old Catholic Communion. What is at stake is the right balance between autonomy and communion.[23]

(d) From this question, Old Catholics have learned that an early exchange of information is essential for developments that may be important to other churches. Apart from improving internal communication, the IBC has recently established new procedures for consultation and reception.[24] The aim is to make sure that whenever important issues are at stake, local churches and the supra-local level are heard, and can perform their duties without encroaching on one another's competences.

(e) Surviving differences of opinion is an essential part of the search for the truth. Nicholas Sagovsky writes: 'Conflict is integral to life in community. It is not the presence of conflict that is unhealthy for communal life, but the premature suppression of conflict in the interests of an inauthentic unity.'[25] Orthodox theologian Thomas Hopko has pleaded for an open debate on the ordination of women on two grounds.[26] Firstly the Orthodox Church does not have an infallible doctrinal authority to decide on questions of Christian faith and practice, so truth can only be found in a debate between members of the church. This is why all believers should be free to express their opinions and be heard, without fear of sanctions or animosity. Secondly history has shown that large groups of believers, sometimes even a majority of them, have supported and defended false doctrines while a minority, including Athanasius and Maximus Confessor, safeguarded the truth.

The discussion about the ordination of women has been testing for the unity of the Old Catholic Churches. This has been a real 'Zerreissprobe' (acid test). The temporary suspension of the German bishop from the IBC after the ordination of the first women priests in 1996 led him to consider the possibility of the German Old Catholic Church joining the Anglican Communion.[27] The Old Catholic churches have largely survived their differences; many members were happy to see the conflict ended and a period of reconciliation within the Union of Utrecht after 1997, a price to which the PNCC contributed through the decision to leave in 2003.

(f) A disruption of eucharistic unity when there is a difference of opinion is as harmful as the suppression of conflict for the sake of a false unity. In the 1870s the lifting of the requirement of priestly celibacy in the Swiss and German Old Catholic churches led to a cooling of relations with the Dutch Old Catholic Church. However, this serious difference of opinion never led to a complete severance, and was followed by an intensified contact, symbolized in the foundation of the Union of Utrecht in 1889. A disruption of the eucharistic community would have been much more harmful than a temporary cooling of relations, and restoration would have been much more difficult. Disrupted eucharistic communion is a severe limitation, and can be an immovable obstacle in the search for truth. However, while there is a community in Christ through the eucharist people will feel a need to settle their conflicts.

(g) The decision in favour of the ordination of women has faced the Church with several consequences and challenges. One is the search for a credible way of involving women in the priestly ministry and dealing with those who oppose this development. The churches have found different solutions for dealing with conscientious objectors to the ordination of women. For some years the Dutch Old Catholic Church announced publicly in any parish whenever a woman priest was to preside at the eucharist, so members who objected could stay away. Recently this decision has been revoked without much resistance. Such a decision will help put an end to double standards for the appreciation of services taken by male or female priests and hopefully also in the appreciation of those priests themselves. It is a sign that reception is progressing: obviously many churchgoers no longer really care whether the priest is male or female.

There was no support in the Old Catholic Church for a far-reaching provision such as the Church of England's Act of Synod, which was opposed on both financial and ecclesiological grounds. The introduction of extra Provincial Episcopal Visitors, or 'flying bishops', was seen as particularly problematic. Anglican theologians also pointed out that careful interpretation was needed to prevent these flying bishops being seen as an alternative episcopal authority, rather than the supplement to normal episcopal authority they were meant to be.

(h) Reception does not simply mean acceptance of the unavoidable. It is a slow process without a fixed outcome which involves distinguishing between the authentic and the spurious, between emotions and theological arguments. It implies the possibility of rejection and is not a legal concept but a relational event, recognizing that major changes 'require space and generosity and a certain amount of elasticity'.[28] Reception is 'an aspect of communion', it is 'a dynamic of giving and receiving', which presupposes 'a partnership in the gospel ... between all who have a stake in the issue that needs to be resolved'.[29]

(i) In 2006 the tenth anniversary of the ordination of the first women priests in the Old Catholic churches was celebrated. Women in office are still a small minority and this is not expected to change soon. This means that women alone do not yet have the power and influence to bring about further changes. They need allies to support their cause, particularly among their male colleagues, leading lay men and women, and among bishops.

The ordination of women as priests, or their consecration as bishops, does not automatically resolve all outstanding questions and may indeed exacerbate them. Yet over the last decade the questions have changed and are no longer about the pros and cons of the ordination of women to the priesthood. Now and in the future it will be a question of the way in which the Old Catholic Church can use the experience and competencies of ordained women, both in practical work and in theological reflection. The decision to include women in the ministry of the Church will have to be reflected in liturgical, legal and other official texts. The reception of the significance of this step, in practice and in theology, is still going on and churches which have ordained women have much to learn from one another.

Bibliography

Amtliches Kirchenblatt des Katholischen Bistums der Alt-Katholiken in Deutschland, ed. Bischöfliches Ordinariat (Bonn: Bischöfliches Ordinariat, 1994 and 1995).

Avis, P., 'Reception. Towards an Anglican Understanding', in P. Avis (ed.), *Seeking the Truth of Change in the Church. Reception, Communion and the Ordination of Women* (London and New York: Continuum/T&T Clark, 2004), pp. 19–39.

Berlis, A., 'Diakonin soll sie sein...!' Die Frauenordination im Gespräch der (alt-katholischen) Kirche', in A. Berlis and K.-D. Gerth (eds), *Christus Spes: Liturgie und Glaube
im ökumenischen Kontext. FS für Bischof Sigisbert Kraft* (Frankfurt a.M.: P. Lang,
1994), pp. 47–62.
——, 'Der Bund alt-katholischer Frauen und sein Engagement für Frauenrechte', in
Muschiol, G. (ed.), *Katholikinnen und Moderne. Katholische Frauenbewegung
zwischen Tradition und Emanzipation* (Münster: Aschendorff, 2003), pp. 199–220.
——, 'Heilige und Heiligenverehrung in der alt-katholischen Kirche', in M. Barnard, P.
Post and E. Rose (eds), *A Cloud of Witness. The Cult of Saints in Past and Present*,
Liturgia Condenda 18 (Louvain: Peeters, 2005), pp. 297–323.
Chaves, M., *Ordaining Women: Culture and Conflict in Religious Organizations*
(Cambridge, MA: Harvard University Press, 1997).
Hopko, T., 'The Debate Continues – 1998', in T. Hopko (ed.), *Women and the Priesthood*,
2nd edn (Crestwood, NY: St Vladimir's Seminary Press, 1999), pp. 249–57.
IBC, 'Communiqué der internationalen alt-katholischen Bischofskonferenz. Sondersession
1. bis 6. Juli 1991 in Wislikofen', *Christen heute*, 35.8 (1991), p. 5.
——, 'Das Communiqué von Wislikofen (1997)', *Christen heute*, 41 (1997), p. 203.
——, Die Erklärung der IBK, *Christen heute*, 41 (1997), pp. 204–5.
Korte, A.-M., 'Erkenning van religieus leiderschap van vrouwen: een "moderne" kwestie?',
Tijdschrift voor Theologie, 43 (2003), pp. 113–23.
Lambeth Commission on Communion, *The Windsor Report* (London: Church House
Publishing, 2004).
Oeyen, C., 'Priesteramt der Frau? Die altkatholische Theologie als Beispiel einer
Denkentwicklung', *Ökumenische Rundschau*, 35 (1986), pp. 254–66.
Parmentier, M., 'Ignaz von Döllinger und Vinzenz von Lerin', *Internationale kirchliche
Zeitschrift*, 81 (1991), pp. 41–58.
Reininger, D., *Diakonat der Frau in der einen Kirche: Diskussionen, Entscheidungen und
pastoral-praktische Erfahrungen in der christlichen Ökumene und ihr Beitrag zur
römisch-katholischen Diskussion* (Ostfildern: Schwabenverlag, 1999).
Sagovsky, N., *Ecumenism, Christian Origins and the Practice of Communion* (Cambridge:
Cambridge University Press, 2000).
Visser, J., 'The Old Catholic Churches of the Union of Utrecht', *International Journal for
the Study of the Christian Church*, 3 (2003), pp. 68–84.
——, 'Die Beziehungen zwischen dem Vatikan und der Utrechter Union aus altkatholischer
Sicht', in H. Gerny, H. Rein and M. Weyermann (eds), *Die Wurzel aller Theologie:
Sentire cum Ecclesia. Festschrift zum 60. Geburtstag von Urs von Arx* (Bern: Stämpfli,
2003), pp. 309–25.
Vobbe, J., Entscheidung zur Frauenordination: Sondersitzung der Internationalen
Bischofskonferenz, *Christen heute*, 41 (1997), pp. 182–3.
——, 'Einheit in der Vielfalt oder Einigkeit im Dissens? Ökumenische Erfahrungen und
Perspektiven aus alt-katholischer Sicht', *KNA Dokumentation*, 10 (27 September
2005), pp. 1–15.
Von Arx, U., 'Die Debatte über die Frauenordination in den Altkatholischen Kirchen der
Utrechter Union', in D. Buser and A. Loretan (eds), *Gleichstellung der Geschlechter
und die Kirchen. Ein Beitrag zur menschenrechtlichen und ökumenischen Diskussion*
(Fribourg: Universitätsverlag, 1999), pp. 165–211.
——, 'The Old Catholic Churches of the Union of Utrecht', in P. Avis (ed.), *The Christian
Church. An Introduction to the Major Traditions* (London: SPCK, 2002), pp. 153–85.
—— (comp.), *The Ordination of Women to the Priesthood. Special Session of the
International Old Catholic Bishops' Conference, July 1–6, 1991, Wislikofen,
Switzerland. Documentation on Behalf of the IBC Commission 'The Position of
Women in the Church'*, English version in part comp. T.A. Schnitker, Berne, May 1991
(published as a manuscript).
Von Arx, U. and Weyermann, M. (eds), 'Statute of the Old Catholic Bishops United in

the Union of Utrecht', *Supplement to the Internationale Kirchliche Zeitschrift*, 91 (2001), pp. 28–42.

Notes

1   Trans. Huub Stegeman, with thanks also to Dr Charlotte Methuen for her help. I would also like to thank the Royal Dutch Academy of Sciences for its financial support.
2   These included Mary the Mother of Jesus, Mary Magdalene, Perpetua and Felicitas, Blandina, Thekla, Makrina, Olympias, Clare of Assisi, Edith Stein, Katharina Staritz and many others. See A. Berlis, 'Heilige und Heiligenverehrung in der Alt-Katholischen Kirche', in M. Barnard, P. Post and E. Rose (eds), *A Cloud of Witness: The Cult of Saints in Past and Present*, Liturgia Condenda 18 (Louvain: Peeters, 2005), pp. 297–323 (321–3).
3   See J. Visser, 'The Old Catholic Churches of the Union of Utrecht', *International Journal for the Study of the Christian Church*, 3 (2003), pp. 68–84; U. von Arx, 'The Old Catholic Churches of the Union of Utrecht', in P. Avis (ed.), *The Christian Church: An Introduction to the Major Traditions* (London: SPCK, 2002), pp. 157–85.
4   U. von Arx, (ed.), *The Ordination of Women to the Priesthood. Special Session of the International Old Catholic Bishops' Conference, July 1–6, 1991, Wislikofen, Switzerland. Documentation on Behalf of the IBC Commission 'The Position of Women in the Church'*, trans. T.A. Schnitker (Berne, May 1991), p. 1.
5   For discussion of women and the diaconate in the Old Catholic Church, see A. Berlis, '"Diakonin soll sie sein...!" Die Frauenordination im Gespräch der (alt-katholischen) Kirche', in A. Berlis and K.-D. Gerth (eds), *Christus Spes: Liturgie und Glaube im ökumenischen Kontext. FS für Bischof Sigisbert Kraft* (Frankfurt a.M.: P. Lang, 1994), pp. 47–62; D. Reininger, *Diakonat der Frau in der einen Kirche: Diskussionen, Entscheidungen und pastoral-praktische Erfahrungen in der christlichen Ökumene und ihr Beitrag zur römisch-katholischen Diskussion* (Ostfildern: Schwabenverlag, 1999), pp. 399–460.
6   Von Arx (ed.), *The Ordination of Women*, p. 3.
7   *Amtliches Kirchenblatt des Katholischen Bistums der Alt-Katholiken in Deutschland* (Bonn: Bischöfliches Ordinariat, 1994), No. 2, p. 7.
8   For women and the priesthood in the Old Catholic Church see C. Oeyen, 'Priesteramt der Frau? Die altkatholische Theologie als Beispiel einer Denkentwicklung', *Ökumenische Rundschau*, 35 (1986), pp. 254–66; U. von Arx, 'Die Debatte über die Frauenordination in den Altkatholischen Kirchen der Utrechter Union', in D. Buser and A. Loretan (eds), *Gleichstellung der Geschlechter und die Kirchen. Ein Beitrag zur menschenrechtlichen und ökumenischen Diskussion* (Fribourg: Universitätsverlag, 1999), pp. 165–211.
9   *Amtliches Kirchenblatt des Katholischen Bistums der Alt-Katholiken in Deutschland* (Bonn: Bischöfliches Ordinariat, 1995), No. 1, p. 3.
10 IBC, 'Communiqué der Internationalen Alt-Katholischen Bischofskonferenz. Sondersession 1. bis 6. Juli 1991 in Wislikofen', *Christen heute*, 35.8 (1991), p. 5 (trans. from the German).
11 Published in German: IBC, 'Das Communiqué von Wislikofen', *Christen heute*, 41 (1997), p. 203.
12 Quoted in J. Vobbe, 'Entscheidung zur Frauenordination: Sondersitzung der Internationalen Bischofskonferenz', *Christen heute*, 41 (1997), pp. 182–3 (182).
13 Statute, B, Art. 1 c., see U. von Arx and M. Weyermann (eds), 'Statute of the Old Catholic Bishops United in the Union of Utrecht', *Supplement to the Internationale Kirchliche Zeitschrift*, 91 (2001), pp. 28–42 (31).
14 IBC, 'Die Erklärung der IBK', *Christen heute*, 41 (1997), pp. 204–5 (204); see also

von Arx, 'Debatte über die Frauenordination', pp. 176–7.

15 'Id teneamus quod ubique, quod semper, quod ab omnibus creditum est: hoc est etenim vere proprieque catholicum.' For a critical appreciation of this, cf. M. Parmentier, 'Ignaz von Döllinger und Vinzenz von Lerin', *Internationale Kirchliche Zeitschrift*, 81 (1991), pp. 41–58.

16 See von Arx, 'Debatte über die Frauenordination', pp. 195–8.

17 This issue re-emerged frequently in discussion on the ordination of women in the Old Catholic Church. See a recent article by German Old Catholic bishop, J. Vobbe, 'Einheit in der Vielfalt oder Einigkeit im Dissens? Ökumenische Erfahrungen und Perspektiven aus alt-katholischer Sicht', *KNA Dokumentation*, 10 (27 September 2005), pp. 1–15 (11).

18 See A. Berlis, 'Der Bund Alt-Katholischer Frauen und sein Engagement für Frauenrechte', in G. Muschiol (ed.), *Katholikinnen und Moderne. Katholische Frauenbewegung zwischen Tradition und Emanzipation* (Münster: Aschendorff, 2003), pp. 199–220.

19 See M. Chaves, *Ordaining Women: Culture and Conflict in Religious Organizations* (Cambridge, MA: Harvard University Press, 1997).

20 For a critical appreciation of Chaves, see A.-M. Korte, 'Erkenning van religieus leiderschap van vrouwen: een "moderne" kwestie?', *Tijdschrift voor Theologie*, 43 (2003), pp. 113–23.

21 In practice this applies also to the episcopate, which has not been explicitly discussed but must be included by virtue of the unity of ordained ministry. Those Old Catholic churches which ordain women to the priesthood include more or less explicitly in their canon law the possibility that all priests who fulfil the requirements may be chosen and consecrated bishop, whether male or female.

22 J. Visser, 'Die Beziehungen zwischen dem Vatikan und der Utrechter Union aus altkatholischer Sicht', in H. Gerny, H. Rein and M. Weyermann (eds), *Die Wurzel aller Theologie: Sentire cum Ecclesia. Festschrift zum 60. Geburtstag von Urs von Arx* (Bern: Stämpfli, 2003), pp. 309–25 (p. 324).

23 See also the Lambeth Commission on Communion, *The Windsor Report* (London: Church House Publishing, 2004), no. 84.

24 See von Arx and Weyermann (eds), 'Statute of the Old Catholic Bishops', pp. 34–5 (B, Art. 6).

25 N. Sagovsky, *Ecumenism, Christian Origins and the Practice of Communion* (Cambridge: Cambridge University Press, 2000), p. 8.

26 T. Hopko, 'The Debate Continues – 1998', in T. Hopko (ed.), *Women and the Priesthood*, 2nd edn (Crestwood, NY: St Vladimir's Seminary Press, 1999), pp. 249–57.

27 Suggested by Bischof Joachim Vobbe on 15 December 2006 at the tenth anniversary celebration in the Poppelsdorfer Schloss, Bonn.

28 P. Avis, 'Reception: Towards an Anglican Understanding', in P. Avis (ed.), *Seeking the Truth of Change in the Church: Reception, Communion and the Ordination of Women* (London and New York: Continuum/T&T Clark, 2004), pp. 19–39 (p. 25).

29 Avis, Reception, p. 26.

Part 3

Sociological Perspectives

11

Forever Pruning? The Path to Ordained Women's Full Participation in the Episcopal Church of the USA

Adair T. Lummis

Introduction: Women priests, rectors and bishops

With the 2006 election of Bishop Katherine Jefferts Schori as Presiding Bishop of the Episcopal Church in the USA, the path to ordained women's full participation might seem to have broadened into a highway. Clearing the path for women's ordination to full clergy status has not been easy, however. The long tradition of only male priests in the Episcopal Church and the Anglican Communion, bolstered by selective references to scripture and confirmed by the legal authority that bishops have over ordination of candidates, are heavy brush through which to start hacking a trail.

Both now and in centuries past, Episcopal lay women have been significantly more involved in worship and programmes of congregations then men, not only in the Episcopal Church but in every other Christian denomination across the world.[1] Yet, 50 years ago no women were allowed to be delegates to General Convention, no women were enrolled in the Master of Divinity programme (typically required for priesthood) at Episcopal seminaries, and in half of the US dioceses women were not even allowed to serve on parish vestries.[2]

Now, women comprise between a third and a half of those entering Master of Divinity programmes in most Episcopal seminaries, are over 20 per cent of the active Episcopal priests,[3] make up 40 per cent of those ordained every year, and 12 women have been elected to the episcopate. Lay women have become a substantial proportion within parish vestries across dioceses; furthermore about two-fifths of the Deputies and First Alternates to General Convention are women, and a laywoman has served as the President of the House of Deputies. These trends would seem to give a good prognosis for continued growth toward full gender equality of ordained women and men in the leadership of the Episcopal Church. However, there are continuing obstacles to achieving gender equality in the Episcopal ordained ministry as well as that of other denominations.

1 Social justice as spur for the ordination of women

Were it not for women's push for social justice, for others and then for themselves, they might never have been ordained. Historians have explored how women's position in Christian churches altered during America's tumultuous early years as it became an independent republic.[4] They focus primarily on the impact of the evangelization movement of the Great Awakening, and its aftermath, both in expanding the numbers of congregations and the definitions of how people qualified to be religious leaders. Changes originating in the religious realm allowed women to gain experience and opportunities to be leaders both within and outside their churches. By the early nineteenth century, some women who had become lay leaders in their congregations were further inspired to become public advocates for major and controversial national causes such as the end of slavery.

The Grimké sisters, Sarah and Angelina, were raised Episcopalian in a Southern slave-holding family, but they abhorred slavery and wanted to work for its eradication. As adults they came north and joined the more liberal Presbyterian Church and then the even more liberal Quakers. Along with other men and women from varying Christian traditions, the sisters were part of what sociologists Young and Cheery describe as the 'confessional protest wave of social movements' in the 1830s.[5] These movements began from religious roots to become organized efforts to denounce as religious 'sins' such behaviour as drinking alcohol and slavery. Thousands of Americans from different denominations and regions of the country united around single-issue causes. Angelina and Sarah Grimké worked very hard for the abolition of slavery, leading to their continued support from adherents to this cause. However, they began to lose affirmation when they insisted on speaking not just to women's assemblies but also to mixed assemblies of women and men. They lost even more supporters and antagonized particularly conservative affiliates when they further demanded that women should have the same rights and responsibilities in society as men. In response the sisters renounced their ties to all formal religious bodies. However, other Episcopal lay women emerged and stayed as leaders in social justice causes, while also advocating women's greater leadership role in the Church.

Throughout the nineteenth century and into the twentieth, these trends of women's activity in sacred and secular places accelerated. More women with official church titles expanded their ministries beyond their local churches and communities. Regional and national, denominational and ecumenical women's organizations came into being. These women's church organizations focused on mission efforts to better the prospects of children and the conditions of the poor: concerns that were deemed within the respectable purview of women. Women within such organizations gained expertise in administration and programme development, as they successfully raised funds for their mission activities. Money is power, and this raised fears that women would take over the Church.[6] The more centralized denominations became on the national level, the less autonomy denominational leaders gave women's boards to deploy funds collected, or even to organize internally.

After the Second World War, stirred by the racial riots in the USA, many women and men became involved in social justice efforts. In this ferment of social change the more liberal women's perspective was not distinctly heard until the mid-1960s. When Betty Friedan published *The Feminine Mystique* in 1963 the Second Wave Feminist Movement was launched, hitting the US churches in the 1970s as no other social movement had in over a century. It most affected the mainline Protestant denominations, those more deeply connected with wider secular society, where women were already making substantial gains in educational attainment and employment. Lay women in the Episcopal Church and other moderate-to-liberal Protestant denominations accordingly had greater opportunity to expand the scope of their leadership than did women in the more conservative charismatic and fundamentalist congregations that set themselves apart from secular society.

By the early 1970s, a number of liberal Christian women had turned their substantial organizational and leadership abilities to promoting women's ordination and placing them in pulpits. Feminist scholars published critiques aimed at changing the male-dominated theological precepts and language used in worship. Coalitions emerged within and among denominations to achieve women's ordination and expand the number of women clergy. Several of these coalitions were connected with the National Council of Churches of Christ (NCCC), which had been formed in the early twentieth century to spread the social gospel through mission activities focused on social justice, racial and economic reform. The NCCC received the bulk of its financial support and operating legitimacy from the national denominational offices of the mainline moderate Protestant denominations, including the Episcopal Church. By the mid-1970s several NCCC subdivisions or associated groups, particularly the Commission on Women in Ministry (COWIM), had begun concerted efforts to end discrimination against women in church leadership positions.[7] These interconnected movements and networks led to more women entering seminaries in the late 1960s and early 1970s, a development that put more pressure on the denominations to ordain these women.

2 Ordination gatekeepers in different denominational polities

Ordination to clergy status indicates that church officials affirm that the aspirant's call from God, spiritual gifts, knowledge, skills and good character are genuine and sufficient to be a leader and interpreter of the faith for a religious community. Can women have such a legitimate call? Some American denominations have ordained women since the mid-nineteenth century, although few women in any denomination were ordained to full clergy status before the latter half of the twentieth century. Some denominations present an easier initial path to ordination than others and even now the ease of the journey varies according to who controls the gates and the rules for getting through them.

In different denominational polities, the primary ordination gatekeepers can be the governing body of a local congregation or the regional and/or national denominational executive. Denominations can be categorized according to where the primary authority for ordination is located, and this classification has consequences for the ordination of women.[8]

Spirit-centred denominations are theologically and socially conservative. They are not traditional in the liturgical sense, however, since their faith focuses on seeing the Holy Spirit at work in new, varied and often charismatic ways. Some of these denominations have ordained women for decades, including the Assemblies of God, Church of God (Anderson), Church of the Nazarene, Free Methodists, Wesleyan and various Pentecostal and Holiness churches. Spirit-centred denominations that do not ordain women include the large historic black denomination the Church of God in Christ and several Pentecostal associations of churches.

The major criterion for ordination in Spirit-centred denominations is an individual, direct, otherworldly spiritual experience of call. Women and men are seen as equally likely to be visited by the Holy Spirit. When first founded, almost all of the Spirit-centred churches ordained women, mainly to fill positions as missionaries, pastoral assistants or to preach in small churches. As these denominations and affiliated congregations grew in size, however, so did their reluctance to grant women any ordained status for their ministries. Regardless of a woman's spiritual authority to prophesy and teach, she would be likely to encounter strong objections to her becoming the ordained preacher and pastor, based on conservative biblical injunctions against women in leadership over men in this world. In the Spirit-centred denominations that do ordain women, the average number of ordained women has actually declined over time.

Congregation-centred denominations view the 'gathered people of God' or the local congregation as the centre of faith and decision-making. In these denominations, congregations are not required to get regional or national church approval for most of their decisions and can call any minister they want, including clergy from another denomination. Such denominations vary in theology and in their acceptance of women in church leadership.

The most liberal denominations on a variety of theological and social issues are the Unitarian-Universalists, the United Church of Christ, the Disciples of Christ and the American Baptists (originally Northern Baptists). For a couple of centuries these denominations, or their pre-merger parent bodies, had lay women preachers and missionaries. This led them to accept women's ordination relatively early and a substantial number of women have been ordained in these denominations.

In sharp contrast another denomination in this cluster, the Southern Baptist Convention, is very conservative theologically. The SBC has recently reaffirmed its strong stance that ordained women are not biblically legitimate, and congregations should never call women as their pastor. However, because the Southern Baptists have a congregational polity, a local church may still ordain and have a woman as pastor. Some more liberal Southern Baptist congregations have done just that. Whether congregation-centred denominations are theologically liberal or conservative, their polity can be a block to women's leadership, since local churches may prefer to hire a male candidate even if he is less qualified than a woman.

Institution-centred denominations have a long tradition of ordered connections between their local, regional and national organizations and officials. In these denominations, ordination is not to a congregation but to the whole denomination. Major decisions with implications for policy concerning ordained orders in the denomination need review not just by local and regional church officials but also by national representative bodies.

Denominations in this group that ordain women include the Episcopal Church, the Presbyterian Church USA, the Evangelical Lutheran Church in America, the Reformed Church in America and the United Methodist Church (UMC). Those that do not ordain women include the Roman Catholic Church and the Lutheran Missouri Synod, the Eastern Orthodox Church, and (at least until very recently), the Christian Reformed Church, as well as churches connected with parts of the Anglican Communion.

The institution-centred denominations that ordain women have done so by sequential steps, such as commissioning, licensing, consecrating or ordaining to a permanent diaconate, and only then to full clergy status. Those who had hoped that permitting women to be deacons would soon lead to them being ordained to the priesthood were disappointed in both the Episcopal Church and Church of England. [9]

In those denominations that ordain women, the power of the regional executive to make final decisions means this body can make it very easy for a woman to be ordained. Conversely, if the executive does not want a particular woman to be ordained – no matter how high her seminary grades or scores on the national exam or how much affirmation she receives from congregational leaders – she will have to seek ordination in another regional judicatory of the denomination or in another denomination.

Checks and balances in the organizational hierarchy of the Episcopal, Anglican and other institution-centred denominations serve to sustain continuity. However, they also make changes in church policy more difficult and are potential causes of greater denominational disruption than would probably arise in Spirit- and congregation-centred denominations.

A lengthy historical tradition of doing things a certain way, combined with a substantial lapse of time between formal legislative meetings and votes, exacerbates the difficulty of changing institutional laws and procedures and gives disproportionate influence to longstanding insiders. [10] However, because institution-centred denominations are interconnected and more centralized, they can often implement new policies faster, further and more firmly than can congregational- and Spirit-centred denominations.

The Episcopal Church and the two denominations that joined to form the Evangelical Lutheran Church did not ordain women to full clergy status until 1976 and 1970 respectively, almost three-quarters of a century after most liberal congregation-centred denominations. However, in part because of their polity, these institution-centred denominations soon matched congregation-centred denominations in proportions of women among their clergy. [11]

3 Continuing resistances to ordained women

Working for social justice through various causes mobilized support for the ordination of women among male and female church leaders during the last half of the twentieth century. Committed Episcopal lay women, ordained and lay men were pivotal in getting women ordained and placed. As Darling writes: 'Until some women could be ordained, all women were second-class in the church; removing the gender test for ordination profoundly altered a central symbol of the tradition.'[12]

A growing number in both the Episcopal Church and the Church of England saw the blocking of women's ordination on grounds of gender as unjust toward humans and a travesty before God. Still, in both churches then and now, as well as in the conservative denominations and congregations, there are those do not want to alter the traditional symbolism of male-only clergy for one or more reasons.

Theological reasons
For the most extreme conservatives, theological objections to the ordination of women are based on biblical injunctions that women should take a secondary role to men in church, home and society. In the USA today some evangelical denominations and independent congregations extend their denial of women's ordination to include all leadership where they would be in positions over men.[13] Such denominations continue to resist any push from the outside culture to ordain women.[14]

Most (but not all) regional and national church executives in the mainline Protestant denominations would probably agree with Harriet Baber that theological objections to the ordination of women rest on 'highly questionable assumptions, including particularly the controversial assumption that there are theologically significant gender differences'.[15] Yet these executives are probably aware of pockets of resistance to clergywomen among their congregations, and so may proceed cautiously in both recommending women for ordination and as clergy for empty pulpits.

Reasons related to preserving unity
One of the major reasons delaying the ordination of women in the Episcopal Church, as well as the Church of England, was purportedly to keep congregations, dioceses or the whole Church together and in good communion with denominations ordaining only men.[16] Preserving the unity of the Anglican Communion is also cited by some diocesan leaders who caution against election of women to the episcopate.

Sensitivity to the objections of those who might leave a congregation or denomination if a woman became their pastor or bishop, particularly in the institution-centred denominations, remains a reason for delaying the ordination or clergy placement of women in the USA. When they hire a man rather than a woman as their pastor, local search committees often assert that though they have no personal objections, others do, and they value church unity more highly than gender equity.[17]

Resistance based on belief that women lead churches less well than men, so should be unpaid

There are stereotypes about women's presumed lesser ability to perform well as top leaders in any organization, especially the Church. Some pastoral search committees fear clergywomen will be less effective in promoting monetary and member vitality and growth, and may even reduce the number of men in active congregational membership. There is no support for either of these apprehensions, as numerous studies have shown.[18] Nevertheless, these stereotypes still block women's ordained leadership in congregations, particularly in senior positions. Church officials responsible for helping congregations to find the right pastor may encounter tension between following denominational anti-discrimination policies for hiring clergy and maintaining congregational satisfaction with the denomination.

During the 1980s and 1990s, ordained women became more visible; at the same time there were fewer paid ministerial posts available. Paula Nesbitt describes the backlash against Episcopal women priests, which started around this time, as being directly proportional to the increase in their numbers and the reduction in parishes needing rectors.[19] Ordained women found wider acceptance as assistant and associate ministers under the direction of senior ordained men. This conditional recognition, while allowing more women priests to serve, damaged their career mobility.[20] By the same token, dioceses might be more welcoming of ordained women in lower orders of the Church hierarchy than in the priesthood. Nesbitt connects the backlash against women priests with the growth of Episcopal women in the permanent diaconate, predominantly an unpaid order from which people do not go on to become priests.[21] Some church officials still prefer women to stay as deacons permanently, and many women ordained to this order appear content not to pursue priesthood.[22] By increasing numbers of women in the permanent diaconate, bishops can claim many more clergywomen in their dioceses, while still reserving the priesthood for the more motivated men.[23] Women's preponderance in unpaid lower orders can also give ammunition to those who claim that they lack the dedication to seek priesthood.

Permanent deacons typically receive ministerial education before their ordination in one- or two-year part-time training programmes run by their diocese. Similar preparation for lay pastors and deacons in other denominations predominantly produces women graduates.[24] In recent years the Episcopal Church has seen a significant rise in the number of women ordained to the vocational or permanent diaconate, a trend Price expects to continue.[25] The major reason these programmes are growing is the need for volunteer clergy, who have some ministerial training, to pastor impoverished congregations.

The resistance to ordained women in top church positions has decreased during the last three decades but it has not disappeared. Episcopal laity and clergy surveyed in 2002 were more approving of women holding church leadership positions than those questioned 15 years earlier. On both occasions, however, church members grew less favourable towards women filling positions the higher these were in the Episcopal hierarchy.[26] This was particularly true of respondents from parishes in the South.[27]

Resistance due to conservative regional culture

The culture of a region can expedite or block the likelihood of women being ordained or paid to be pastors. Denominations with a substantial proportion of congregations in the South were less likely to ordain women, or slower to do so, than denominations concentrated elsewhere. Chaves says this is because in the South-eastern states there was less acceptance of the ideal of equality between women and men in almost every occupation or social arena, including the church.[28] A recent national study confirmed that the South is the most politically and socially conservative area of the USA on a variety of issues.[29] Social opposition to legal marriages between same-sex partners is greater in the South, as is religious resistance to considering the ordination of openly gay or lesbian people. The South is also the most 'churched' region of the USA and where the larger, wealthier congregations are. Philip Jenkins shows these trends hold for the global South as well, both in more conservative theology and greater church growth for all denominations, including Anglican and Episcopal churches.[30]

In the Episcopal Church, the initial resistance to women's ordination came from dioceses in the Southern USA and the more Anglo-Catholic dioceses of the lower Midwest 'Biretta Belt'. Compared to men, fewer women are ordained yearly in these dioceses, and are less likely to acquire the better clergy positions and accompanying salaries.[31]

Resistance because clergywomen are too liberal

There are congregations that would not welcome ordained women even in subordinate positions, for fear they might use inclusive language in worship, support the ordination of homosexuals and involve the Church in social justice causes, particularly those involving political advocacy. Many clergy-women ordained in the 1970s and 1980s held these values, considered 'feminist' at the time.[32] The 1993 'Re-Imagining Conference' in Minneapolis exacerbated fears among conservative factions in several mainline denominations that clergywomen might espouse feminist theology from the pulpit.[33] This conference got extensive publicity in the secular press, largely because of its worship celebrations emphasizing Sophia as the female aspect of God. Although nearly forgotten over a decade later, there may still be suspicions that clergywomen are predominantly more liberal than their male colleagues in terms of church and social activism.

Clergy surveyed in several mainline Protestant denominations show this to be true. In 2003 Deckman *et al.* found that clergywomen held far more liberal values than did clergymen on women's legal rights (including the right to an abortion) and on civil rights for homosexuals, as well as being more politically active in their communities.[34] Olson, Crawford and Deckman subsequently interviewed women pastors, concluding that most believed they had a sacred calling to speak out and act locally in trying to change policies and community conditions that kept some groups economically and socially disadvantaged.[35]

Episcopal clergywomen follow this pattern of activism more than clergymen do.[36] They were found to be more likely than clergymen or lay members to use inclusive language in worship both for humans[37] and for God.[38] Further, if people are members of a congregation with a woman priest on the pastoral staff they are also more likely to approve of inclusive language.

Not all clergywomen who endorse a particular justice issue necessarily act on or promote it. About a third of those women pastors interviewed by Olsen and her colleagues in 2005 felt constrained in acting on their values, sometimes because of anticipated objections from denominational officials or lay leaders. Attitudinal divisions on justice issues within the congregations, was the greatest deterrent to clergywomen, however, since taking any stance that might divide their congregation further would not be good ministry. Similarly, Episcopal female priests were more likely to advocate taking action on political or social causes than male priests or laity,[39] unless they saw their congregation as predominantly conservative. As already noted, the Episcopal clergy and laypersons least likely to undertake social advocacy were in the South.[40]

4 Why women want to be ordained

Given these continuing obstacles to parish deployment of clergywomen, the main reason why women want to be ordained in the USA as elsewhere is because this is 'more than just a job'.[41] Women may have different priorities for ordination than men, and these may change with time. In 1980 ordained women from mainline Protestant denominations in the USA were preaching in pulpits where no woman had preached before, and in locations where church members of other denominations were unlikely to have seen a woman pastor either. A decade later, many towns and cities had at least one congregation headed by an ordained woman. Did this make a difference to reasons for seeking ordination?

Conviction of God's call
A sense of God's call was a central motivation for the great majority of both women and men in deciding to seek ordination, according to cross-denominational surveys in 1980–81 and 1993–94.[42] Women may have been less sure that their call was to ordained ministry, though, often lacking the amount of social support that men received for pursuing a sense of vocation. This may be one reason why clergywomen enter seminary at later ages on average than do men.[43] Clergywomen's delay in acting on a sense of call has also been found in the Church of England, for similar reasons.[44]

Desire to exercise priesthood and/or be recognized as legitimate ministers
Only clergy may perform certain actions in worship, particularly in institution-centred denominations. In 1981 Episcopal clergywomen had long been barred from administering the sacraments and were more likely than

the total sample of clergy across denominations to cite as an important reason for seeking ordination a 'desire to administer the sacraments and perform other priestly acts'. Many were lay women, doing much of the active ministry in congregations, yet their ministries were not accepted or recognized as valuable. Gaining acceptance for their ministry by legitimization through ordination was more important for all clergy in the 1980–81 survey, particularly women for whom this was a novelty; whereas nearly a generation later almost all these figures fell, as depicted in Table 1.

Table 1: **Priestly ministry and acceptance motivations**

Motivations to seek ordination (% 'quite important')		Episcopal clergy Women Men		Total clergy Women Men	
To administer sacraments and other priestly acts	1980–81	84%	55%	56%	35%
	1993–94	67%	58%	42%	25%
Greater acceptance of my ministry by ordination	1980–81	42%	32%	56%	47%
	1993–94	17%	21%	40%	30%

Women's concern to diminish sexism

Despite the role of 1970s Second Wave Feminism in the USA in lifting the injustice of denying women ordination, there was no united feminist front among the supporters of women clergy. Internal divisions existed over whether women are equal, inferior, or superior to men in various qualities deemed important for ordained ministry, both generally[45] and even among feminist women. Another source of division arose from ordination gatekeepers who gave preference to ordaining as priests women who eschewed the term 'feminist'.[46] In England and the USA only a minority of women sought ordination 'to change the sexist nature of the Church'. This was particularly true in the 1990s when women pastors had become far more visible in US congregations.

Table 2: **Women clergy ordained to change the sexist nature of the Church**

	Episcopal clergywomen		Total clergywomen (seven denominations)	
	1980–81	1993–94	1980–81	1993–94
Quite important	23%	7%	27%	10%
Somewhat important	39%	26%	29%	25%
Somewhat–quite important	62%	33%	56%	35%

Women's need for paid pastoral positions
Full ordination is required for most positions as rector of a self-supporting
parish, and is often an advantage in getting a professional position in other
church-connected organizations. Yet in 1993–94 fewer Episcopal clergy
than those of other denominations surveyed said that being better able to get
clergy positions was important in their seeking ordination. Those eagerly
entering seminary may never have considered the possibility that they might
not become full-time paid rectors.

Table 3: **Clergy who wanted ordination for church position**

1993–94	Episcopal Women	Clergy Men	Clergy (15 denominations) Women	Men
Quite important	7%	6%	21%	13%
Somewhat important	15%	18%	24%	25%
Somewhat–quite important	22%	24%	45%	38%

The clergy job market may actually deter more people from ordination
than it attracts. The average age of seminarians entering training or being
ordained, particularly women, has increased by a decade since 1970 in the
Episcopal Church, and in seminaries of other mainline Protestant denominations.[47] Some research indicates that students with initial interests in
ordination may decide against this in part because of the better career
prospects with a degree in a secular field.[48]

5 Continuing obstacles to women being ordained

More women are training for ministry than ever before, yet Association of
Theological Schools statistics indicate that over twice as many men (4,293)
as women (2,121) completed their Master of Divinity degree at ATS
seminaries in 2005. This includes seminarians in denominations that do not
ordain women, but the statistics are sobering, even for mainline Protestant
denominations.

Of those women who finish training, some may have decided against
considering ordination or a ministerial career by their senior year or earlier,
through lack of support from faculty and denominational officials. Barbara
Finlay followed students in a Presbyterian seminary and describes how the
faculty and others discouraged women from considering parish ministry.[49]
She warns:

> If we were to count the number of women who wanted to pursue
> ministry but were discouraged by their pastors; plus the number who in
> seminary became discouraged by the discrimination and resistance they
> experience; our estimate of the number of women who have left the

religious calling for other work would be much greater than has been recognized.[50]

When getting a church position is part of being ordained to full ministerial status, as it is in most institution-centred denominations, this makes ordination even more difficult, particularly for women. There were many more women in seminary and leading worship in the mainline denominations during the latter part of the twentieth century, but this did not seem to make it easier than before for them to be ordained; quite the contrary.

In the late 1970s, soon after the ordination of women became legal in most Episcopal Church dioceses, the majority of women had some difficulty in becoming priests. The next five years saw a climate of affirmation for women's ordination, so much so that women had an easier time becoming priests than did men in many dioceses. By the late 1980s a backlash had begun and positions were reversed, as shown in Table 4, based on a 1993–94 survey of clergy perceptions.

Table 4: **Ease of ordination by gender and year**

Percentage saying 'Somewhat to quite difficult' to be ordained to full ministerial status	*Episcopal clergy*		*Total clergy*	
	Women	*Men*	*Women*	*Men*
Year of ordination 1980 and before	67%	36%	25%	17%
1981–85	42%	63%	26%	34%
1986–94	53%	32%	36%	34%

Twenty-first-century women and social justice

National women's church organizations
Success can bring premature complacency. By the start of this century, women's ministry was neither a major priority of the National Council of Churches nor its supporting denominations: churches that individually and collectively had done much to advance the ordination of women. In 2003 a conference in Hartford Seminary of the Justice for Women's Working Group (the only remaining National Council office focused on fairness for women in Church and society) discussed its ever-diminishing finance and loss of active younger women members.

Leaders attributed these crises to the fact that the women's movement had already attained many of its goals, leaving women to ask why they should support these organizations with their money or time. It was said that women are now too busy to give much time to causes outside their jobs and families. Furthermore, younger women are primarily oriented to what some call 'Third Wave Feminism' and do not now see women becoming leaders as problematic. If they attend church they usually have minimal interest in changing the language to include female images of humans and of God. Third Wave feminists are interested in the impact of social issues and global factors on people of every race, nationality and sexual orientation.

Church executives and national commissions have downsized or disbanded women's boards and agencies on the premise that combining women with men into one larger committee is more 'inclusive'.[51] 'Inclusivity', however, does not necessarily mean 'equality'. Leaders of national women's denominational organizations, who had believed their fight for full women's participation in the Church had almost been won, were taken off guard.

Matters were much the same in the women's organizations of the Episcopal Church. Lay and ordained women on national church staff or committees had a broader church view than those in the dioceses. They saw the need to keep open the ECUSA path to full participation by women, both as clergy and professional staff, and to continue education and work for women's concerns. Over the last 15 years the Women's Ministries Office at the Episcopal Church Center has run countrywide programmes for women's leadership. In 2001 the Committee on Status of Women of the Executive Council of the Episcopal Church began a national research project to assess the attitudes toward and extent of women's church leadership, following a survey nearly 15 years earlier. This research was to help national and diocesan committees decide how they could increase the leadership of women in the Episcopal Church.[52]

Clergywomen's continuing and new social justice concerns
Concern about justice for others has always been pivotal to the ministry of clergywomen in the mainline denominations. In 2002 Episcopal clergywomen were significantly more likely than clergymen or lay people to affirm that all levels of the Church should be working with families affected by welfare reform and medical care legislation, should be involved in ecology and the environment, should combat homophobia and heterosexism, and help to end racial or ethnic discrimination.[53] Of these four mission areas, Episcopal clergy and laity of both genders agreed that the priority was the elimination of racial and ethnic discrimination in ordination and in church employment policy. The greatest discrepancy in perceived importance was for reducing homophobia in church and society. Clergywomen said this was the second most significant mission area, whereas clergymen and lay people saw it as least important.

Those Episcopal clergywomen most concerned with reducing homophobia are also more likely to endorse all three other mission areas. They are the clergywomen most supportive of inclusive language in church services, who firmly believe that the Episcopal Church at all levels should strengthen deployment and compensation of female priests and lay professionals.[54] For these women priests, eradicating homophobia is part of their concern for justice as a whole, not a single issue.

Those who most want the Episcopal Church to focus on reducing homophobia are also those most open to women in all church leadership positions. They are usually the same people who endorse the Church's involvement in addressing other justice concerns. This leaves an opposite cluster of those who do not want their congregation, diocese or the national Episcopal Church to work for justice in any of these areas. They are dispro-portionately clergy and lay men, along with lay women in the South.

Some might suggest that clergywomen would do better to keep away from social advocacy or including disenfranchised groups in the Church, and instead concern themselves with otherworldly matters and the spiritual health of their congregations. The experience of the Spirit-centred denomi-nations, where the numbers and status of ordained women have declined over time, argues against that however. Faith, combined with striving for social justice in this world, appears to be a strong bulwark against the growth of institutional sexism in the churches.

More women or more ethnic minority priests?

When three different studies have asked Episcopal priests whether more women should be ordained, male priests have responded less enthusiastically than women clergy. Whereas 44 per cent of male clergy agreed with the suggestion in 1980–81, by 1993–94 this figure had fallen to 38 per cent and in 2002 was 36 per cent. The figures for women clergy also fell, from 81 per cent in 1980–81, to 69 per cent in 1993–94 and 59 per cent in 2002.

Episcopal women surveyed in 2002, both lay and ordained, saw other more pressing justice issues than women's ordination and church leadership. A majority of Episcopal clergy and laity surveyed, both women and men, said it was of greater importance to ordain more people from ethnic minorities.[55] A need to increase the numbers of racial and ethnic minority priests does not, however, have to conflict with the ordination of more women. Women seeking ordination in the Episcopal Church may be of Asian, Black or Hispanic ethnicity, either immigrants or US-born. Those dioceses with less support for ordaining women also lag behind in ordaining candidates from racial and ethnic minorities, another contrast between the North-east and the South.[56]

A fair reward for labour?

Becoming ordained is only the first step for clergywomen's full participation in ministry. Over the last decade in the Episcopal Church, as in other denom-inations, parishes have paid ordained women consistently less than ordained men, partly because they are less likely to be senior pastors.[57] An unknown, but probably substantial, number of seminary-educated women have been unable to find full-time or paid clergy positions of any sort. Episcopal Church statistics indicate that clergywomen's median salary is $10,000 less than that of clergymen in parish ministry, and that clergywomen are dispro-portionately found in associate, assistant and curate positions. Even the relatively few clergywomen (14 per cent) who become senior rectors make about $13,000 a year less than do their male counterparts.[58] These condi-tions continue to block the path to women's full participation in the ministry of the Church.

Postscript

The emphasis on social justice, held by women and those men who support them, has given them the strength to cut the path to the women's ordination, and the persistence to continue pruning the undergrowth. Those who pursue social justice goals may not always be highly diplomatic, and without care their words and actions may sometimes divide a congregation, a diocese, a denomination and a communion. Yet the challenge of achieving women's full participation remains, in provinces throughout the Anglican Communion and in other denominations. What is needed is to hold fast to the value of social justice for women, and for all those who are disenfranchised now, so they can be brought fully into the life and leadership of the churches.

Bibliography

Books and articles
Baber, H., 'What Women's Ordination Entails. A Logical Investigation', *Theology*, C11.806 (March/April 1999).
Barker, L.R. and Martin, B.E., *Alternatives in Theological Education* (New Brighton, MN: United Theological Seminary, 2000).
Beit-Hallahmi, B., 'Religion, Religiosity and Gender', in C. Ember (ed.), *The Encyclopedia of Sex and Gender* (Boston, MA: Kluwer, 2003), pp. 117–27.
Carroll, J.W, *God's Potters: Pastoral Leadership in the Shaping of Congregations* (Grand Rapids, MI: Eerdmans, 2006).
Carroll, J.W., Hargrove, B. and Lummis, A.T., *Women of the Cloth: A New Opportunity for Churches* (San Francisco, CA: Harper & Row, 1983).
Chaves, M., *Ordaining Women: Culture and Conflict in Religious Organizations* (Cambridge, MA: Harvard University Press, 1997).
Committee on the Status of Women in the Episcopal Church, *Reaching Toward Wholeness II; The 21st Century Survey* (New York: Episcopal Church Center, 2003).
Darling, P., *New Wine: The Story of Women Transforming Leadership and Power in the Episcopal Church* (Boston, MA: Cowley, 1994).
Deckman, M.M., Crawford, S.E., Olson, L.R., Green, J.C., 'Clergy and the Politics of Gender', *Journal for the Scientific Study of Religion*, 42 (2003), pp. 621–31.
Donovan, M., *Women Priests in the Episcopal Church: The Experience of the First Decade* (Cincinnati, OH: Forward Movement Publications, 1998).
Finlay, B., *Facing the Stained Glass Ceiling: Gender in a Protestant Seminary* (Lanham, MD: University Press of America, 2003).
Francis, L.J., and Robbins, M., *The Long Diaconate 1987–1994 Women Deacons and the Delayed Journey to Priesthood* (Leominster: Gracewing, 1999).
Gallagher, S., 'The Marginalization of Evangelical Feminism', *Sociology of Religion*, 65 (2004), pp. 215–37.
Hartmann, S.M., 'Expanding Feminism's Field and Focus: Activism in the National Council of Churches in the 1960s and 1970s', in M.L. Bendroth and V.L. Brereton (eds), *Women in Twentieth Century Protestantism* (Champaign, IL: University of Illinois Press, 2002), pp. 49–69.
Hiatt, S.R., 'Women's Ordination in the Anglican Communion: Can this Church be Saved?', in C. Wessinger (ed.), *Religious Institutions and Women's Leadership: New Roles Inside the Mainstream* (Columbia, SC: University of South Carolina Press, 1996), pp. 210–27.

Jenkins, P., *The Next Christendom: The Coming of Global Christianity* (Oxford: Oxford University Press, 2002).

Jones, I., *Women and Priesthood in the Church of England: Ten Years On* (London: Church House Publishing, 2004).

Lehman, E.C., *Women's Path into Ministry: Six Major Studies* (Durham, NC: Duke Divinity, Pulpit and Pew reports, 2002).

Lindley, S.H., *You Have Stept out of Your Place: A History of Women and Religion in America* (Louisville, KY: Westminster John Knox Press, 1996).

Lummis, A.T., *What Do Lay People Want in Pastors? Answers from Lay Search Committee Chairs and Regional Judicatory Leaders* (Durham, NC: Duke Divinity, Pulpit and Pew reports, 2003).

——, 'A Research Note: Real Men and Church Participation', *Review of Religious Research*, 25 (2004), pp. 404–14.

Nesbitt, P., *Feminization of the Clergy in America: Occupational and Organizational Perspectives* (New York: Oxford University Press, 1997).

——, 'Women's Ordination: Problems and Possibilities. Five Lessons from Episcopal Women Clergy', Plenary address, Women's Ordination Conference, 2002.

Olson, L.R., Crawford, S.E.S. and Deckman, M.M., *Women with a Mission: Religion, Gender and the Politics of Women Clergy* (Tuscaloosa, AL: University of Alabama Press, 2005).

Price, M.J., *The 2004 Church Compensation Report* (New York: Church Pension Group, 2005).

——, 'The State of the Clergy 2006' (New York: Church Pension Group, 2006).

Schneider, C.J. and Schneider, D., *In their Own Right: The History of American Clergywomen* (New York: Crossroad, 1997).

Silk, M., 'Religion and Region in American Public Life', *Journal for the Scientific Study of Religion*, 44 (2005), pp. 265–90.

Sullins, P., 'The Stained Glass Ceiling: Career Attainment for Women Clergy', *Sociology of Religion*, 61 (2006), pp. 243–66.

Taves, A., 'Feminization Revisited: Protestantism and Gender at the Turn of the Century', in M.L. Bendroth and V.L. Brereton (eds), *Women in Twentieth Century Protestantism* (Champaign, IL: University of Illinois Press, 2002), pp. 304–24.

Wheeler, B.G., 'Is there a Problem? Theological Students and Religious Leadership for the Future', *Auburn Studies*, 8 (New York: Auburn Seminary, 2001).

Wind, J.P. and Gilbert, R.R., *The Leadership Situation Facing American Congregations* (Bethesda, MD: Alban Institute, 2001).

Woolever, C., Bruce, D., Wulff, K. and Smith-Williams, I., 'The Gender Ratio in the Pews: Consequences for Congregational Vitality', *Journal of Beliefs and Values*, 27 (2006), pp. 25–38.

Young, M.P., and Cheery, S.M., 'The Secularization of Confessional Protests: The Role of Religious Processes of Rationalization and Differentiation', *Journal for the Scientific Study of Religion*, 44 (December 2005), pp. 373–95.

Zikmund, B.B., Lummis, A.T. and Chang, P.M.Y., *Clergy Women: An Uphill Calling* (Louisville, KY: Westminster John Knox Press, 1998).

Websites
http://newark.rutgers.edu/~lcrew/womenpr.html

Notes

1   See B. Beit-Hallahmi, 'Religion, Religiosity and Gender' in C. Ember, (ed.), *The Encyclopedia of Sex and Gender* (Boston, MA: Kluwer, 2003), pp. 117–27 (117–18).

2   See M. Donovan, *Women Priests in the Episcopal Church: The Experience of the First*

Decade (Cincinnati, OH: Forward Movement Publications, 1998) and P. Darling, *New Wine: The Story of Women Transforming Leadership and Power in the Episcopal Church* (Boston, MA: Cowley, 1994).

3   See Louie Crew's website http://newark.rutgers.edu/~lcrew/womenpr.html for statistics on women priests and bishops and updates on ordinations of women by Matthew Price of the Church Pension Group.

4   See S.H. Lindley, *You Have Stept Out of Your Place: A History of Women and Religion in America* (Louisville, KY: Westminster John Knox Press, 1996) and C.J. Schneider and D. Schneider, *In their Own Right: The History of American Clergywomen* (New York: Crossroad, 1997).

5   M.P. Young and S.M. Cheery, 'The Secularization of Confessional Protests: The Role of Religious Processes of Rationalization and Differentiation', *Journal for the Scientific Study of Religion*, 44 (December 2005), pp. 373–95.

6   See A. Taves, 'Feminization Revisited: Protestantism and Gender at the Turn of the Century' in M.L. Bendroth and V.L. Brereton (eds), *Women in Twentieth Century Protestantism* (Champaign, IL: University of Illinois Press, 2002), pp. 304–24.

7   S.M. Hartmann, 'Expanding Feminism's Field and Focus: Activism in the National Council of Churches in the 1960s and 1970s', in M.L. Bendroth and V.L. Brereton (eds), *Women in Twentieth Century Protestantism* (Champaign, IL: University of Illinois Press, 2002), pp. 49–69.

8   Barbara Brown Zikmund developed this polity schema, see: B.B. Zikmund, A.T. Lummis and P.M.Y. Chang, *Clergy Women: An Uphill Calling* (Louisville, KY: Westminster John Knox Press, 1998), pp. 6–15.

9   See P. Darling, *New Wine: The Story of Women Transforming Leadership and Power in the Episcopal Church* (Boston, MA: Cowley, 1994); L.J. Francis and M. Robbins, *The Long Diaconate 1987–1994 Women Deacons and the Delayed Journey to Priesthood* (Leominster: Gracewing, 1999), and I. Jones, *Women and Priesthood in the Church of England: Ten Years On* (London: Church House Publishing, 2004).

10   Darling, *New Wine*, pp. 219–20.

11   Proportion of women clergy in 2000: congregation-centred denominations, which first ordained women in the nineteenth century, American Baptist Church 1,032 (13 per cent); Disciples of Christ 1,564 (22 per cent). Institution-centred denominations, which first ordained women in the last quarter of the twentieth century, Episcopal Church 3,482 (20 per cent); Evangelical Lutheran Church in America 2,358 (13 per cent).

12   Darling, *New Wine*, pp. 230 also Donovan, *Women Priests* and P. Nesbitt, *Feminization of the Clergy in America: Occupational and Organizational Perspectives* (New York: Oxford University Press, 1997).

13   S. Gallagher, 'The Marginalization of Evangelical Feminism', *Sociology of Religion*, 65 (2004), pp. 215–37.

14   M. Chaves, *Ordaining Women: Culture and Conflict in Religious Organizations* (Cambridge, MA: Harvard University Press, 1997), pp. 96, 174, *et passim*.

15   H. Baber, 'What Women's Ordination Entails. A Logical Investigation', *Theology*, CII.806 (March/April 1999), p. 1.

16   Jones, *Women and Priesthood*, pp. 71–3.

17   See J.W. Carroll, B. Hargrove and A.T. Lummis, *Women of the Cloth: A New Opportunity for Churches* (San Francisco, CA: Harper & Row, 1983); Chaves, *Ordaining Women*; E.C. Lehman, *Women's Path into Ministry: Six Major Studies* (Durham, NC: Duke Divinity, Pulpit and Pew research reports, 2002); and Zikmund, Lummis and Chang, *Clergy Women*. Two studies conducted in 1987 and 2002 found Episcopal Church lay and clergy in dioceses across the country were significantly more likely to say they would accept a woman in top church leadership than they thought was true of most in their congregations; Committee on the Status of Women in the Episcopal Church, *Reaching Toward Wholeness II; The 21st Century Survey* (New

York: Episcopal Church Center, 2003), p. 17.

18 See Lehman, *Women's Path*; A.T. Lummis, *What Do Lay People Want in Pastors? Answers from Lay Search Committee Chairs and Regional Judicatory Leaders* (Durham, NC: Duke Divinity, Pulpit and Pew Reports, 2003); A.T. Lummis, 'A Research Note: Real Men and Church Participation', *Review of Religious Research*, 25 (2004), pp. 404–14 and C. Woolever, D. Bruce, K. Wulff and I. Smith-Williams, 'The Gender Ratio in the Pews: Consequences for Congregational Vitality', *Journal of Beliefs and Values*, 27 (2006), pp. 25–38.

19 Nesbitt, *Feminization of the Clergy*, pp. 109, 117–22.

20 P. Sullins, 'The Stained Glass Ceiling: Career Attainment for Women Clergy', *Sociology of Religion*, 61 (2006), pp. 243–66.

21 Nesbitt, *Feminization of the Clergy*, pp. 118–20. Some Episcopal dioceses call the permanent diaconate the 'vocational' or 'perpetual diaconate'. These names distinguish it from the 'transitional diaconate' leading to priesthood.

22 In some dioceses, permanent deacons are raised up from and serve only in their home congregation or are bishop's deacons, sent to help congregations where needed. They are often older persons or women who are not employed outside the home.

23 P. Nesbitt, 'Women's Ordination: Problems and Possibilities. Five Lessons from Episcopal Women Clergy' plenary address, Women's Ordination Conference, 2002. For research on women 'permanent NSMs' in the Church of England see Jones, *Women and Priesthood*, pp. 113–15.

24 For a study of lay pastors in small churches see J.P. Wind and R.R. Gilbert, *The Leadership Situation Facing American Congregations* (Bethesda, MD: Alban Institute, 2001). L.R. Barker and B.E. Martin, *Alternatives in Theological Education* (New Brighton, MN: United Theological Seminary, 2000) studied programmes in six Protestant denominations preparing graduates to serve as lay pastors and permanent deacons They found that about 60 per cent of the advanced students and graduates of these programmes are women, typically women over 50.

25 M.J. Price, 'The State of the Clergy 2006' (New York: Church Pension Group, 2006).

26 Those 'very willing' to have a woman senior warden in their congregation were 75 per cent in 1987 and 87 per cent in 2002; 'very willing' to have a woman assistant minister about 63 per cent in 1987 and 80 per cent in 2002; 'very willing' to have a woman rector 43 per cent in 1987 rising to 70 per cent in 2002; and a woman diocesan bishop 34 per cent in 1987 rising to 63 per cent in 2002.

27 In 2002 those 'very willing' to have a woman as their rector were North-east 79 per cent and South 45 per cent; as their bishop, North-east 79 per cent and South 40 per cent.

28 Chaves, *Ordaining Women*, pp. 135–9.

29 M. Silk, 'Religion and Region in American Public Life', *Journal for the Scientific Study of Religion*, 44 (2005), pp. 265–90.

30 P. Jenkins, *The Next Christendom: The Coming of Global Christianity* (Oxford: Oxford University Press, 2002), pp. 7–8.

31 See Price, 'The State of the Clergy 2006'.

32 See Carroll, Hargrove and Lummis, *Women of the Cloth* and Zikmund, Lummis and Chang, *Clergy Women*.

33 Some 2,000 women, representing 16 denominations, attended this conference celebrating the midpoint of the WCC Ecumenical Decade of Churches in Solidarity with Women 1988–1998. It created a backlash against liberal theology and clergy-women in the conservative factions of mainline denominations, particularly PCUSA and UMC. See Schneider and Schneider, *In Their Own Right*, pp. 232–44.

34 M.M. Deckman, S.E.S. Crawford, L.R. Olson and J.C. Green, 'Clergy and the Politics of Gender', *Journal for the Scientific Study of Religion*, 42 (2003), pp. 621–31.

35 L.R. Olson, S.E.S. Crawford and M.M. Deckman, *Women with a Mission: Religion, Gender and the Politics of Women Clergy* (Tuscaloosa, AL: University of Alabama

Press, 2005).
36 Survey evidence is presented in the report by the Committee on the Status of Women, *Reaching Toward Wholeness II* (2003), p. 21.
37 Clergy in 2002 who agreed with inclusive language referring to 'men and women' rather than just 'men': Episcopal clergywomen 84 per cent and clergymen 65 per cent; lay women 49 per cent and men 45 per cent.
38 Comfortable using female nouns for God: clergywomen 66 per cent and clergymen 43 per cent; lay women 30 per cent and lay men 24 per cent.
39 Committee on the Status of Women, *Reaching Toward Wholeness II* (2003), pp. 32–44.
40 Only 36 per cent of the survey respondents in the South had been involved in any social advocacy during the last few years, compared to 45 per cent in the North-central, 47 per cent in the West, and 53 per cent in the North-east.
41 See Jones, *Women and Priesthood*, pp. 68–70 on motives for ordination in the Church of England.
42 Carroll, Hargrove and Lummis, *Women of the Cloth* and Zikmund, Lummis and Chang, *Clergy Women* are based on these surveys.
43 Zikmund, Lummis and Chang, *Clergy Women*, pp. 98–9.
44 Jones, *Women and Priesthood*, pp. 61–2.
45 Lindley, *You Have Stept*, pp. 425–6.
46 S.R. Hiatt, 'Women's Ordination in the Anglican Communion: Can this Church be Saved?', in C. Wessinger (ed.), *Religious Institutions and Women's Leadership: New Roles inside the Mainstream* (Columbia, SC: University of South Carolina Press, 1996), pp. 210–27.
47 See Price, 'The State of the Clergy 2003', and 'The State of the Clergy 2006' and Zikmund, Lummis and Chang, *Clergy Women*.
48 B.G. Wheeler, 'Is there a Problem? Theological Students and Religious Leadership for the Future', *Auburn Studies*, 8 (New York: Auburn Seminary, 2001).
49 B. Finlay, *Facing the Stained Glass Ceiling: Gender in a Protestant Seminary* (Lanham, MD: University Press of America, 2003).
50 Finlay, *Facing the Stained Glass Ceiling*, pp. 127–8.
51 See several chapters in Bendroth and Brereton (eds), *Women in Twentieth Century Protestantism*.
52 The 2002 survey owes a great deal to three lay women: Marjorie Burke (project chair), Sally Bucklee (chair of the committee) and Marge Christie (consultant for the committee, who recently chaired the US caucus to the 50th UN Commission on the Status of Women).
53 These indices are based on additive scales of three items for each of the four mission areas. Survey respondents were asked to prioritize each issue for the national church, their diocese and congregation.
54 All the statements quoted are based on statistically significant correlations between these advocacy scales and other attitudes, identified among clergywomen, clergymen, lay women and lay men from the diocesan survey data collected by the Episcopal Committee on Status of Women (2003).
55 Committee on the Status of Women, p. 19. Those who agreed 'More ethnic minorities should be ordained': clergywomen 86 per cent, clergymen 70 per cent; lay women 58 per cent and lay men 51 per cent.
56 In the 2002 survey, 61 per cent in the North-east wanted more ethnic minorities ordained compared to 47 per cent for more women ordained; in the South, these percentages were 46 per cent and 38 per cent respectively.
57 For studies of clergy position and/or salary and gender see Zikmund, Lummis and Chang, *Clergy Women*; J.W. Carroll, *God's Potters: Pastoral Leadership in the Shaping of Congregations* (Grand Rapids, MI: Eerdmans, 2006); Nesbitt, *Feminization of the Clergy*; and Sullins, 'The Stained Glass Ceiling'.

58 M.J. Price, *The 2004 Church Compensation Report* (New York: Church Pension
    Group, 2005) reports these statistics. Louie Crew posts on his website that male
    Episcopal priests are 75 per cent more likely than female priests to be rectors of
    parishes with over 1,000 congregants; only about five women priests are rectors of
    parishes of this size. The 2003 research report of the Episcopal Committee on the
    Status of Women has similar statistics.

12

The Feminization and Professionalization of Ordained Ministry within the Mâ'ohi Protestant Church in French Polynesia[1]

Gwendoline Malogne-Fer

The Evangelical Church of French Polynesia (EEPF) – renamed the Mâ'ohi Protestant Church (EPM)[2] in 2004 – makes up approximately 40 per cent of the population (estimated at 250,000 inhabitants in 2002) despite a relative decline in church membership and a pluralization of the Polynesian religious landscape. It is a Protestant church in the Reformed tradition, whose origins are found in the London Missionary Society (1797–1863) and the Paris Society for Evangelical Missions (1863–1963). While the mission field afforded French women an opportunity to exercise significant responsibility, the arrival of Protestantism in Polynesia had effects upon the position of Polynesian women which were both paradoxical and hard to evaluate: on the one hand emancipation through equal access to instruction and baptism; on the other reinforced control of sexuality and family norms.

The decision to authorize women to become ministers is a recent one (1995), but has met with a certain degree of success, since of the last four cohorts of trainee ministers at theological college, women make up more than half of their number (10 out of 18). I propose to study here the conditions in which the debate on women's ordained ministry has come to light in French Polynesia, the attendant consequences in terms of the modification of the exercise of ordained ministry, and the incomplete nature of the process.[3] In French Polynesia, women's ordination has to be understood within a twofold dynamic: the Protestant Church's autonomy in relation to French missionaries and women's equal access to the different ministries recognized by the Church.[4] Women's access to ordained ministry should also be considered within the wider context of far-reaching institutional, economic and social changes taking place in Polynesian society.

Since the 1960s, and the establishment of the Pacific Nuclear Centre at Moruroa and Fangataufa (in the Tuamotu Gambier archipelago), an economy which was previously based on agriculture and fishing has now become dependent on tertiary activities (such as tourism, commerce and administration) and state subsidies. The development of these tertiary sectors, both private and public, which provide a large amount of employment for women, has facilitated a rapid increase in women's salaries.[5] This increase has been accompanied by an improvement in the level of education and a sharp decline in the birth rate within a short space of time.[6]

The admission of women to ordained ministry within the Mâ'ohi Protestant Church

Regional and international context
The EEPF achieved autonomy in 1963, which meant that it was no longer overseen by French missionaries but by Polynesian ministers. Church autonomy formed part of a global process of decolonization (the autonomy of churches having a duty to anticipate and accompany colonial independence) a process which, in French Polynesia, has not been completed due to the setting up of the Pacific nuclear testing centre. Within the contemporary Protestant Church its autonomous position encouraged a stance against the French presence on Polynesian soil.[7]

The church's organizational autonomy allowed it to sit as a fully-fledged church on different international or regional bodies, notably the World Council of Churches (WCC) and the Pacific Conference of Churches (PCFC) established in 1966, which brings together the Protestant and Anglican churches in the Pacific region.

The Church's autonomy led to a greater involvement in the ecumenical movement. The WCC, whose mission is to bring churches together and foster reconciliation between them, is also very active in relation to gender equality. In 1969 the WCC urged churches to send women to represent member churches, and this enabled some ministers' wives to attend ecumenical meetings and to become aware of the legitimacy of equality demands. It was at these international meetings that the ministers' wives discovered that some churches in the Pacific region, culturally and geographically close to their own, had ordained women as ministers; the first church to ordain women was the United Church of Papua New Guinea and the Solomon Islands in 1976.[8] Throughout the 1980s and 1990s a number of other Protestant churches allowed women to become ministers: the Kiribati Protestant Church (1984)[9], the Free Wesleyan Church of Tonga (1990) and in particular the Evangelical Church of New Caledonia and the Loyalty Islands (in 1991), with which the EPM maintains close relations due to the strong Tahitian Protestant community in Nouméa.[10]

The accession of women to the ordained ministry: a debate between two moments in history (1981 and 1995)
The question of women's ordained ministry was first raised in 1981 in connection with one particular case, that of a minister's wife who had obtained the same theology degree as her husband from the Pacific Theological College in Fiji.[11] At the time of the husband's ordination, the synod took the decision not to ordain his wife because this dual ordination would have upset the traditional functioning of the 'pastoral couple' (*le couple pastoral*). In 1995 the EEPF synod – under pressure from some

ministers' wives active in the ecumenical movement – authorized the admission of women to the ministry, arguing that 'nothing in the Bible forbids women from becoming ministers'.[12] This position led to the arguments of those opposed to women's ordination being classed as culturally rather than theologically based, and hence inadmissible.

In fact, those ministers who came out in favour of women's ordination tended to see their own position as proof of their theological prowess, and that it was thanks to the teaching they had received at theological college that they understood and accepted the Church's decision. The reactions of clergy wives (not all of whom were involved in ecumenical organizations) were much more qualified because some saw in this a direct competition with the wife's ministry, which up to 1995 was the sole channel by which women could attain the highest levels of responsibility within the Church. The accession of women to ordained ministry reinforced the tensions between the older church members, attached to traditional interpretations of the Bible and the younger generation, notably young clergy, keen to promote a more contextualized reading of the Bible.

The conditions in which the question of women's ordination was raised emphasize that access to degree-level theological training constituted an essential step for the admission of women to ordained ministry. In France, the work of Jean-Paul Willaime demonstrated that in Reformed and Lutheran Protestantism, women's admission to ordained ministry came about thanks to women's admission to theology faculties.[13] These conclusions are akin to the work of Catherine Marry, who noted that in numerous professional spheres, higher education was key to the feminization of higher-level professions.[14] The fact that women were eligible to study theology, albeit initially justified by their involvement as wives in their husbands' ministries, subsequently played an instrumental role in the transformation of a derived ministry into a fully-fledged one.

Challenge to the traditional 'pastoral couple'

The decision taken in 1995 authorizing women to become ministers only partially challenges that of 1981, in so far as the Church (whilst upholding the obligation for ministers to marry) refused to allow both members of a couple to become ordained ministers. The obligation to marry dates from 1806, from the requirement for missionaries of the London Missionary Society to marry before departing for Tahiti, to prevent marriages between Englishmen and Tahitian women.[15] Marriage subsequently became a requirement for those Polynesians wishing to convert to Protestantism and become `etâretia (church members). Thus it was proof of a successful conversion no less than of the stability of conjugal relations.

Today, the obligation to marry remains in place for ministers, who have a duty to be a role model for their parishioners. The pastoral couple is widely believed to be the only model able to ensure the proper running of the parish, with the minister's wife overseeing the women of the parish while the minister looks after the whole parish. Wives are neither ordained nor paid by the Church but nevertheless carry out a 'derived ministry' not linked to

their ecclesiastical status (they are lay people) but rather to their marital
status. The ordination ceremony is meaningful in two senses – the minister
is ordained, but his wife (who is generally involved in every stage of her
husband's vocation and training, and who accompanies him at the
ceremony), is not ordained. Throughout the 1980s ministers' wives built up
their 'derived ministry', through access to the same classes as their husbands
at theological college (1977), through attendance at clergy meetings and also
because some of them carried out duties which were paid by the Church (as
manager of young women's accommodation, or as teachers or librarians in
Protestant primary and secondary schools). At the same time, the institution-
alization of women's activities at parish level reinforced the position of
ministers' and deacons' wives – most commonly as Chair of the Women's
Committee, which is responsible in every parish for organizing the annual
meeting of women church members and for Women's Sunday (every third
Sunday). The ordination of women thus challenges the functioning of the
traditional 'pastoral couple': where a woman becomes an ordained minister,
there is no defined role for her husband. This change affects marital relations
as well as the *modus operandi* of ordained ministry.

The feminization and professionalization of ordained ministry

A further important development was the professionalization of the ordained
ministry to which women were seeking access. As Jean-Paul Willaime has
written, professionalization is defined as

> le processus par lequel un métier s'autonomise par rapport à l'institution
> dans laquelle il s'exerce et s'auto-légitime à partir de la competence
> qu'il met en œuvre. Le professionel est un expert dans un domaine
> spécialisée et c'est sa qualité d'expert qui est la principale source de
> légitimité [the process by which a profession becomes autonomous in
> relation to the institution in which it is performed and defines its own
> legitimacy by the competence it displays. The professional is an expert
> in a specialized field and it is this expert quality which is the primary
> means of legitimacy].[16]

In the past three decades, the EEPF has instigated just such a process of
professionalization in ordained ministry. The first stage of this process
began during the 1970s with the untangling of family and parochial interests.
No longer did pastors minister in their home parish, or continue to work on
the land alongside their pastoral duties as a 'pastor-farmer'. Instead they
became full-time ministers, with their authority derived from their theological
college training rather than their family connections. However, if the professionalization of ordained ministry in the EEPF did not actually begin with
women's ordination, the entry of women to the ministry did (as in France)[17]
mark a new stage in the process. This has been manifested in the raising of

educational standards, the emergence of specialized ministries and the exclusion from political office of those in church leadership positions.

Pastoral training rather than parish support
In 1995 the EEPF authorized women to become ordained ministers. In 1997 the first candidate entered theological college and was ordained in August 2003 after spending four years at theological college and two years on work-placement in a parish. The admission of women to ordained ministry in 1995 coincided with greater priority being given to pastoral training and a change in theological college entrance requirements. Since 1996, entry into theological college has required the baccalauréat, whilst a parallel entry process or probationary year is provided for those without a baccalauréat. The latter must attend evening classes for a year and take an exam which is more or less selective depending on the numbers of direct entrants to the theological college. The backgrounds of the students differ along gender lines: young women entrants tend to be single and baccalauréat-holders, while men are married, without a baccalauréat, and sent by their home parish.

Table 1: **Theological college entrants**

Students	Women	Men
1997–2001 (total)	1	3
Baccalauréat candidates	1	-
Single candidates	1	-
1999–2003 (total)	3	2
Baccalauréat candidates	3	-
Single candidates	3	-
2001–5 (total)	3	2
Baccalauréat candidates	2	1
Single candidates	3	1
2003–7 (total)	3	1
Baccalauréat candidates	2	-
Single candidates	3	-

These differences should be viewed in light of the higher level of academic success being achieved by girls – not only in French Polynesia but in many countries – which may be explained by a number of factors: girls adjust better to school work, have a greater respect for discipline, and work harder as a means of avoiding domestic chores during adolescence when, in Polynesian homes, parental pressure to help with housework is exerted more strongly on girls than on boys.[18]

The requirement of the baccalauréat for entry into theological college is a source of argument and discontent in the parish since it is perceived to favour young women. The transformation of scholarly capital into social capital recognized by parishes is not a given. The question asked by many parishioners – 'is vocation about faith or about qualifications?' – sets faith in opposition to the academic knowledge being delivered by the French education system. By implication, young women who place value upon their school education are, at the same time, distancing themselves from their parish activities. The debate over whether vocation is a matter of academic knowledge or personal faith serves to undermine young women. The admission of women to ordained ministry is felt to pose an intellectualizing threat to church ministry. Women with the baccalauréat on the other hand, view their academic success as a confirmation of a vocation which is not recognized by their parish.

Non-parish ministry: ideally feminine ministries?

Non-parish ministries target communities which cannot be defined in terms of geography and which are not involved in any parish: young people in schools, hospital patients, prisoners, etc. The emergence of these ministries is one factor challenging the parish framework as the exclusive model for ecclesiastical organization in the context of heavy migration (from the archipelagos to Tahiti) and increasing urbanization in Tahiti, which now accounts for up to 70 per cent of the population.[19] In many cases non-parish ministry suits female ministers particularly well for at least two reasons, the first is entirely negative: women's ordained ministry is by no means accepted in parishes and is potentially fraught with difficulties. Non-parish ministry provides an opportunity to balance the opposition between the synod authorization of women's ordination and the marked apprehension of parishioners. The second reason is that non-parish ministry – such as school and hospital chaplaincy – corresponds with the activities and sectors traditionally open to women, such as the education of young children and care for the sick. As such, in 2005, three out of the first seven women ministers (ordained or on placement), carried out non-parish ministry (journalist, accountant, chaplain) and one was a minister in one of French Polynesia's two non-geographical parishes: which serves the *hakka*-speaking Protestant Chinese community in Tahiti. The Church's very first ordained woman minister is currently the chaplain at the Pirae Protestant high-school, thus tying her back into her former role as a primary school teacher. Moreover, when women are asked about their professional aspirations, the most common answer is to be a theological college teacher.

The separation of political and religious spheres

The professionalization of ordained ministry was reinforced by a ruling of the synod, applied for the first time in 2001, which required church ministers to choose between their church position and their political position. This ruling was taken initially in 1996 when church leaders called for a peaceful demonstration against the resumption of nuclear testing. They then realized that a significant number of deacons, who were also territorial or municipal counsellors in the Gaston Flosse political party, were not able to take part in the demonstration. Once church leaders realized how much political parties were making use of church structures (in particular the *'âmuira'a*, parish subgroups bringing together parishioners according to geography or family background), they ruled for a separation of political involvement and official church positions. In the main this decision was poorly received since it undermined both the traditional position of those who held the dual roles of deacon and municipal counsellor, and the way of life on the Austral Islands where church and village interests were closely intertwined.

An incomplete process

The feminization of ordained ministry is an incomplete process which has encountered three major obstacles: 'Doublebind' mechanisms or contradictory demands; potential institutional marginalization; and lastly a theological and cultural renewal, initiated by the Church's Theological Commission, which is at odds with the process of ministerial professionalization.

Differentialists vs. egalitarians – the insoluble dilemma

As women assume the same ecclesiastical responsibilities as men, the tension inherent in the dialogue between equality and difference becomes highly visible. Eleni Varikas recalls the dilemma facing women when they attain positions which were previously exclusively male domains: i.e. to adapt to masculine norms and run the risk of 'becoming' (*'devenir'*) like the men or to bring to bear a feminine specificity which condemns them to be simply 'imperfect men' (*'hommes imparfaits'*).[20]

The accession of women to ordained ministry was at the outset claimed by clergy wives on egalitarian grounds: equal access to ministerial training and equal capability of men and women. On the other hand, male ministers, and in particular the Church's leaders charged with representing and also reforming the Church as an institution, insist on the promotion of gender difference: women are expected to be ministers in a different way, working in closer relationship with and more attentive to their parishioners; to embody a new, less authoritative and more relational form of ministry. The promotion of their gender identity means that female theological students are called to remain different from their male counterparts despite undertaking the same responsibilities as them.

This call conflicts with the expectations of parishioners, who continue to want a married man, assisted by his wife. They cite parish organization (more particularly the existence of a Women's Committee, usually chaired by the minister's wife) as the justification for keeping the traditional 'pastoral couple'.

The conflicting expectations between parish integration and the demand for a feminine identity are being played out at the level of dress-codes, which play a determining role in the process of integration or exclusion in parishes. The parishioners of Papeete, who did not wish to receive female theological students on work-placement in their parish, expressed their disagreement by asking the students not to dress like a minister – in navy-blue suit – but in a white dress like a woman; in fact, like a minister's wife. The theological students meanwhile waver between the desire to display a certain femininity, and due respect for traditional dress-codes. The issue of hat-wearing seems to have been the most awkward for these young women, who associate it with the clothes worn by elderly people. All this has led to some delicate negotiations.

Institutional marginalization

Ordained women ministers are frequently responsible for non-parish ministries (school chaplaincy, accountancy and/or church journalism) or for non-Polynesian parishes. Consequently they are more rarely to be found within the leadership structures of the Church, elected by parishioners, than their colleagues. They are similarly absent from the Theological Commission. The fact that women are marginalized within the institution causes them to identify (and be identified) more closely with new forms of religious practice which are themselves less institutionalized.

In contrast to church leaders who desire women to have a 'different' kind of ministry, women ministers themselves are more preoccupied with matters such as being accepted by parishioners rather than with reforming the church institution early in their ministry. However, there are some female ministers who have combined the desire for institutional renewal, with another more personal objective, that of staying true to themselves, and thus are developing another, radically desacralized vision, of pastoral ministry and the Church. Women are frequently responsible for managing relations with non-Polynesian or non-Christian communities in French Polynesia and often find themselves, as a result, on the margins of the Church as institution. And yet, this precarious position reflects the religious pluralization which is a mark of contemporary familial evolution – including at the level of the individual family unit.[21] These women, as a result of their background and their marital situation, are already familiar with interfamily religious plurality (their husbands are sometimes non-practising or, more rarely, non-believers). They thus develop a more ecumenical approach in their ministry, mixing more easily with non-Protestant people (school chaplaincy lessons are delivered to all pupils irrespective of their religion) or non-practising people. They are also keen to accept invitations from other churches, notably Protestant ones (Pentecostals and Adventists).

Theological tensions: liberation of the Mâ'ohi people/liberation of the Mâ'ohi women

The feminization of the clergy is accompanied by a transformation in both the *modus operandi* and the legitimization of church ministries, which come into conflict with the Church's official theological position. While the profession-alization of ministry places emphasis on theological training and heralds the deterritorialization of religious belonging, recent work carried out by the

Theological Commission advocates a return to the land (*te fenua*) and to the Tahitian language (*Reo Mâ'ohi*) as the only way to an authentic Polynesian Protestantism.

Since 1988 the Theological Commission, chaired by a lay person, Turo Raapoto (a doctor in linguistics), has been producing pamphlets which sketch the contours for a 'theology of liberation' or 'theology of the land' which are based around Mâ'ohi culture, Mâ'ohi land and the Mâ'ohi language. Whilst translating the Bible into Tahitian, English missionaries recognized that the language had an almost sacred quality and this was the proof that God wanted to meet the Mâ'ohi people in their language and their culture.[22] This theological renewal goes beyond the initial objective, which was to 'decolonize' the theologies of the South by promoting the emergence of contextual theologies. This theological position does not stop at the promotion of cultural expressions since it accords a religious dimension to an exclusively cultural process. By multiplying the references to the pre-missionary period, a period during which women did not have access to the *marae* (open-air cultic sites at that time), the theological renewal lends weight to the opinions of those opposed to women's ordination who find reasons from within this cultural register for disqualifying women from ministerial ordination. In this way, the question of equality between men and women becomes an imported issue, which places the emancipation of women at the heart of the process of acculturation.

The approach of the Theological Commission, composed almost exclusively of men, underlines the impossibility of simultaneously considering the liberation of the Mâ'ohi people and that of Mâ'ohi women. This commission is composed essentially of male ministers who work in Tahitian language parishes and go from parish to parish teaching in *Reo Mâ'ohi*. So whilst from the early missionary days women have had access to biblical knowledge and to the transmission of that knowledge, notably by becoming Sunday School teachers, the work of the Theological Commission reveals that women still do not have full access to the creation of new theological knowledge.

Conclusion

At its most basic level, the feminization of the clergy simply means the numerical presence of women ministers in roles which were hitherto undertaken exclusively by men. However, at another level this term also points to a transformation of the ways in which ordained ministry is exercised. Women ministers particularly move away from the traditional pastoral couple model – which required the wife to carry out unpaid voluntary work alongside her spouse – in that their husbands play little or no part in their wives' pastoral mininstries.

At the same time as giving women entry to ordained ministry, the Church made the baccalauréat an entry criterion for theological college. This move to professionalize the ministry, favouring academic training over parish support and developing non-parish ministry, is at odds with the Church's ways of working and with parishioners' expectations.

At an institutional level, pastors not based in a parish remain the most often marginalized, if for no other reason than their exclusion from decision-making processes, which continue to operate along the lines of territorial-based representation. Above all professionalization of mininstry should in principle have been accompanied by a refocusing around the heart of the profession, i.e. theological training. However, women ministers, more of whom have the baccalauréat than their male counterparts, have had no opportunity to be involved in the work of the Theological Commission. The uncomfortable position of women ministers – holders of a French qualification but felt to lack parish experience – underlines the Church's ambiguous position on education. Whilst it requires the baccalauréat the Church is promoting the knowledge delivered by an education system rooted in a colonial context which it otherwise rejects.

At parish level, most parishioners continue to prefer their future ministers to be married men. Debates surrounding the conjugal status of women ministers (questions of celibacy, marriage, role of the husband) underline the tensions between a privatization of women ministers' conjugal lives and the maintenance of traditional models of authority based on the marital exemplar. Women ministers challenge the pastoral couple model by overturning the very hierarchy of the sexes which underpins it. Henceforth the requirement for them to marrry before they may be ordained is losing legitimacy and is the focus for disquiet and debate.

The Church, conscious of these contradictions, remains for now hesitant in the light of two radically different options. The first of these, the product of a pastoral seminar in 2005, aims to strengthen the traditional pastoral couple model via the reintroduction of the requirement for all entrants to theological college to be married. The second option, discussed at the August 2006 synod, relates to a relaxation of the rules to enable the ordination of both marriage partners, thereby substituting (or juxtaposing) the 'couple pastoral' model with that of the 'couple de pasteurs'. Discussions relating to the marital situation of ministers are thus at present ongoing.

Bibliography

Davies, J., *The History of the Tahitian Mission, 1799–1830*, ed. C.W. Newbury (Cambridge: Cambridge University Press, 1961).

Forman, C., *The Island Churches of the South Pacific* (New York: Orbis, 1982).

——, 'Women in the Churches of Oceania', in D. O'Brien and S. Tiffany (eds), *Rethinking Women's Roles. Perspectives from the Pacific* (Berkeley and Los Angeles, CA: University of California Press, 1984), pp. 153–72.

Kutimeni Tenten, M., 'The Relationship between Katekateka and Women's Ordination in the Kiribati Protestant Church', in K. Johnson and J. -A. Filemoni-Tofaeono (eds), *Weavings: Women Doing Theology in Oceania* (Suva, Fiji: Weavers, South Association of Theological Schools and Institute of Pacific Studies, University of the South Pacific, 2003), pp. 32–42.

ISPF (Institut statistique de la Polynésie française) et ministère polynésien du tourisme, de l'environnement et de la condition féminine, *Vahine en chiffres* (Papeete: ISPF, 2002).

——, *Année 2004 des résultats incertains* (Papeete: ISPF, 2005), p. 67.

Malogne-Fer, G., 'L'EEPF. et les essais nucléaires: de la prise de conscience chrétienne à la prise de position publique (1963–1982)', in J.M. Regnault (ed.), *François Mitterrand et les territoires français du Pacifique (1981–1988)* (Paris: Les indes savants, 2003), pp. 205–14.

——, 'Quand les femmes prennent la parole: démocratisation institutionnelle et professionnalisation des ministères au sein de l'église évangélique de Polynésie française', unpublished doctoral dissertation, Paris: l'Ecole des hautes etudes en sciences sociales, 2005.

——, *Les femmes dans l'église protestante mâ'ohi: religion, genre et pouvoir en Polynésie française* (Paris: Editions Karthala, 2007).

Marry, C., *Les Femmes ingénieurs. Une révolution silencieuse* (Paris: Belin, 2004).

Nicole, J., *Au Pied de l'écriture, histoire de la traduction de la Bible en tahitien* (Papeete: Haere po no Tahiti, 1988).

Varikas, E., 'Egalité', in H. Hirata, F. Laborie *et al.* (eds), *Dictionnaire critique du féminisme* (Paris: Presses Universitaires de France, 2000), pp. 54–60.

Wete, T., 'Women as "Life-Giver": Toward a renewed understanding of women's ministry and leadership in the Evangelical Church of New Caledonia and the Loyalty Islands', unpublished Masters dissertation, Suva, Fiji: Pacific Theological College, 2003.

Willaime, J.-P., *Profession: pasteur. Sociologie de la condition du clerc à la fin du XXᵉ siècle* (Geneva: Labor et Fides, 1986).

——, 'L'Accès des femmes au pastorat et la sécularisation du rôle du clerc dans le protestantisme', *Archives de sciences sociales des religions*, 95 (1996), pp. 29–45.

——, 'Les Pasteures et les mutations contemporaines du rôle du clerc', *CLIO: Histoire, femmes et sociétés* 15 (2002), pp. 69–83.

Notes

1   The original conference paper upon which this chapter is based was translated from the French by Stephen Brown. Additional translation for this revised version was by Alison Jones.

2   EEPF: L'église évangélique de Polynésie française; EPM: L'église protestante mâ'ohi.

3   This communication stems from a sociological thesis carried out under the supervision of Danièle Hervieu-Léger and defended in June 2005 at the Ecole des hautes études en sciences sociales in Paris. The method deployed is that of semi-directed interviews carried out in Tahiti between October 2000 and August 2002.

4   Women already had access to the diaconal ministry (since 1947) and the ministry of evangelist (the officializing of this ministry dates from the 1970s). Whilst many women have become evangelists, very few have chosen diaconal ministry, which is essentially defined as a ministry of authority (the council of deacons being the sole decision-making body in the parish).

5   The level of employment previously at 28 per cent in 1962 had increased to 47 per cent by 1996, a figure which is close to that of mainland France. (ISPF [Institut statistique de la Polynésie française] et ministère polynésien du tourisme, de l'environnement et de la condition féminine, *Vahine en chiffres* (Papeete: ISPF, 2002).)

6   The average number of children per woman which stood at 4.2 at the beginning of the 1960s had reduced to 2.1 by 2004 (ISPF, *Année 2004 des résultants incertains* (Papeete: ISPF, 2004), p. 67.

7   G. Malogne-Fer, 'L'EEPF et les essais nucléaires: de la prise de conscience chrétienne à la prise de position publique (1963–1982)', in J.-M. Regnault (ed.), *François Mitterrand et les territoires français du Pacifique (1981–1988)* (Paris: Les indes savants, 2003), pp. 205–14.

8   This is the first church in the Pacific region, apart from the churches of Australia and New Zealand. (See C. Forman, 'Women in the Churches of Oceania', in D. O'Brien and S.

Tiffany (eds), *Rethinking Women's Roles. Perspectives from the Pacific* (Berkeley and Los Angeles, CA: University of California Press, 1984), pp. 153–72 (p. 169).

9   M.K. Tenten, 'The Relationship between Katekateka and Women's Ordination in the Kiribati Protestant Church', in K. Johnson and J.A. Filemoni-Tofaeono (eds), *Weavings: Women Doing Theology in Oceania* (Suva, Fiji: Weavers, South Association of Theological Schools and Institute of Pacific Studies University of the South Pacific, 2003), pp. 32–42.

10 T. Wete, 'Women as "Life-Giver": Toward a Renewed Understanding of Women's Ministry and Leadership in the Evangelical Church of New Caledonia and the Loyalty Islands', unpublished Masters dissertation, Pacific Theological College, Suva, Fiji, 2003.

11 The Pacific Theological College was established as part of the PCFC initiative: from 1966 the college has trained future ministers from the Oceania region.

12 Paraphrase taken from an interview with John Doom, previous church general secretary, on 3 May 2001. The full quotation reads: 'L'accession des femmes au ministère pastoral n'est pas une décision de l'église mais un réflexion théologique, il n'y a aucun texte qui interdit les femmes au ministère pastoral' [The accession of women to pastoral ministry is not a decision for the church to make but rather a theological reflection, there is no text which forbids women from becoming ministers].

13 J.-P. Willaime, 'L'Accès des femmes au pastorat et la sécularisation du rôle du clerc dans le protestantisme', *Archives de sciences sociales des religions*, 95 (1996), pp. 29–45.

14 C. Marry, *Les Femmes ingénieurs: Une révolution silencieuse* (Paris: Belin, 2004).

15 J. Davies, *The History of the Tahitian Mission, 1799–1830*, ed. C.W. Newbury (Cambridge: Cambridge University Press, 1961), pp. xxxix, 91.

16 J.-P. Willaime, *Profession: pasteur. Sociologie de la condition du clerc à la fin du XXᵉ siècle* (Genève: Labor et Fides, 1986), p. 217.

17 J.-P. Willaime, 'Les Pasteures et les mutations contemporaines du rôle du clerc', *CLIO: Histoire, femmes et sociétés*, 15 (2002), pp. 69–83 (p. 77).

18 In the 20–29 age group included in the census of 1996, young women holding the baccalaureate or a higher education degree represented 21.7 per cent of the total of young women in this bracket as opposed to 16.7 per cent for boys. In 2002 the figures were 34.3 per cent for young women and 23 per cent for young men respectively (Source: ISPF).

19 ISPF, 2003.

20 E. Varikas, 'Egalité', in H. Hirata, F. Laborie *et al.* (eds), *Dictionnaire critique du féminisme* (Paris: Presses Universitaires de France, 2000), pp. 54–60 (p. 56).

21 Within Polynesian families, the coexistence of different religions has increased markedly within the generation: a survey carried out in 2000 in Tahiti by the Louis Harris Institute and published in *La Tahiti dépêche de Tahiti* in September 2000 shows that 55 per cent of present-day couples have the same religion, whilst the percentage was 84 per cent for the parents of those questioned.

22 For a history of translation of the Bible into Tahitian see J. Nicole, *Au Pied de l'écriture, histoire de la traduction de la Bible en tahitien* (Papeete: Haere po no Tahiti, 1988).

13

Neither Male nor Female: Tradition, Ordination and Female Leadership in the Nigerian New Generation Churches

Bolaji Olukemi Bateye

Introduction

Female Religious Leaders (FRLs) are becoming forces to reckon with in contemporary Nigerian society. Who are these FRLs? What do they stand for? What are their styles of leadership and what are their views concerning the issue of women and ordination? How have they 'negotiated' the quicksand of patriarchal traditions and what are their prospects for the future Nigerian ecclesial landscape? This essay raises questions and seeks to answer them by evidence gleaned from specifically selected experienced FRLs of New Generation Churches in southwestern Nigeria. It examines the perspectives of three outstanding FRLs on issues of women and ordination, and probes the general acceptability of the feminine presence in their ordained ministry, congregations and communities.

Women in traditional Yoruba religion and culture

Generally the African woman's worldview, in keeping with Yoruba culture, is not detached from her social and cultural contexts. According to Chris Manus:

> African peoples are naturally community living people. The African epistemology and ontology is anthropologically expressed in the African's understanding of his or her being in the world with others. Unlike the Cartesian individualism [*cogito, ergo sum*] – *cognatus sum, ergo sum* – meaning 'because I am related to others, I do exist'. This is to say, an African is human in so far as he/she is integrated into a community. The community is a communion made up of the living and the dead, with some kind of a hierarchical order.[1]

Specifically the Yoruba of southwestern Nigeria are culturally patriarchal and androcentric. Individuals are close-knit as each person is seen as a constituent of the society. The people's traditional religion is equally an integral part of their culture, for all aspects of life virtually from 'womb to tomb' have a religious basis and are therefore celebrated – for example, birth, puberty, marriage, chieftaincy, death etc. Social roles are ascribed to different categories of people in the community. Otite and Ogionwo define social roles as, 'a regular way of acting expected of all persons occupying a given position in the social order of people'.[2]

My purpose in discussing traditional religion in the first instance is for us to have a better grasp of the contexts from which these Yoruba Christian women have emerged. It is generally accepted that there is hardly any family in Yoruba society that does not have its own household traditional religion. As a matter of fact the prefixes and suffixes to people's names will inform one about their background. Names such as Ogunwale, Ogunbiyi and Ogunsola, for example, show that they (or more likely their forebears) were 'Ogun' worshippers.

Although the goddess tradition has gone a long way in projecting an image of emancipation of women in Yoruba traditional religion, the place of women in the Yoruba traditional society has largely been dismal. The power of culture has been used to render the greater part of a woman's life invisible. Women have suffered exploitation arising from discriminatory sex roles, unequal property rights and power-sharing. In some cases, women are regarded as mere chattels and subservient to men. Among the evils associated with the sex-roles of women are subjection to the degrading humiliation of polygamy, submission to the dominance of the husband and taking full responsibility for barrenness and all ills associated with procreation, including the stigma of the menstrual flow, which is more often than not associated with uncleanness. A woman who refuses to participate in certain repressive rituals is often blamed for any misfortunes in her family. For example, a woman who failed to carry out the *oro ile* (literally, family rites), Levirate marriage and practices associated with widowhood would incur the wrath of both her immediate and extended family. The following is a popular song usually sung as a satire on such practices:

Awa yio s'oro ile wa o
Awa yio s'oro ile wa o
Esin ka nope, oo eh
Esin kan o pe, k'awa ma s'oro
Awa yio s'oro ile wa o.

[We will perform the rites of our home
We will perform the rites of our home
No religion states (that)
We should not perform the rites of our home.
We will perform the rites of our home.]

Traditional religion has a strong hold on the people's way of life. The efforts made by Christianity and Muslim proselytization have not deterred people from performing certain family and communal rituals.

New Generation Churches (NGCs)

An historical overview of the New Generation Churches (NGCs) situates their presence within the context of the advent of Christianity in Yorubaland. This dates from the coming of the mission churches to the emergence of the African independent churches. O.U. Kalu (1978), J.A. Omoyajowo, J.D.Y. Peel and B.O. Bateye, among others, have written on this issue.[3] These works address the empowering nature of Christianity especially with regard to women in the NGCs.

The missionaries regarded African culture as barbaric and prohibited African cultural practices in the Church. Hence European culture to the early African converts was synonymous with the practices of the Church and was therefore given a divine mandate as supposedly being Bible-based. This situation had profound implications with regard to women. European culture was considered liberating in some ways to women, especially in its condemnation of the polygamy that was generally the cause of much suffering. However, it also transplanted the biases and prejudices of European culture with regard to male–female relationships to Yoruba society. During the nineteenth century the prevailing idea was that men were superior beings meant by God and nature to dominate the world, while women were meant to obey and serve.[4] Thus there was a kind of ambivalence in the stance of the African women converts towards European culture.

Nevertheless, for many the belief was that European culture was more liberating than oppressive for the African woman, and that the demands of the European missionary church culture on them were less rigorous than those of African culture. Women's experience in Africa was that of perpetual servitude to the male. Thus they did not question the apparent misuse of scripture to justify the exclusion of women from leadership roles in the Church.

Pentecostal-style churches are prominent in the contemporary ecclesial scene in Nigeria. Many of them are relatively newly established. Rosalind Hackett characterizes them as

> the 'new generation' or 'new breed' Churches. They are distinguished not by their denominational labels and heritage, but rather by their commitment to a 'full gospel', highly evangelistic, Bible-centered, not forcibly, but leaning toward, literalist religious orientations. They readily distinguish between those who subscribe to such a worldview – often referred to as 'born-again' – and those who do not. The latter may be disparagingly labeled as 'dead Christians' or 'unsaved'.[5]

Women who had been excluded from the clergy and participation in leadership roles in the early mission churches began to assume paramount roles in the NGCs. A number of these churches were established by women. It is intriguing to note that in spite of the patriarchal and androcentric attitudes that prevail in Yorubaland these women have a large following and command respect from wider society.

Female religious leaders and the ordained ministry[6]

We shall examine the perspectives on women and ordained ministry of three women church founders and leaders of NGCs in the Yoruba area of Nigeria: Dorcas Olaniyi, Stella Ajisebutu and Remilekun Batire. The nature of their circumstances and their calling make them typical examples of church founders among the NGCs in Yorubaland.

Archbishop Dorcas Olaniyi is enjoying a great deal of popularity among the Nigerian Yoruba public and has become almost an international figure, with branches of her church abroad. Stella Ajisebutu is respected among a narrow circle of intellectuals in Yorubaland, although she shies away from publicity. Remi Batire is well known in the environs of Akure town and has also established a highly successful branch of her church in London.

Dorcas Olaniyi, the founder of Agbala Daniel Church, was born on 12 February 1934 into a polygamous family. Her early childhood experience included visions and being put in the care of white missionaries for a period of 12 years. The turning-point in Olaniyi's life occurred in 1950 when she received a calling as a prophet in a vision from God. In the vision Olaniyi reported, 'I went to Kaduna where the Lord told me I was a prophetess, I saw myself buried in a pit. Jesus and Joseph brought me out'.[7] She embarked on an ambitious independent ministry after a vision on 17 November 1979 urging her to establish a church to be named the Agbala Daniel Church (ADC). This was accomplished in Ibadan in 1983; her reputation as a prophetess and evangelist spread and her ministry has grown with branches in Nigeria, Britain and the USA.

The ADC adheres to a number of basic tenets. It upholds the doctrine of the Trinity and teaches the triune God. The ADC accepts the atonement, the virgin birth of Jesus Christ, the forgiveness of sins, the death and resurrection of Jesus and the judgement of the faithful and the unfaithful. The church also believes in the efficacy of prayer and fasting and in miracles. The practice of baptism by immersion, belief in the baptism of the Holy Spirit and the operation of the gifts of the Holy Spirit are hallmarks of the church. The making of disciples and evangelism are carried out with zeal. Olaniyi is forthright in her advocacy for empowerment of women. Her crusade is to get all, both men and women, involved in discipleship.

Dr Stella Ajisebutu was born on 10 February 1942. She, as with the case of Dorcas Olaniyi, was also the product of a polygamous home. Before her birth, her father had received a prophecy that his child would be a great prophet. He therefore assumed that such a child would be a boy and gave her masculine names Oluwafeyijimi Olukunle that she would later drop on the day of her wedding. It was in 1988 that a turning-point occurred in Ajisebutu's life that ushered her into the Christian ministry. She received a vision, in which the Lord instructed her to name the prayer-meeting she conducted in a friend's house as the Faith Clinic. The name of the Faith Clinic was later at the instance of the Lord changed to Water from the Rock. This was to remind her of how Moses struck the rock in the desert and water came out for the Israelites.

Stella Ajisebutu's main motivation for ministry stems from a divine calling, nevertheless she emphasizes the importance of role models and mentors. The implication of this attitude gives an insight into factors that influence her perspectives on what accounts for good leadership.

Remilekun Batire is the founder of Christ Miracle Christian Centre, Akure. She was born about 50 years ago and came from a monogamous Christian family background. She claimed she received a miraculous calling from God to the status of prophetess. She also claimed that God gave her a special gift of healing and made a covenant with her that sickness brought to her would be cured.

Batire, like Olaniyi, also hails from a Christ Apostolic Church (CAC) background.[8] It is perhaps for this reason that the styles of her worship sessions are similar to those of Agbala Daniel. She however claimed that her favourite Bible passages, which God gave her at the time of her calling, were: Jer. 32.27: 'Behold, I am the LORD, the God of all flesh: is there any thing too hard for me?'; Mk 10.27: 'And Jesus looking upon them saith, With men it is impossible, but not with God: for with God all things are possible'; and Lk. 1.37-38: 'For with God nothing shall be impossible. And Mary said, Behold the handmaid of the Lord; be it unto me according to thy word. And the angel departed from her.'[9]

Rereading the Bible

The FRLs in question identified traditional biblical criticism as being andro-centric. They insist that all hands must be on deck when it comes to biblical reading and interpretation, especially in an African setting. They unanimously concur with Schneider's summation in her articulation of guidelines for doing feminist hermeneutics, as cited by Susan Rakoczy, that asks:

> … how an intrinsically oppressive text, one that is actually morally offensive in some respects, can function normatively in and for the believing community? In what sense can one regard as the word of God that which, in some respects at least, cannot possibly be attributed to God without rendering God the enemy and oppressor of some human beings?[10]

In this wise they reflect what many feminist theologians refer to as the perspective of the white, Western middle-class male which effectively subordinates women and makes them invisible. Mary Daly (1968), Elisabeth Schüssler Fiorenza (1983, 1996), Rosemary Ruether (1972), Letty Russell (1974) and the Cornwall Collective (1980),[11] among others, have written extensively on the issue of women's ordination and the challenges facing women from feminist theological perspectives. There have also been attempts by African female scholars and theologians to reread the Bible especially taking into cognizance the social location and realities that African women face. Efforts such as these are chiefly documented in the works of the Circle of Concerned African Women Theologians.[12]

The exclusion of women, the FRLs recognize, has become a distinguishing feature of Christianity. Individual personal names of women are suppressed. There is an attempt to bury the roles of women under the dominant, official memory of mainstream Christian patriarchal tradition. Chris Manus laments that:

> the obliteration of the memories of women appears a conscious art by the Synoptics (Mk 7.24-30; 12.41-44; 14.3-9). In these passages and others, the evangelists suppress individual personal names while narrating female stories of wholeness, courage, discipleship and inclusivity in the early church communities. They attempt to bury the roles of women under the dominant, official memory of mainstream Christian patriarchal tradition.[13]

There is further degrading of women by the attitude of some orthodox Jewish men that offer prayers of thanks to God for not being of the feminine gender. G. Kittel *et al.* captioned this as follows: 'Praise be He (Yahweh) that he did not create me as a heathen, as an ignorant man, or as a woman.[14]

Apart from the portrayal of women as a voiceless subordinate group, the FRLs also point out that the narratives of the Bible are told from the male perspective as men and not women wrote them. This, they argue, leaves room for biases and prejudices as in such accounts women are wrongly portrayed as morally weak and misguided beings and ultimately as the source of evil. The FRLs' reponses to this portrayal are in conformity to Nyambura Njoroge's admonition about 'rereading the Bible with new eyes'.[15] By this is meant reading from the female perspective in general and also, where it is deemed expedient, from the perspective of the oppressed, of which women form the majority.

Ordination of women

Ordination has a long history in biblical tradition. Writing from a Protestant-Evangelical background, Peter Hobson asserts: 'Ordination is normally thought of as the recognition and appointment of someone to a Church office'.[16] This is also in agreement with the general understanding of ordination by mainline and independent Churches in Nigeria. It is the laying of hands by the bishop on candidates in order that they might be empowered to perform priestly and prophetic functions in the Church and wider society.

The ordination of women figures prominently in the thinking of the FRLs as in feminist literature. Both Myrtle Langley and Elisabeth Schüssler Fiorenza eloquently proffer arguments that cite scripture as women's basis for equality.[17] Again both scholars present the notion that patriarchal domination results from compromise of the true practices of the Early Church with their surrounding social contexts in later times. In a later work,[18] Myrtle Langley presents Jesus as having no problem whatsoever in relating to the status and position of women. She affirms that women and men are created equal. In the same vein, Chris U. Manus[19] discussed the egalitarian principle encoded in Paul's teaching in Gal. 3.28: 'in Christ there is neither Jew nor Greek, slave nor free, male nor female'. He argues that while Paul did not envisage a society without masters and slaves, Paul nevertheless laid emphasis on 'people to people relationship'. This is a radical challenge to Christian conscience that calls all Christians irrespective of their ethnic backgrounds to sink their differences in Christ. Such personal relationship, Manus argues, extends to the liberation of women from oppressive androcentric structures.

In a later article Manus reiterates his position on Gal. 3.28 by instilling critical attitudes towards gender-related issues encoded in African religious myths *vis-à-vis* the New Testament texts' sexist orientations.[20] According to him, such texts and the interpretations given them lend value to the traditional sexist interpretation, exclusivist and abusive language fashioned to depersonify women in the men's world of the Yoruba and the Igbo.

The FRLs identify some common elements in the arguments of opponents to women's ordination. These are countered as follows:

(a) The maleness of Jesus

It is because Jesus was a man that it is reasoned that only a male can take on the role of priest. Langley presents this argument as follows:

> If the Priest represents Christ to the Church, he must necessarily be the icon or image of Christ – *an alter Christus* – it is reasoned that if a woman were allowed to be an *alter Christus*, then the very concept of God would be threatened. If God became incarnate in Christ so as to represent all human kind, then it is His humanity and not His maleness, which is operative for salvation; otherwise the female sex is excluded from the scope of salvation.[21]

In response to this argument, the FRLs present the submission that 'the first exaltation of woman came from God as we can see in Gen. 1.27: 'So God created man in his own image, in the image of God created he him; male and female created he them.' According to Olaniyi, 'This is where the love of God for woman started. God did not create females different from the males – he created us equally.'[22]

(b) Baptism

The confession that in baptism 'there is neither Jew nor Greek, slave nor free, male nor female' (Gal. 3.26-28), many argue, is in matters of salvation not in exercising authority. However, according to FRLs, at baptism all Christians, irrespective of their gender, receive prophetic gifts to operate as priests and priestesses, prophets and prophetesses. Each of these offices for the FRLs has credence in the salvific work of Christ. At baptism women and men are empowered to 'speak forth' the good news and to teach others. By this is implied that in baptism there is equality in empowerment for men and women in the ordained ministry.

(c) *Prophetic/Apostolic Tradition*

From the scriptures, it is argued that the original Apostles were men. Jesus himself acknowledged that God chose them for him, e.g. in Jn 17.6, 9, 12, 24, and therefore it would be against the culture of the time for women to continue the apostolic tradition. An opposing viewpoint by the FRLs is that women as well as men receive divine revelation and can therefore transmit the good and divine news. Jesus's command to Mary Magdalene to witness to his disciples of his resurrection and ascension to his father is used in support of this conviction.[23] They hold on to a vision of oneness in Christ derived from the Pauline egalitarian principle of 'neither male nor female'.[24] There was a general consensus among all the female leaders that were interviewed on the issue of apostolic tradition.

(d) *Teaching*

The conviction exists that women should not teach or have authority over men, which means that women are forbidden to teach mixed congregations. Accordingly women are not permitted to assume the office of teacher in such congregations. The FRLs argue, however, that Priscilla along with her husband Aquila both taught Apollos, a recognized man of God.[25] To protest that this was permissible because they operated as a husband and wife and that in that sense Priscilla could operate under her husband's authority would prompt the question as to whether it would be considered acceptable for women to teach provided their husbands were with them! It is an uncontested fact that Priscilla did teach Apollos. The controversy borders on reasons proffered as to why this should be. It is instructive to note that the Bible did not make any adverse comment on this particular incident. God is sovereign in his choice of roles of individuals regardless of gender. Stella Ajisebutu affirms, 'Women anointed by God's Spirit can do anything men can do.'[26] In a studio interview with Dr Stella Ajisebutu on 15 August 2006 at the Obafemi Awolowo University educational technology studio, she asserted that ordination to the ministry was not limited to any gender.

(e) *Leadership*

A favourite resort to scripture by those opposing women in leadership positions is the Pauline injunction in 1 Cor. 11.3 where it is stated that man is the head of woman. It is the duty of the priest to assume the leadership roles in the Church, and by implication that must be a man as women are subordinate to men. Furthermore, scriptural teaching on the posts of bishops insists that they have wives, thus implying again that they must be men: 1 Tim. 3.1-2: 'This is a true saying, If a man desires the office of a bishop, he desireth a good work. A bishop then must be blameless, the husband of one wife, vigilant, sober, of good behaviour, given to hospitality, apt to teach.'

However, the FRLs insist that Deborah took up the leadership role as a judge in Israel. She is further identified not merely as a wife but as a prophetess. Dorcas Olaniyi points out that 'Women like Deborah had a calling ... There are lots of women today who God is using and I am among them. God is using me as the leader in Agbala Daniel Church in Nigeria.'[27]

(f) Keeping silence
In 1 Cor. 14.34-36, Paul commanded:

> Let your women keep silence in the churches: for it is not permitted unto them to speak; but they are commanded to be under obedience, as also saith the law. And if they will learn anything, let them ask their husbands at home: for it is a shame for women to speak in the church. What! Came the word of God out from you? Or came it unto you only?

Stella Ajisebutu believes that this command is not binding on the churches today. It was made to keep order in a particular congregation at that time. Remilekun Batire corroborates this assertion but goes on to add that people do not understand Paul and the Bible. In one verse Paul seems to be saying women are to keep silence in the church, but in another he gives instruction as to how they should pray and prophesy in the churches.[28] Why should women be asked to consult their husbands at home rather than debate issues in the Church? Furthermore in an exegetical study of this short but polemic pericope, Chris Manus opines that

> In Hellenistic Judaism, this 'master–wife', relationship between man and woman was considered normative and in Hellenistic Christianity also seems to have incurred much resistance on the part of the male membership against any form of feminist pressure in the community. It was probably at this period that Jewish separation of the sexes at worship was breaking down in the newly founded Gentile churches. The 'order' was probably promulgated to address this problem.[29]

In all and to reiterate the FRLs' position, women irrespective of their status are not barred from breaking loose from social and cultural conventions that prohibit them from speaking in the Church. Paul's injunction has been misinterpreted.

Congregations under female leadership

From the foregoing it can be seen that a meaningful enquiry into the activities of female religious leaders must take cognizance of their followers and congregations. Pertinent questions in this regard relate to their understanding of scripture on the question of women. This study addresses this issue with respect to the female followers.

Questionnaires were administered randomly to selected women congregational members totalling 180 respondents in six churches/denominations, each from a different denomination and state in the Yoruba area of Nigeria. (Stella Ajisebutu and Dorcas Olaniyi both have churches located at Ile-Ife, and for this reason only one of them – Dorcas Olaniyi's church – was selected). The selected churches are indicated in Table 1 below:

Table 1: **Hermeneutics of the Bible on Behalf of Women**[30]

	Denomination	Do women alongside men reflect the image of God?	Are women not inferior but equal to men?	Should women be ordained to the priesthood?	Can women be preachers?	Can women be pastors?
A	Christ Miracle Christian Centre, Danjuma Road, Akure	69.2	57.7	61.5	69.2	76.9
B	The Last Days Deliverance Ministry Iloo, Ilesha (aka Mama Tolu Sako-Igbala)	60	60	73.3	80	73.3
C	Agbala Daniel Church, Ile-Ife Branch	77.8	66.7	55.6	77.8	61
D	Power Pentecostal Church (aka Agbala Olorun Kii ba ti Power of God Never Fails), Lagos	81.8	54.5	81.8	81.8	72.7
E	Erinmo Great Temple Church, Ori Iyanrin Road, Abeokuta	68.2	81.8	68.2	63.6	54.5
F	Christ the Messiah Church, Coca-cola Road, Ilorin	52.6	47.4	73.7	73.7	58.4

* Figures indicate 'Yes' response in percentage.

Of the 180 questionnaires that were disseminated, 111 (about 62 per cent) were returned to the researcher – a good return rate. The questionnaire is structured on the basis of 'Yes', 'No' and 'Uncertain' answers. According to the survey in Table 1, all the churches approved the ordination of women to priesthood and believed that women could be pastors and preachers. However, concerning the issue of women reflecting the image of God and the equality of men and women, there was a marked contrast between Church F and the others. The low ratings of Church F (52 per cent and 47.4 per cent respectively) could be on account of its location in a predominantly Muslim area and therefore being subject to the Islamic influence on gender. (It is significant, regarding the issue of ordination, preaching and pastoring of women that Church F has the second highest rating in support of women preachers. This no doubt testifies to the personality and impact of the particular Church founder.) Perhaps most revealing is the fact that Church D situated in Lagos, Nigeria's most populous city, that has the highest approval 70 per cent to 80 per cent in virtually all but one issue should fall to a relatively low 54.5 per cent approval on gender equality! Could this paradox be due to hidden biases acting on the women's self-image in that particular church? Its 70 per cent to 80 per cent approval on other issues could be due to its belonging to a cosmopolitan and predominantly Christian society such as Lagos. In all, from the foregoing, it is apparent that while the FRLs have an impact on their female congregations, *they do not have a blank cheque in this regard!*

Conclusion

The above accounts may be seen as sufficient to present the thinking of the FRLs concerned on the question of women and ordination. It is apparent that in matters concerning the Church and in spiritual matters these women believe and act according to their belief that there is no distinction between men and women. For them it can be said in agreement with Myrtle Langley that

> The New Testament writings and early Christian practice ... speak of the people of God collectively as a holy priesthood who are to offer spiritual sacrifices made acceptable to God through Jesus Christ (I Pet. 2.5) and as a royal priesthood who are to sing the praise of God who called them out of darkness to his wonderful light.[31]

The FRLs regard the Bible as highly liberating and not restrictive to women. Women in the congregations of the churches headed by FRLs were supportive of women exercising a continuous and ordained ministry in the Church. They rejected the notion that women be limited under the cloak of tradition to the roles of wives and mothers.

Bibliography

Ajayi, S.A., 'The Planting of Baptist Mission Work among the Yoruba 1850–1960: A Religio-Cultural Conflict', in *Ife Annals of the Institute of Cultural Studies*, 5 (Obafemi Institute of Cultural Studies, Awolowo University, Ile-Ife, 1994), pp. 45–56.

Ajisebutu, S., *At Eventide* (Ibadan: Yadah, 2000).

Ayandele, E.A., *The Missionary Impact on Modern Nigeria 1892–1914: A Political and Social Analysis* (London: Longman, 1966).

Bateye, B.O., 'Female Leaders of New Generation Churches as Change Agents in Yoruba Land', unpublished Ph.D. thesis, Dept Religious Studies, Obafemi Awolowo University, Ile-Ife, 2001.

The Cornwall Collective, *Your Daughters Shall Prophesy: Feminist Alternatives in Theological Education* (New York: Pilgrim Press, 1980).

Daly, M., *The Church and the Second Sex* (New York: Harper & Row, 1968).

Fiorenza, E.S., *In Memory of Her: A Feminist Theological Reconstruction of Christian*

Origins, (London and New York: SCM Press, 1983).

——, *Discipleship of Equals: A Critical Feminist Ekklēsia-logy of Liberation* (New York: Crossroad, 1994).

——, (ed.) *The Power of Naming: A Concilium Reader in Feminist Liberation Theology* (New York: Orbis/SCM Press, 1996).

Hackett, R.I.J., 'Charismatic/Pentecostal Appropriation of Media Technologies in Nigeria and Ghana', *Journal of Religion in Africa*, 28.3 (1998), pp. 258–77.

——, (ed.), *New Religious Movement in Nigeria* (Lewiston: Edwin Mellen, 1987).

Hobson, P., *Head-Covering and Lady Pastor-Teachers* (Malaysia: Bethlehem, 1997).

Kalu, O.U. (ed.), *Christianity in West Africa: The Nigerian Story* (Ibadan: Daystar, 1978).

Karamaga, A., 'Selfhood of the Church in Africa', 27 December 1994 (Geneva: WCC), pp. 41–8.

Kittel, G. *et al.*, *Theological Dictionary of the New Testament*, vol. I (Grand Rapids, MI: Eerdmans, 1968).

Lane, P., *Radicals and Reformers* (London: Batsford, 1973).

Langley, M.S., *Equal Woman: A Christian Feminist Perspective* (Southampton: Marshalls, 1983).

——, 'One Baptism, One Ministry: The Ordination of Women and Unity in Christ', in *Transformation: An International Dialogue of Evangelical Social Ethics*, 6.2 (April/June 1989), pp. 27–31.

Mckenzie, V.M., *Not without a Struggle: Leadership Development for African American Women in Ministry* (Cleveland, OH: United Church, 1996).

Manus, C.U., 'Gal. 3.28 – A Study of Paul's Attitude towards Ethnicity: its Relevance for Contemporary Nigeria', *Ife Journal of Religion*, 11 (1982), pp. 18–26.

——, 'The Subordination of the Women in the Church. 1 Cor. 14.33b-36 Reconsidered', in *Revue africaine de théologie*, 8.6 (October 1984), pp. 183–95.

——, 'New Testament Perspectives on Human Rights in African Contexts: Some Historical–Theological Reflections', *Ministerial Formation*, 84 (January 1999), pp. 11–28.

——, 'Rereading Androcentric Religious Language of the Sacred Tales of the African Traditional Religion', *African Journal of Biblical Studies* (April, 2000).

——, unpublished lecture Notes for REL 405: Ethics, Obafemi Awolowo University, Harmattan semester, 2004, pp. 1–10.

Njoroge, N., 'African Women Doing Theology and Ministry', *Ministerial Formation*, 62 (July 1993), pp. 8–12.

Njoroge, N. and Dube, M. (eds), *Talitha cum! Theologies of African Women* (Pietermaritzburg: Cluster, 2001).

Oduyoye, M.A., 'Biblical Interpretation and the Social Location of the Interpreter: African Women's Reading of the Bible', in F.F. Segovia and M.A. Tolbert (eds), *Reading from this Place: Social Location and Biblical Interpretation in Global Perspective* (Minneapolis, MN: Fortress Press, 1995), pp. 33–51.

Ojo, J.R.O., 'The Position of Women in Yoruba Traditional Society', in *Seminar Papers* (History Dept, University of Ife, 1979), pp. 115–38.

Olaniyi, D.S., *'Woman, I Condemn you Not' Says Jesus: John 8.11* (Ibadan: ADC, 1988).

Olayinka, B.O., 'A Feminist-Hermeneutical Approach to Understanding the Roles of some Old Testament Valiant Women', unpublished MA Thesis (Dept Religious Studies, Obafemi Awolowo University, Ile-Ife, Nigeria, 1992). (Author's name is now B.O. Bateye.)

Okure, T., 'Feminist Interpretation in Africa', in E.S. Fiorenza (ed.), *Searching the Scriptures: A Feminist Introduction*, Vol. 1 (New York: Crossroad, 1993), pp. 76–85.

Omoyajowo, J.A., *Cherubim and Seraphim: The History of an African Independent Church* (New York: NOK, 1982).

——, 'The Role of Women in African Traditional Religions and among the Yoruba', in

J.K.O. Olupona (ed.), *African Traditional Religion in Contemporary Society* (New York: Paragon House, 1991).

Otite, X. and Ogionwo, W., *An Introduction to Sociological Studies* (Ibadan: Heinemann Educational, 1979).

Peel, J.D.Y., *Aladura: A Religious Movement among the Yoruba* (Oxford: Oxford University Press, 1968).

Peel, J.D.Y., *Religious Encounter and the Making of the Yoruba* (Bloomington: Indian University Press, 2000).

——, 'Gender in Yoruba Religious Change' in D. Maxwell (ed.), *The Journal of Religion in Africa* (Leiden: Brill Academic Publishers), 3.2 (2000), pp. 136–66.

Rakoczy, S., *In Her Name: Women Doing Theology* (Pietermaritzburg: Cluster, 2004).

Ruether, R. (ed.), *Liberation Theology* (New York: Paulist Press, 1972).

Russell, L., *Human Liberation in a Feminist Perspective – A Theology* (Philadelphia, PA: Westminster Press, 1974).

Smith, P.O., 'Feminism in Cross-Cultural Perspective: Women in Africa', *Transformation: An International Dialogue of Evangelical Social Ethics*, 6.2 (April/June, 1989), pp. 11–17.

Notes

1   Chris U. Manus, unpublished lecture notes for the Ethics course, Obafemi Awolowo University, Harmattan semester 2004, pp. 6–7.

2   X. Otite and W. Ogionwo, *An Introduction to Sociological Studies* (Ibadan: Heinemann Educational Books, 1979), p. 253.

3   O.U. Kalu (ed.), *Christianity in West Africa: The Nigerian Story* (Ibadan: Daystar, 1978); J.A. Omoyajowo, 'The Role of Women in African Traditional Religions and among the Yoruba', in J.K.O. Olupona (ed.), *African Traditional Religion in Contemporary Society* (New York: Paragon House, 1991); J.D.Y. Peel, *Religious Encounter and the Making of the Yoruba* (Bloomington, IN: Indiana University Press, 2000); J.D.Y. Peel, 'Gender in Yoruba Religious Change', in D. Maxwell (ed.), *The Journal of Religion in Africa*, 3.2 (2002), pp. 136–66; B.O. Bateye, 'Female Leaders of New Generation Churches as Change Agents in Yoruba Land', unpublished Ph.D. thesis submitted to the Department of Religious Studies, Obafemi Awolowo University, Ile-Ife, 2001.

4   P. Lane, *Radicals and Reformers* (London: Batsford, 1973), p. 67.

5   R.I.J. Hackett, 'Charismatic/Pentecostal Appropriation of Media Technologies in Nigeria and Ghana', *Journal of Religion in Africa*, 27.3 (1998), pp. 258–77 (p. 262).

6   Interviews with the FRLs in question were carried out during the course of fieldwork and participant observation in the selected congregations from 1997 to 2000. This formed the major bulk of my doctoral thesis, 'Female Leaders of New Generation Churches as Change-Agents in Yoruba Land'.

7   Bateye, 'Female Leaders of New Generation Churches', p. 141.

8   Christ Apostolic Church (CAC), an African Independent Church, is a type of Aladura church popularly known as the praying group.

9   All biblical quotations are KJV.

10 Susan Rakoczy, *In Her Name: Women Doing Theology* (Pietermaritzburg: Cluster, 2004), p. 155.

11 Mary Daly, *The Church and the Second Sex* (New York: Harper & Row, 1968); Elisabeth Schüssler Fiorenza, *In Memory of Her: A Feminist Theological Reconstruction of Christian Origins* (London and New York: SCM Press, 1983); Elisabeth Schüssler Fiorenza (ed.), *The Power of Naming: A Concilium Reader in Feminist Liberation Theology* (New York and London: Orbis/SCM Press, 1996); Rosemary Radford Ruether (ed.), *Liberation Theology* (New York: Paulist Press,

1972); Letty Russell, *Human Liberation in a Feminist Perspective – A Theology* (Philadelphia, PA: Westminster Press, 1974); the Cornwall Collective, *Your Daughters Shall Prophesy: Feminist Alternatives in Theological Education* (New York: Pilgrim Press, 1980).

12 M.A. Oduyoye, 'Biblical Interpretation and the Social Location of the Interpreter: African Women's Reading of the Bible', in F.F. Segovia and M.A. Tolbert (eds), *Reading from this Place: Social Location and Biblical Interpretation in Global Perspective* (Minneapolis, MN: Fortress Press, 1995), pp. 33–51; T. Okure, 'Feminist Interpretation in Africa' in E.S. Fiorenza (ed.), *Searching the Scriptures: A Feminist Introduction*, Vol. 1 (New York: Crossroad, 1993), pp. 76–85; N. Njoroge and M. Dube (eds), *Talitha cum! Theologies of African Women* (Pietermaritzburg: Cluster, 2001)

13 C.U. Manus, 'New Testament Perspectives on Human Rights in African Contexts: Some Historical – Theological Reflections', *Ministerial Formation*, 84 (January 1999), pp. 11–28, pp. 22–3.

14 G. Kittel *et al.*, *Theological Dictionary of the New Testament*, Vol. 1 (Grand Rapids, MI: Eerdmans, 1968), p. 777. This is a popular prayer in Judaism, in the Talmud, which men of Israel recite with pride. This anti-feminist prayer was representative and characteristic of the patriarchal age in Israel and among the Persians and Greeks at that time.

15 N. Njoroge, 'African Women doing Theology and Ministry', *Ministerial Formation*, 62 (July 1993), pp. 8–12, p. 12.

16 P. Hobson, *Head-Covering and Lady Pastor-Teachers* (Malaysia: Bethlehem, 1997), p. 66.

17 M.S. Langley, *Equal Woman: A Christian Feminist Perspective* (Southampton: Marshalls Press, 1983); Elisabeth Schüssler Fiorenza, *In Memory of Her: A Feminist Theological Reconstruction of Christian Origins* (New York and London: SCM Press, 1983).

18 M.S. Langley, 'One Baptism, One Ministry: The Ordination of Women and Unity in Christ', *Transformation: An International Dialogue of Evangelical Social Ethics*, 6.2 (April/June 1989), pp. 27–31.

19 C.U. Manus, 'Gal. 3:28 – A Study of Paul's Attitude towards Ethnicity: its Relevance for Contemporary Nigeria', *Ife Journal of Religion*, 11 (1982), pp. 18–26.

20 C.U. Manus, 'New Testament Perspectives on Human Rights in African Contexts: Some Historical – Theological Reflections', *Ministerial Formation*, 84 (January 1999), pp. 11–28.

21 Langley, 'One Baptism, One Ministry', p. 28.

22 Bateye, 'Female Leaders of New Generation Churches', p. 142.

23 Jn 20.17.

24 Gal. 3.26-28.

25 Acts 18.25-26.

26 See also, Bolaji Bateye, 'Female Leaders of New Generation Churches'.

27 Bateye, 'Female Leaders of New Generation Churches', p. 150.

28 Bateye, 'Female Leaders of New Generation Churches', p. 183.

29 C.U. Manus, 'The Subordination of the Women in the Church. 1 Cor. 14: 33b-36 Reconsidered', *Revue africaine de théologie*, 8.6 (October, 1984), p. 188.

30 The female-founded and led churches selected for this study were six, categorized as follows: Christ Miracle Christian Centre, Akure (founded by Pastor/Prophetess Remilekun Batire); The Last Days Deliverance Ministry International Iloo, Ilesha (founded by Pastor Bola Taiwo); Agbala Daniel Church, headquarters at Ibadan (founded by Archbishop Dorcas Siyanbola Olaniyi: Ile-Ife branch was also used for the purpose of this survey); Power Pentecostal Church (aka) Agbala Agbara Olorun kii ba ti (Power of God Never Fails.), Okota Lagos (founded by Bishop Bola Odeleke); Erinmo Great Temple Church, Ori Iyanrin Road, Abeokuta (founded by Revd

Apostolic Mother Olufunmilayo Lawanson); and Christ the Messiah Church Coca-cola Road, Ilorin (founded by Prophetess (Dr) G.I. Aimila). A detailed analysis of these churches can also be found in Bateye, 'Female Leaders of New Generation Churches'.

31 Langley, *Equal Woman: A Christian Feminist Perspective*, p.176.

14

One Ministry, Separate Spheres:
The Experiences of Ordained Women in
Senior Leadership in the Salvation Army in
the United Kingdom

Helen Cameron and Gillian Jackson

Introduction

The Salvation Army is unusual amongst UK Christian denominations in having equality for men and women in ordained ministry written into its founding documents.[1] Throughout its history over half of its ministers have been women.

This chapter seeks to explore the experiences of senior ordained women in the Salvation Army in the UK by interviewing a sample of women who currently hold positions of leadership. The first section sets the context by looking briefly at the historical development of women's ministry in the Salvation Army and its understanding of ministry. Following that, the method used to gather the data is explained and the views of the women interviewed presented. We then discuss these views, identifying three cross-cutting themes. Finally, we draw some conclusions based on what the experiences of the senior women have disclosed.

The Salvation Army is an international evangelical Protestant denomination which also undertakes substantial charitable social work. It works in 111 countries and has 17,131 ordained officers, 1,062,453 soldier members, 180,214 adherent members and 106,695 employees. In the UK it has 692 local churches (called corps) and 105 residential social service centres,[2] as well as many community-based services. The UK and the Republic of Ireland form a single territory with a headquarters in London and 18 regional (called divisional) headquarters. As will be evident from this chapter, the term 'leader' can refer to a position held as an individual or, for a married woman, it can refer to a position held jointly with her husband.

Historical and theological context

The Salvation Army grew out of the ministry of a Methodist minister, William Booth, and his wife Catherine. In letters exchanged between them before they married, Catherine made her approval of women's ministry clear. However, it was not until five years after they married that she first preached, shortly afterwards she undertook many of her husband's duties as Superintendent while he was unwell. After leaving Methodism, William and Catherine supported their growing family by preaching at revivalist meetings. In 1865 William was invited to take charge of a nondenominational mission in the East End of London. In July 1877 its magazine said of female preachers:

> As it is manifest from the Scripture of the Old and especially the New Testament that God has sanctioned the labours of Godly women in His church; Godly women possessing the necessary gifts and qualifications, shall be employed as preachers itinerant or otherwise and class leaders and as such shall have appointments given to them on the preacher's plan; and they shall be eligible for any office, and to speak and vote at all official meetings.[3]

In 1878 the Christian Mission changed its name to the Salvation Army, with William Booth becoming its General and other manifestations of the military metaphor, such as uniforms and flags, following quickly.

Catherine Booth died in 1890, 12 years before her husband, but that did not diminish the formal commitment to women's ministry. Orders and Regulations for Staff Officers, dated 1895 stated:

> In the Army men and women are alike eligible for all ranks, authorities and duties, all positions being open to both alike. In the Orders therefore, the words 'man', 'he' or 'his' must be understood to refer to person of either sex, unless otherwise indicated or evidently impossible.[4]

Given the limited options open to working-class women in Victorian England, it was not surprising that becoming a Salvation Army officer was attractive. It involved a public role, the possibility of mobility around the country and an opportunity to lead. A rule was introduced at an early stage restricting officers' choice of marriage partners to other officers.[5] However, as Eason's study shows, married women soon occupied roles auxiliary to those of their husbands and, when their husbands worked 'on headquarters', ceased to have an appointment of their own. Single women officers were largely confined to social work for women clients and to running smaller corps (local churches). Some women officers were commissioned to serve in 'goodwill' or community work, a development of work started in the slums of large cities in the 1880s. It was unusual, although not unknown, for women to have positions of authority over men.

Eason's analysis suggests that it was the evangelical theology and Victorian cultural assumptions of sexual difference that led to this inequality in practice.

> Masculinity was centred around reason and authority; whereas femininity was associated with passion, persuasion and sacrificial service. Apart from preaching, where reason and emotion could coexist, the roles assigned to officers were determined primarily on the basis of gender.[6]

Harold Hill[7] has shown that the Salvation Army's theology of ministry also contains gaps between theory and practice. Such was the controversy that accompanied the rapid early growth of the Salvation Army in the 1880s that there would have been no thought of describing its officers as 'ordained', particularly as so many of them were women. The focus was on the urgency of the mission rather than the status of those who undertook it.[8]

In 1978 the then General, Arnold Brown, introduced the word 'ordain' into the internationally required rubric for the commissioning of Salvation Army officers. This was done with the aim of securing for officers the same status as ministers of other denominations, a concern that had become particularly evident in North America.[9] Alongside this rather shaky ecclesiology had grown the practice, in most territories, of treating officers as ministers and reserving to them particular tasks such as the leading of worship, officiating at lifecycle rituals and enrolling soldiers. From the outset, only officers had held senior leadership positions, with no voice, as of right, for soldiers, in the running of the movement. Hill concludes that whatever the debates about theology, in practice, the Salvation Army has become a highly clericalized denomination.

Very few women officers have served as national and international leaders. Two single women have served as General: Evangeline Booth (William and Catherine's fourth daughter), during 1934–39 and Eva Burrows from 1986 to 1993. The other 15 have been married men. In 2006 a single woman, Robin Dunster, was appointed as second-in-command to the General. Within the UK territory no women have served as Territorial Commander or as Chief Secretary (second-in-command). This means that there is little autobiographical literature available for senior women compared with senior men: hence the need for empirical research for this chapter.

One of the few books to address directly the issues faced by senior ordained women is *Living at the Edge: Sacrament and Solidarity in Leadership*[10] by Penny Jamieson, the first Anglican woman bishop, ordained bishop in Dunedin, New Zealand, in 1989. A key difference between Jamieson and the women described in this chapter is that she became bishop by election. She argues that election makes it easier for the bishop, and so for a woman, to assume authority because the diocese has been part of the process of choosing them. All Salvation Army officers are appointed to their positions. There is no system of applying for positions and only the General is elected and that by a 'High Council' comprising only those officers who lead territories. Jamieson[11] makes the theological point that those in senior leadership tend to see their authority emanating from God the Father 'as a given', and so lose sight of the more embodied and collaborative models of authority suggested by the Incarnation and the Holy Spirit.

Given the radical attitude displayed by the early Salvation Army, it is surprising that there has been no engagement with the feminist theology that has developed since the 1960s. However, in more recent years there have been some signs of engagement, despite the fact that many women do not identify with the term feminist. An internal conference paper,[12] offers a rationale for women's leadership based upon a theology of new creation in which the gendered order instigated at the Fall is redeemed by Christ in whom there is neither male nor female.

The interviews

One of the authors of this chapter, Gillian Jackson, interviewed a sample of ten women who are currently in, or are about to enter, senior leadership in the Salvation Army. Senior leadership was defined as leadership or directorship within a divisional or territorial headquarters. Data collected in spring 2006 indicated there were 15 women in senior leadership roles in divisional headquarters (13 with their husbands) and nine in territorial headquarters (three with their husbands). At this level, there are only three married women leaders holding senior leadership positions apart from their husbands. The sample of women included both married and single women, covering the age range from 39 to 61 years old. These women also included varying degrees of experience as Salvation Army officers ranging from eight to 40 years.

Jackson undertook the interviews because it was felt that, as an officer, she would gain a better rapport with the interviewees. However, she was aware of the bias she might bring to the interviews as a married woman.

The data amassed from these interviews were considerable as the women took the opportunity to share openly their own experience, particularly in face-to-face interviews (rather than the three conducted by telephone), and this was both inspiring and humbling to listen to. It may also suggest that this was a welcome opportunity to discuss an issue which is rarely highlighted in the organization. It also became apparent in the interviews, mainly due to the reflection of the women themselves, that many more questions could have been asked: for example, 'How do women in senior leadership help develop other women in leadership?'

Whilst this essay cannot begin to make an analysis of all the data, nevertheless we will attempt to present a selection of the comments in order to give a picture of the experiences of some women in senior leadership in the Salvation Army.

What Katy Did

Although the majority of Salvation Army officers are female, there had never been a forum to encourage dialogue about women in ministry. The 'What Katy Did' course (organized by the William Booth College) ran three times during 2003–4.[13] A number of those interviewed had attended and commented on its effectiveness:

> It encouraged a wider group of women to start thinking about women in leadership and made it OK for us to be thinking about it and not that it was something offbeat or not right. Also it helped us to see that we are not feminist because we think like this, and this was an acceptable arena to discuss these issues.

One thing it did raise was that there was almost as big a dichotomy between single women and married women as there is between men and women.

Good dialogue between married and single women and how they could understand each other. For example, married mothers stress out when they have to leave children behind for a few days; single officers have had to leave motherhood behind.

Gaining respect and equality
Married women are in many cases perceived to be in supportive roles, that is, supportive to their husbands, and therefore are not deemed to have the same authority. This can mean a male officer receives all communication from headquarters. As one married woman said: 'At Divisional Headquarters level I have had to fight for equality, for example, after a year of them writing to my husband about finance, which I did, he had to write to them to tell them to direct the correspondence to me.'

Women in senior leadership may find themselves disadvantaged because they simply do not behave in the same way as men do at that level. One single woman says of her experience:

At this level in leadership there are a set of games that men play that I can't play. 'You've got to be good at poker.' There are games with rules and I don't know the rules. Some women might be able to play them. I am more extrovert and lay my cards on the table.

There is also the experience of having to work twice as hard as a man does to prove yourself, as 'for men, people criticize skill rather than gender'. These inequalities were explained in most of the interviews with reference to the inter-nationalism of the Salvation Army, which can be restrictive not least because 'the international Army's tradition and culture does not allow for women to be over their husbands'.

The old model and the new models
It has been traditional practice within the Salvation Army that married people have been appointed to their roles together, but in recent years there has been a move towards recognizing an individual's abilities through separate appoint-ments. Views on this development fell into three categories.

1 That sharing together in ministry was a privilege and the opportunity to do so should always be available.
2 Where couples agree to it, then separate appointments should be given on the individual's merit.
3 Couples when offering for ministry within The Salvation Army should be made aware that serving together is not guaranteed.

As one might expect, moving from a rather static model to a number of models will create its own opportunities and challenges. As one interviewee commented:

'I have no problem with different models but it is when one model is accepted as the norm you have to work harder to move out of it – again 150 years of history.' One of those challenges is when a married woman is appointed as assistant to her husband: should she challenge the appointment? 'I do question if it is worth fighting it, this is because when a woman does fight they can be seen as a radical feminist or the husband is seen as a weaker man or henpecked husband. The reality is, my husband supports equality.'

At times women have been too comfortable in the supportive role, to the detriment of their own development. One woman commented: 'In the early days when I was working in a team with my husband it was possible to hide away in our 'coupleness'. Now I have to take responsibility for who I am and the decisions that I make.'

Parenting

As one might imagine, if couples are treated equally and are developed to their own potential, the woman cannot remain in a 'supportive' role, and this raises other issues concerning family. Are there equal expectations placed on husband and wife to share childcare? Responses to this were varied:

Expectations from others are that the woman will be the main childcarer. There needs to be more role modelling of joint childcare.

It can't be done. This is one of the sensitive things I have to deal with. There is extra pressure on women by getting their own salary.

The last comment refers to changes made in the last seven years which mean women now have an equal allowance to men, previously this had been a 60/40 split, the man receiving the larger portion. Neither spouse has the option to work part-time, and the allowance paid to them is not sufficient for only one spouse to work and the other to choose not to.

The response to the expectations suggests that while both officers, particularly at senior level, are expected to fulfil the role, little help is given in order for both parents to fulfil their roles, and ultimately the woman reverts back to being the main childcarer. The consequences of this are acknowledged: 'Many women focus on the family and when the time comes for their husbands to move into a different job they simply have missed out the steps and have not had the development. This means even though they are capable they are not ready.'

Lack of development

Responses to the questions from the more experienced officers suggest that there have been great strides made in valuing women in ministry. Older officers recalled that 'In early officership a woman was only acknowledged as an asterisk beside her husband's name' and 'I was advised at one stage not to outshine my husband.' However, it was also acknowledged that there is a long way to go:

At grass-roots level there has been a change in perception since my early officership and the battle for equality has been won at that level.

However, senior leadership is governed more by the dictates of the Salvation Army whose structure has not necessarily moved within the cultural context. This may be due to restrictions in certain cultures, affecting how we work internationally.

Women also acknowledge skills they have missed out on:

Men have had the experience of being on business boards and learning skills of sifting information, making decisions, challenging one another, project management, time management and objectivity. Whereas women have developed a greater ability for support.

A number of women who are now in senior leadership endeavour to make the most of their opportunities to contribute and not just support:

We have worked out a shared role within the division. In that we both do Sunday ministry, preach, appraisals, pastoral care council meetings and both take a key role in divisional meetings. Both of us are on all the boards and I make sure I am at all the boards.

Discussion

In this section we identify three themes that emerged from the data and link them back to issues raised earlier in the essay.

The interaction between gender and culture

Many interviewees offered as an explanation for the lack of individual leadership opportunities for women officers that it would not be acceptable in many of the other cultures in which the Salvation Army works internationally. This raises the issue of the relationship between gender and culture. Historically, the Salvation Army is a denomination that has both adopted cultural forms to convey the gospel and rejected cultural forms that seemed to disadvantage those it served. William and Catherine Booth were happy to endorse and institutionalize women's ministry even though it led to their movement being seen as outside respectable religion.

However, the discourse from our interviewees suggests that culture fixes gender and so changes in women's leadership are contingent upon leaders in developing countries whose culture is neither changing nor amenable to change. This rather colonial view is at odds with much Salvationist theology which would have a much more dialogical approach to culture.[14]

At times, there may be a perception that the Salvation Army leads the way in equality of women's ministry, and this is misleading. The difference between being a pioneer and continuing to lead practice is not always understood or appreciated by male senior leaders.

The relationship between the marriage covenant and the officer covenant
The different experiences of married and single women are evident from the interviews. Married women have experience working alongside their husbands in an auxiliary capacity and some of them have had their own appointments. However, the suggestion is that married women will only have appointments senior to their husbands if this does not jeopardize their marriage. This can only be assumed to mean that it does not go against their husbands' wishes. It is also a tacit acknowledgement that there are men who would be concerned about undertaking their work without their wife's day-to-day support. This is aside from the domestic and emotional support which men often rely upon from women.[15] Nevertheless, the socialization into auxiliary roles means that by the time women reach a point in their ministry where they could be considered for senior leadership they have neither the experience nor the confidence to lead on their own. Thus it can be seen that the marriage covenant 'trumps' the officer covenant when it comes to full development of the woman's abilities. This is at odds with the mutuality found in the Salvation Army marriage covenant undertaken by soldiers as well as officers:

> We do solemnly declare that, although we enter into this marriage for reasons of personal happiness and fulfilment, we will do our utmost to ensure that our married status and relationship will deepen our commitment to God and enhance the effectiveness of our service as soldiers of Jesus Christ in the Salvation Army.[16]

For some married women, it is sufficient that their husbands privately regard them as their equals, rather than it being manifest in the status of their appointments.

The tensions between married and single women
The different experiences of officership open to married and single women have produced tensions and lack of sympathy between them. A key outcome of the three 'What Katy Did' conferences for women officers was a greater mutual understanding between the two groups. Some single women resented married women's access to senior leadership, albeit alongside their husbands. Some married women resented single women's sole command of a corps or social service centre. Single women resented the fact that married women were given the opportunity to hold appointments in their own right before single women were given the right to marry non-officers. The lack of mutual understanding may also be explained by many women officers' aversion to 'women-only' events which the Salvation Army holds under the 'Home and Family' label. For married women these events resonated with their being stereotyped as primarily concerned with home and family. For single women these events resonated with their being stereotyped as having no home or family life. Thus the limited opportunities for women officers to meet and compare notes were the last places in which they wanted to reflect upon their gender.

Conclusion

The Salvation Army has a clearly defined ordained leadership which is entered through a period of training, the signing of a covenant with God and undertakings towards the Salvation Army. However, this essay has shown that women officers have experiences which define their ministry according to their gender.

In seeking to understand the differences between men and women in ministry we have found it helpful to draw upon Croft's[17] threefold classification of ministry as *diakonia*, presbyter and episcope. It is evident from the interviews that the first two are seen as more suitable for women than the third. Officer roles that involve practical service have often been associated with single women and this has restricted their ministry to smaller corps and centres where a liturgical role will be combined with hands-on tasks such as cooking for lunch clubs. The presbyteral roles of preaching and pastoral care are widely accepted, although women in joint appointments with their husbands would sometimes take a less prominent public role. Roles which involved significant elements of episcope would normally be undertaken by men, exceptionally by single women and almost never by married women. Married women achieve positions of considerable influence, but this is because of being married to a senior male leader and not related to their individual abilities or lack of them.

The variety of roles held by the women we interviewed indicates that the clarity of distinction between married and single women is breaking down. However, all agreed that the traditional model of a married man being supported by his wife in an auxiliary role must be retained for those who prefer it. Because the Salvation Army is a major provider of state-funded services and because a growing number of officers have had prior careers, there is the growth of an equal opportunities culture which questions why certain leadership roles are not available to women as well as men. Because officers are appointed rather than applying for positions, change is occurring only at the pace at which the senior leaders who have the power of appointment initiate it. The primary concern seems to be whether the married male officer is content for his wife to have a leadership position independent of his own. A younger generation of officers contains some men who feel strongly about their wives developing their full potential and who would not want to have their wives working with them as anything other than a recognized equal. At present, the appointments system does not offer this possibility at senior leadership level, nor has it produced a man working in a role auxiliary to his wife. Because there are a growing number of women in individual appointments with possible opportunities to progress to senior leadership, the pressures to change may grow.

In a number of denominations there are concerns about the proportion of women in ordained ministry. This essay indicates that even where women are in the majority, if there are cultural and theological assumptions about separate gendered spheres, women are unlikely to enter positions of senior leadership in significant numbers.

Bibliography

Croft, S., *Ministry in Three Dimensions: Ordination and Leadership in the Local Church* (London: Darton, Longman & Todd, 1999).

Eason, A.M., *Women in God's Army: Gender and Equality in the Early Salvation Army* (Waterloo, Ont.: Wilfrid Laurier University Press, 2003).

Hill, H., *Leadership in The Salvation Army: A Case Study in Clericalisation* (Milton Keynes: Paternoster Press, 2006).

Jamieson, P., *Living at the Edge: Sacrament and Solidarity in Leadership* (London: Mowbrays, 1997).

Needham, P., *Community in Mission: A Salvationist Ecclesiology* (London: Salvation Army, 1987).

Parkin, C., 'A Theology of Women in Leadership', unpublished paper given at 'What Katy Did' session, William Booth College, London, 2003.

Roper, M., *Masculinity and the British Organization: Man since 1945* (Oxford: Oxford University Press, 1994).

Notes

1   A.M. Eason, *Women in God's Army: Gender and Equality in the Early Salvation Army* (Waterloo, Ont.: Wilfrid Laurier University Press, 2003).

2   Statistics taken from *The Salvation Army Year Book* (London: Salvation Army, 2007).

3   *The Christian Mission Magazine* (July 1877), pp. 182–3 quoted in Harold Hill, *Leadership in the Salvation Army: A Case Study in Clericalisation* (Milton Keynes: Paternoster Press, 2006), p. 236.

4   'The Orders and Regulations for Field Officers' (1886), facing p. v, quoted in Hill, *Leadership in the Salvation Army*, p. 237.

5   This rule was changed in 2002, and in the UK and some other countries officers are now permitted to be married to non-officers.

6   Eason, *Women in God's Army*, p. 154.

7   Hill, *Leadership in the Salvation Army*.

8   Officers received residential training in London before being commissioned and appointed to whichever part of the world their leaders deployed them. The soldiers' 'Articles of War' and officers' 'Covenant' contained no suggestion that becoming an officer was to adopt a distinct religious status or ontology but rather that officership was to make oneself available for fulltime service and deployment anywhere at anytime.

9   This innovation was not welcomed in all territories. In some there was the difficulty of translating the word 'ordain', in others there were theological concerns that the Salvation Army was aligning itself with the churches and losing sight of its founding vision as a mission.

10 Penny Jamieson, *Living at the Edge: Sacrament and Solidarity in Leadership* (London, Mowbrays, 1997).

11 Jamieson, *Living at the Edge*, p. 131.

12 C. Parkin, 'A Theology of Women in Leadership', unpublished paper given at 'What Katy Did', William Booth College: London, 2003.

13 'What Katy Did' derived its name from the co-founder of the Salvation Army, Catherine Booth. The objective of this conference was for women to be encouraged, empowered, affirmed and inspired as women, and women in ministry.

14 P. Needham, *Community in Mission: A Salvationist Ecclesiology* (London: Salvation Army, 1987).

15 Michael Roper, *Masculinity and the British Organization: Man since 1945* (Oxford:

Oxford University Press, 1994).

16 *Salvation Army Ceremonies* (London: Salvation Army, 1993), p. 16.

17 S. Croft, *Ministry in Three Dimensions: Ordination and Leadership in the Local Church* (London: Darton, Longman & Todd, 1999).

15

Daughters of Jerusalem, Mothers of Salem: Caribbean Women in the Ministry of the Anglican Church[1]

Rachele E. Vernon

Introduction

Sonia Hinds and Beverly Sealy-Knight were the first women to be ordained priests in the Church in the Province of the West Indies on 31 May 1996. A great crowd of witnesses from across the Caribbean overflowed from the Cathedral Church of St Michael and All Angels, Bridgetown, Barbados, as Bishop Rufus Broome performed this historic ceremony. But what did this ordination mean for the Anglican Church in the Caribbean and for these women? Why had the Church taken more than 300 years from its arrival with the English colonists to admit Caribbean women to the priesthood? What issues now faced the Church as a consequence of their ordination? How would they and their sisters be accepted by their brother clergy and by the laity? Were these matters only of concern to these women and their local church communities or were they significant in light of Caribbean gender concerns and theological issues related to the role of women within the ordained ministry?

This essay emerges from a PhD project aiming to fill a significant gap in research about the stories of the first women ordained priests in the Church in the Province of the West Indies.[2] In alignment with Elisabeth Schüssler Fiorenza's assertion that 'historical objectivity can only be approached by reflecting critically on and naming one's theoretical presuppositions and political allegiances',[3] I attest that I am passionately interested in the answers to the issues related to the ordination of Anglican women to the priesthood in the Caribbean, as I am a deaconess in this province. In doing this research, I discovered very little written and almost no published material about the ministry of Caribbean women of any denomination. A few BA research papers on the ministry of the Anglican deaconess order and on the theology of female ordination seemed to be the total collection. To overcome this lack of evidence, I interviewed some of the women pioneers in ordained Anglican ministry, priests, deacons and deaconesses, as well as some of their male counterparts, to address some of these issues in their own words. The women interviewed ranged in age from mid-20s to late 70s. Some were married with young children and others were single. Some had run large parishes, while others were just starting their ministries. The men were senior priests who had worked for many years in the diocese of Jamaica. The Caribbean is relatively small, and the issues are touchy, so I have sought to protect the identities of the interviewees by changing their names and some of their identifying details.

Historical background

The Province of the West Indies was established in 1893. It now consists of eight Anglican dioceses: Barbados, Belize, Guyana, Jamaica and the Cayman Islands, Nassau and the Bahamas, the northeast Caribbean and Aruba and Trinidad and Tobago and the Windward Islands, a chain of islands and mainland territories, nearly all of which were former British colonies in the Caribbean. These dioceses reflect the full spectrum of Anglican church-manship and ideology. Anglican churches in these territories have had to adjust to a situation where they are no longer the majority church, nor the unquestioned choice of the élite.

The territories served by the Province of the West Indies share a legacy of British imperialism and slavery. Colour and class continue to play subtle but important roles in Caribbean society. The political directorate, the civil service, the judiciary and the clergy are dominated by the educated descen-dants of the former African slaves; and, in Trinidad and Tobago and Guyana the descendants of the former indentured labourers from India. The powerful private sector is still controlled by the white or lighter-coloured descendants of the white planters, although there is a growing contingent of black, Indian and Chinese business leaders. The Anglican Church of the twenty-first-century Caribbean is largely controlled by the black and brown middle and working classes and most clergy come from these groups. It is still, however, identified in the minds of many with the upper classes, although few if any clergy come from that class.

Caribbean society is ambivalent about the status of women. In most terri-tories, more females than males are enrolled in secondary and tertiary education, but more women than men are unemployed.[4] Women have served at the highest levels in Caribbean governments and in the judiciary. Up to 2007, there have been two female governors-general, two female prime ministers and three female chief justices in the region, but women are under-represented in the parliaments and in the top leadership of business, and overrepresented among those most affected by violence, poverty and HIV.[5] The Caribbean Church is as ambivalent as the wider society about the role of women in leadership positions. Women make up the majority of congre-gations, and in indigenous, African-derived traditions such as Revival and the Spiritual Baptists, they have long occupied leadership roles. The more European-derived churches have been slower to ordain women, with the Methodists and Reform traditions waiting until the 1980s, and the Baptists until the early 1990s to do so.

The road to the ordination of Caribbean women

God calls people to the priesthood. This is central to Anglican theologies of ordained ministry. This call is perceived within the self, but it ultimately comes from the soul's communion with the Spirit of God. The Holy Spirit must then move the whole community of faith, both the members of the Church's hierarchy and of the wider community of the laity, to accept and validate each person's call to the ordained ministry.[6] Over the years, Caribbean people of diverse ethnicities and of both genders have experienced inward urgings to join in the formal ministry of the Anglican Church. The end of the twentieth century saw both the church authorities and the people of God at last accepting that all persons may truly have a vocation to priesthood, regardless of race, ethnicity or gender. The journey has been long and hard. Men of colour and women of all backgrounds were barred from the ordained ministry on the grounds that they were biologically and spiritually unsuitable and that there was no historical precedent for their acceptance. Nonetheless they found the courage to offer themselves for service in the Church through the inspiration of people of faith and by the active mentorship of wise guides, long before the church authorities and the church community accounted them worthy.

The church hierarchy eventually accepted that race was not an inherent obstacle to ordination. In or around 1865, Mr John Duport of St Kitts, and Messrs Robert Gordon and J.S. Wiltshire of Jamaica, all of African descent, were ordained to Anglican ministry. Gender proved to be a more intractable barrier. Women served as full-time workers in the Anglican Church in the Caribbean from 1890, when Bishop Enos Nuttall brought the deaconess order to Jamaica. Later women joined the Church Army in Jamaica and two orders of sisters, the Order of St John in Barbados and Guyana, and the Order of St Margaret's in Haiti.[7] The diocese of Jamaica voted to ordain women to the priesthood in 1974, but opted to wait for the agreement of the rest of the province before actually ordaining four women: Sybil Morris, Judith Daniel, Vivette Jennings and Patricia Johnson in December 1996. However, the diocese of Barbados pre-empted Jamaica by ordaining two women as priests in May of that year. There are now 25 women priests in the diocese of Jamaica and several others all across the Caribbean. The remainder of this essay recounts these women's attitudes and experiences under three main headings: theological issues, social issues and the impact of women's ordination in the Anglican Church of the Caribbean.

Theological issues

Until the latter part of the twentieth century, the Anglican Church in the Caribbean used long-established patriarchal arguments to justify its reluctance to ordain women to the priesthood. These included the view of Tertullian that women were the bringers of sin, and the contention of Dionysius that women were sexually unclean. It was also argued, as in the

Roman Catholic document *Inter Signiores*, that women do not have an inherent resemblance to Christ.[8] By the 1990s, however, the majority of members of the Province of the West Indies were convinced that it was not only correct, but theologically necessary to ordain women to the priesthood, perhaps because of reasoning such as that used by Archbishop of Canterbury Robert Runcie, when he said, 'Because the humanity of Christ our High Priest includes male and female ... thus ... the ministerial priesthood should now be opened up to women in order the more perfectly to represent Christ's inclusive High Priesthood.'[9] Though majority votes in diocesan and provincial synods allowed Caribbean women to be ordained to the priesthood, a significant minority continue to hold to the traditional view that women ought only to serve as members of the laity. How have these disparate views affected the treatment of ordained women by the male clergy and by the laity?

Laity
The laity have been generally very supportive of women's ministry. Emily Williams, one of the first Jamaicans to be made a deaconess, speaks of the freedom she experienced in her work in the dreaded inner-city communities of western Kingston. 'They respected me, you know. In Majesty Pen, I could go into any home. I was led by the children. Places where not any and anybody could go ... I found myself going all down there. Everybody knew me. You could go down there any hour of the night.'[10] People in the country areas were just as positive:

> I went to work in [rural Jamaica], and that was rewarding. I found that there were times when there was no rector, and it gave me the opportunity of proving that a woman can be a minister, a priest. I remember this old man who said, 'If you are doing all this, why can they not allow you to do the whole thing? Why can they not ordain you?' I never said anything, but that little old man [who one would have thought rejected women] ... it was never there with him. And it gave me the sort of confidence that what I'm doing is no different from what the men were doing.[11]

Those women who became priests occasionally encountered a small number of people who stayed away from communion, or otherwise expressed displeasure in women's ministry; they might express it aloud, but this was rare. Ingrid Taylor, a young Barbadian priest, had one negative encounter with a woman in her congregation. 'There was one lady who spoke to me and said, "I'm so happy for you; however, I hope that too many women don't decide that they want to go into the ministry because that would mean that I would have to find another church to attend."'[12] Sharon Lesley, also a Barbadian, says that the people of the first parish where she served as priest-in-charge were quite definite that they wanted a woman. 'They asked for one of the women to be sent ... They sent for either Stephanie or Sharon, and they didn't know either of us ... But it didn't matter to them which of us came.'[13]

Male clergy

Male members of the clergy came from all points in the spectrum in terms of their support (or otherwise) of the women. Some men had no hesitation in sharing their positive feelings about women in ministry: Canon Wesley Granger has always been an enthusiastic supporter of the ministry of women. I have seen him happily arrange services at his church where one woman has preached, another has presided at the eucharist, and a third has assisted with the chalice. These are his words on the subject:

> I don't know what the church would be today if it were not for women. And they hold positions in every part of the church. And today we have reached where we now ordain women to the priesthood. I totally endorse it. I totally agree. I am all for it ... The women in the church will continue to play their part, as they played their part when Jesus was on earth. He was always having women around him giving ministry. And the ordination of women is taking place and it is going to feed us. In the States we have women bishops and I am looking forward to the day when we have women bishops in Jamaica and in the Province of the West Indies.[14]

Some men, such as Archdeacon Ian Wong of Jamaica, were converts. They started out opposing the ministry of women, but seeing them *in situ* caused them to change their minds. Archdeacon Wong tells his own story:

> At first, I was thoroughly against it. My reason is that I didn't see anywhere in the Bible where women were called to that high office. But when Deaconess Lewis was ordained, Sandra McKenzie was the preacher. And Sandra's sermon was 'Go. Tell!' And that was the message the angel gave to that woman, 'Go. Tell!' And she emphasized it and it convinced me. That message was given to women, 'Go, tell!' To tell the joy of the resurrection and what the resurrection means to the world. And I was convinced from there that there was a call for women. And I really support the ordination of women.[15]

On the other hand, some men were, and continue to be, downright hostile to women in ministry, especially to women in the priesthood, or even diaconate. There were at least two instances in the early 1990s where Jamaican women who had served in churches as lay persons were compelled by their rectors to leave the church when they were going to be ordained as deacons. Sharon Lesley recalls that some of her fellow students at Codrington College, Barbados, did not make it easy for her. However, she used her negative experiences to achieve personal growth:

> Most of it was negative. The funny thing is that I didn't even know that I wasn't supposed to be there. I just thought that I, like you, am here because God had called me to be a priest. Only to meet up with this resistance and people giving me reasons why I am there. One person said

I'm there because I want power, another person said I'm following a North American agenda. And to tell the truth I went in there so naïve that if I had given it more serious thought, I would have not gone in.

Actually, the experiences at Codrington forced me to learn a bit more about women. It opened my eyes to the whole feminism thing. So I would say, in a strange kind of twist of fate, Codrington College caused me to be a feminist.[16]

Indeed, instances of continued discrimination also appear to have heightened awareness of patriarchy amongst other ordained women. Deaconess Williams says she had felt no feeling of inferiority while she was in training in the 1960s, but she admits, 'I more feel it now. Not inferiority, but the rejection of the men.'[17] Indeed, instances of continued discrimination also appear to have heightened awareness of patriarchy amongst other ordained women.

Social issues

Class and colour

The women encountered special challenges because of common Caribbean perceptions about social class and the Anglican ministry. In the past, Anglican priests had mostly come from the lighter-coloured upper classes, with European-type features and hair. Even up to the 1980s some persons appeared to be disturbed by candidates who did not fit that pattern. Brenda Barnes, now a deacon in Jamaica, found that although she had been immersed in church life, running youth organizations and camps, there was some resistance to her candidacy for ministry. She attributed this to her colour and her African-type hair and features. To be eligible for admission as a candidate for the deaconess order in the 1980s, she was advised that she first needed to get other professional qualifications although this was not the norm. Brenda tried to get into a teachers training college run by the diocese of Jamaica. That was when her difficulties began:

Having applied to Church Teachers' College I was turned down more than once because I never had long hair and I wasn't brown. [light-coloured] But that never deterred me … I went with this friend of mine … for the interview the same day. I was much more qualified than she was. She got through and I never got through. She had long hair and beauty.[18]

Brenda was readily accepted into another teachers' college. She did not give up her dream of becoming a deaconess, but received little support from her priest. When she asked him for the necessary recommendation, he was annoyed that she had dared to approach him. 'He [said] that he should have been the one to see that I was the kind of person who should become a deaconess and recommend me, not me coming now to him and asking him.'[19]

Sexuality and ministry

Another set of issues centred around the sexuality of the minister: how should women in ministry deal with their sexuality? Should a woman minister endeavour to look as sexless as possible? Should she be celibate? What about the pregnant priest? Could a woman manage a family and a congregation at the same time? Many church families and many individuals have found it difficult to reconcile their notions of sexuality with their notions of the sacred. In the past, churches tended to tackle this discomfort by requiring women in ministry to disguise their sexual identity as far as possible. Until the 1960s, religious sisters wore habits which completely covered and concealed the body, with a wimple hiding the hair and most of the face. Pictures of the early Anglican deaconesses in the Caribbean showed them wearing habit-like garments including wimples.

Times have, of course, changed, and even Roman Catholic sisters regularly wear mufti. In the Caribbean, any gathering of women ministers will find them dressed in whatever takes their fancy, from sober, more traditional outfits to multicoloured silk clericals made entirely of lace. They may define a feminine appearance in different ways, but each one has no doubt about her identity as a woman. It seems clear that the Caribbean woman minister rejoices in her femininity. Stephanie Sydney, a young Barbadian, was determined that she needed to continue to retain her feminine identity as she chose to define it. 'I dress now to reflect who I am and also to reflect that I am a woman. I am a woman and I am an individual.'[20] Some church families (i.e. denominations) dealt with the issue of sexuality by ruling that their women ministers must remain unmarried, even though their male ministers had no such restrictions. General concerns seemed to have been about the propriety of having a pregnant minister performing liturgical services, or of the ability of a woman to manage both a family of young children and a parish. From the outset, Anglican deaconesses were allowed to marry, but Moravians, Methodists and Baptists kept their deaconesses celibate until the 1970s.

The vision of a pregnant minister has not scandalized congregations as much as church leaders once feared. In Barbados, Stephanie Sydney had the privilege of being the first Caribbean woman priest to become pregnant and to give birth. She spoke of her experiences:

> Well, at my first church where I was curate, there were some people ... who definitely had a problem with it, who even said it to me. But by the end of the pregnancy ... some of them came back and admitted that it was not what they had at all expected, and they were able to deal with it afterwards. Sometimes it's just for them to go through it – they can't imagine it before and they need to go through it ... From the time women come into ministry, these are the kinds of things they should all anticipate. They may get married and have children.[21]

The women thought the uneasiness related to their ability to manage both a parish and a family of young children was misplaced for two reasons. In the first place, Caribbean women in many professions have long been juggling both family and their career with fair success, so women priests ought to be no different. On the other hand, they argue that the concerns actually need to be broadened to include male clergy, because men were now playing greater roles in the upbringing of their children. Stephanie found the members of her parish very supportive of her role as wife and mother. 'When I moved into my new parish people were most accommodating, very helpful and that made things easy … people recognized that I had a family and I still had to take care of them, so sometimes you'd hear people say, "Ok now Stephanie, it's time you go home to your husband and your children."' However, she felt that with the changing roles in society, her male colleagues were just as much involved in the care and nurture of their children as she was:

> But when I talk to most of the male colleagues, they're doing just as much in terms of child care. Whether you're a priest or whatever, your spouse expects you to participate in an important role, and the other thing is that the spouses are working. In the past, one of the expectations would have been that the spouse is at home, but it's different now. So a lot of the males are doing just as much in terms of childcare as I am. But it is still to an extent how people perceive motherhood and the role women are expected to play in child-rearing and being wife and all that.[22]

Stephanie recognized that while there was certainly need for the Church to be concerned for the nurture of children and families, this concern should more properly be addressed to making sure that all children in all families received quality time and attention from both parents, and that the Church itself needed to become a family for all. 'If we say that we are a family, then if we have children in that family, we can't just ignore the children … And I would like to imagine that members have grown to the point where they recognize that children have a powerful part to play in the church and if we keep ignoring them or dismissing them, then you're going to lose them.'

The effect of the ordination of women on the Anglican Church in the Caribbean

What impact has the entry of women into the Anglican priesthood of the Caribbean had on the Church? Have women brought anything different to the priesthood simply because they are women? It is difficult to find concrete indicators to demonstrate that the Anglican Church of the Caribbean has been more actively involved in issues such as poverty, health and the active participation of women in governance, labelled as critical by the CARICOM report on the status of women after the 1995 UN Conference on Women held in Beijing. At diocesan and provincial levels there have been initiatives to deal with HIV and AIDS, but little else. Perhaps a more detailed study would reveal considerable activity at the local level. It is not encouraging to note that an examination of the Jamaica synod journal for 2005 revealed that of the 40 boards and committees reported on, only four were chaired by women. Perhaps ten years is not long enough for women to make a major difference.

Even so, the women interviewed felt that what they brought was an awareness that women were able to participate fully in ministry and a greater inclusiveness, 'drawing out of people some of their own creativity.[23] It would seem that the real achievement of the ordination of women and blacks to the priesthood of the Anglican Church in the Caribbean has been the opening up the priesthood to a wider variety of human beings to make it possible for the Church to access the range of talents and perspectives available. The admission of women to the threefold order of ministry does far more than change the face of the Anglican priesthood. It profoundly alters the entire anatomy of ministry. Having a woman celebrate at the altar affects the entire concept of holiness and the notion of the sacred. The menstruating woman and the pregnant woman, far from being barred from the altar, become sacraments of Christ's indwelling.

Bibliography

Bicknell, E.J., *A Theological Introduction to the Thirty-nine Articles of the Church of England* (London: Longmans, Green, 1919), p. 421.

Correspondence between Canterbury and Rome, 1984–86 (http://www.womenpriests.org/church/cant2.htm, downloaded 5 May 2001).

Dionysius, 'Epistle to Bishop Basilides' Canon II (ANF 6.96) quoted in R.A. Tucker and W. Liefield, *Daughters of the Church: Women and Ministry from New Testament Times to the Present* (Grand Rapids, MI: Zondervan, 1987), p. 111.

Evans, E.L., *A History of the Diocese of Jamaica* (Kingston: Diocese of Jamaica c. 1976).

Fiorenza, E. Schüssler, *In Memory of Her: A Feminist Reconstruction of Christian Origins* (London: SCM Press, 1983).

'*Inter Signiores*: Declaration of the Sacred Congregation for the Doctrine of the Faith on the question of the admission of women to the ministerial priesthood' http://www.womenpriests.org/church/interlet.htm

Lightfoot, J.B., *The Church Ministry* (Wilton, CT: Moorehouse Barlow, 1983).

Tang Nain, G. and Bailey, B. (eds), *Gender Equality in the Caribbean: Reality or Illusion* (Kingston: Ian Randle/CARICOM Secretariat, UNIFEM Caribbean Office, 2003).

Tertullian 'The Apparel of Women', Book 1, Ch. 1. Made available to the net by Paul Halsall (Halsall@murray.fordham.edu).

Vernon, R.E., 'Black Priests, Women Priests: The Changing Face of the Anglican Clergy in the Caribbean', unpublished doctoral dissertation, University of the West Indies, 2005.

Interviews

Barnes, Revd Brenda, author interview, 18 August 1998, Kingston, Jamaica.

Granger, Revd Canon Wesley, author interview, May 1999, Kingston, Jamaica.

Leslie, Revd Sharon, author interview, September 2000, Barbados.

Martin, Very Revd Canon Patrick, author interview, 6 May 1999, Kingston, Jamaica.

Sydney, Revd Stephanie, author interview, 9 September 2000, Bridgetown, Barbados.

Taylor, Revd Ingrid, author interview, 9 September 2000, Bridgetown, Barbados.

Williams, Deaconess Emily, author interview, 17 August 1998, Kingston, Jamaica.

Notes

1 The title refers to a custom at the United Theological College of the West Indies in Jamaica where second-year female students are referred to as 'daughters of Jerusalem' and third-years are called 'mothers of Salem'.

2 R.E. Vernon, 'Black Priests, Women Priests: The Changing Face of the Anglican Clergy in the Caribbean', unpublished doctoral dissertation, University of the West Indies, 2005.

3 E. Schüssler Fiorenza, *In Memory of Her: A Feminist Reconstruction of Christian Origins* (London: SCM Press, 1983), p. xvii.

4 B. Bailey, 'The Search for Gender Equity and Empowerment', in G. Tang Nain and B. Bailey (eds), *Gender Equality in the Caribbean: Reality or Illusion* (Kingston: Ian Randle/CARICOM Secretariat, UNIFEM Caribbean Office, 2003), pp. 108–45 (pp. 113, 123).

5 L. Vassell, 'Women, Power and Decision-making', in Tang Nain and Bailey (eds), *Gender Equality in the Caribbean*, pp. 1–38.

6 E.J. Bicknell, *A Theological Introduction to the Thirty-nine Articles of the Church of England* (London: Longmans, Green, 1919), p. 421; J.B. Lightfoot, *The Church Ministry* (Wilton, CT: Moorehouse Barlow, 1983), p. 114.

7 E.L. Evans, *A History of the Diocese of Jamaica* (Kingston: Diocese of Jamaica, c. 1976).

8 Tertullian, 'The Apparel of Women', Book 1, Ch. 1, made available to the net by Paul Halsall, Halsall@murray.fordham.edu.; Dionysius, 'Epistle to Bishop Basilides', Canon II (ANF 6.96) quoted in R.A. Tucker and W. Liefield, *Daughters of the Church: Women and Ministry from New Testament Times to the Present* (Grand Rapids, MI: Zondervan, 1987), p. 111, 'Inter Signiores: Declaration of the Sacred Congregation for the Doctrine of the Faith on the question of the admission of women to the ministerial priesthood' (http://www.womenpriests.org/church/interlet.htm).

9 Letter of Robert Runcie to Pope John Paul II, 11 December 1985, in *Correspondence between Canterbury and Rome, 1984–1986* (www.womenpriests.org/church/cant2.htm).

10 Emily Williams, author interview, 17 August 1998.

11 Williams interview.

12 Ingrid Taylor, author interview, 9 September 2000.

13 Sharon Lesley, author interview, 9 September 2000.

14 Wesley Granger, author interview, May 1999.

15 Ian Wong, author interview, May 1999.

16 Lesley interview.

17 Williams interview.

18 Brenda Barnes, author interview, 18 August 1998.

19 Barnes interview.

20 Stephanie Sydney, author interview, 9 September 2000.

21 Sydney interview.

22 Sydney interview.

23 Sydney interview.

24 Sydney interview.

Afterword

Ian Jones

Rather than seeking to argue the case for women's ordination *per se*, this book has sought to understand and set out something of the current experience and status of ordained women by the beginning of the twenty-first century. Rather than attempting an exhaustive global survey, it has offered a range of different windows onto the past and present experience of women in ordained ministry, and has viewed these through a range of different lenses – denominational, geographical, thematic; historical, theological and sociological. Yet in so doing, it emphasizes the significant contribution to ordained Christian ministry that women are making. New insights have emerged into the nature of the ministerial task and the nature of preparation for it; women and men are learning new things about Jesus Christ as Lord and about the nature of Christian personhood through seeing women at the altar, the pulpit and the drop-in centre; deep-rooted assumptions about the respective roles of women and men are being challenged and new patterns of ministry explored. Those requiring further evidence should look again at the 'Notes on contributors' at the beginning of this book. Far from being a vanity exercise, this list demonstrates in very specific terms the contributions women (and here, ordained women in particular) are making to Church and society: here are leading ecumenists, biblical scholars, theological college teachers and principals, ministerial development advisers, clergy with senior pastoral responsibility and seasoned campaigners for social justice, to pick out just a few.

At the same time as the book highlights the distance women and their churches have travelled, these perspectives also highlight the degree of continued resistance to women's presence amongst the ranks of the ordained. Many of the sources of this resistance are familiar suspects: theological arguments for the subordination of women; cultural expectations of patriarchal superiority; more subtle suggestions that women are insufficiently experienced, called to a different kind of ministry, or just 'equal but different'. Not all barriers are erected out of active hostility: satisfaction that women's ordination has been achieved and is in many places 'reassuringly normal' can conceal the challenges that ordained women continue to face: lack of access to senior positions of responsibility, church systems and cultures that continue to privilege masculinist perspectives, or the difficulty of shaking off that gender prefix – 'women priests' or 'female ministers' – special cases rather than full equals in clerical status.

Indeed, the question of how to respond to continued opposition has been a very prominent theme in both the original conference and this subsequent book. A variety of stances have been adopted, from the patient and prayerful waiting of some to the more active 'ministry of irritation' exercised by others; from the acceptance of limited access to ordained ministry in the hope of being able to dismantle the remaining barriers in due course, to the tough decision to wait until a full measure of parity is granted. Whilst those who disagree with women's ordination have often characterized ordained women and their supporters as a single 'lobby', the accounts given here strongly emphasize the sheer diversity of ways in which women have chosen to exercise their ministry and cope with continued opposition. Conversely, the continued existence of opposition to women's ordained ministry also suggests a pressing need to subject the attitudes and experiences of those who oppose it to the same critical scrutiny as women's own attitudes and experiences. Attachment to a male-only model of ordained ministry/priesthood is similarly diverse. Engaging with particular reservations, rather than with a generalized 'opposition' may make for more constructive discussion all round.

The book also suggests the need for further research and reflection on the experiences and consequences of women's ministry. In his 1997 study of denominational journeys towards women's ordination in the USA, Mark Chaves has highlighted intriguing similarities between churches ordaining women at roughly the same time period and on similar ecclesiological grounds. A comparative study of this kind on a global scale would be an intriguing and illuminating prospect. Indeed, it is remarkable how many contributors to this book have enlisted Chaves' sociological-organizational approach to enable them to contextualize their own case-studies and provide an added analytical dimension.[1] Amongst the most interesting features of the perspectives presented here are the disruptions, continuities and evolutions which occur as one church's debates on women's ordination are transplanted into another geographical or denominational context – be that the arrival of the first women Congregationalist ministers in Australia, the indigenization of the French Protestant pastorate in Polynesia or the spread of support for Catholic women's ordination from key centres in Europe and North America. More than 54 years after Kathleen Bliss first surveyed women's ordination across the churches, and 27 years after Constance Parvey's landmark report for the WCC, there is need for a successor with an added analytical edge. In this book, we have 'sampled' a range of cases and experiences and have suggested some intriguing connections between them. We now invite you, the reader, to explore those patterns and trends in greater depth.

In drawing this collection to a close it is also instructive to consider the silences in the book – the unsaid and the absent voices. For one thing, only one of the original conference speakers, and only one of the contributors to this book, is male. Of course, there have been many dedicated men who have campaigned hard for women's ordination, and several notable male theologians and sociologists who have researched and reflected on women's experience as ministers and priests. It also seems perfectly fitting for women's voices to predominate in this collection, given subject matter and the historic dominance of male voices in Christian history. However, something important is lost if women's ordination is regarded primarily as a question of interest only to women (or perhaps also to the minority of men who are opposed to women's ordination). Further consideration should therefore be given to the ways in which women's ordination has shaped men's understandings of ministry and of their own identity, alongside the experience of women themselves. There is also important work to be done envisaging the shape of ordained Christian ministry with both women and men fully included. If the focus of reflection remains solely on women, it risks perpetuating a situation where women priests and ministers are the unusual phenomenon to be 'researched', and male perspectives are assumed to be the unproblematic 'norm'. In this respect, research on women and ordination perhaps parallels the state of black theology 20 years previously: of interest to a certain constituency but needing to become the subject of much wider conversation for a large-scale transformation of attitudes to take place.

A second 'silence' in the collection which points towards a future research agenda is the absence of contributions from women and men in the churches of Latin America, the Middle East and South and South-East Asia. The book has covered a diverse array of perspectives from countries where Christianity is or has been the predominant religion, but what have been the experiences of women seeking ordination in countries where the Church is a minority presence? For example, how do debates about women's ordination, and the exercise of ordained ministry by women, play out in those Muslim-majority countries where women may not have religious authority over men, or in those South-East Asian countries where parallel debates have taken place within Buddhism over the ordination of women from religious orders? There is a similar need for further understanding about the experience of women's pastoral and ministerial leadership in the fastest-growing branch of the Christian family: the Pentecostal and Charismatic. In the late twentieth-century West, the spectre of secularization has hovered behind most debates over women's ordination: rightly or wrongly, ordaining women has often been seen as a response to institutional decline. But how is women's ordained ministry regarded in Brazil or China, where the Church is growing, with Pentecostal and Charismatic Christians at the forefront? Bolaji Bateye's account of the 'New Generation' churches in Nigeria gives us some tantalizing hints, but more research is still needed.

The context is constantly changing: at the time this afterword was first written (early November 2007), BBC radio ran a report that for the first time, my own denomination (the Church of England) has ordained more new women to the priesthood than men.[2] By 2006, one in four of all Church of England clergy were women, and the proportion continues to rise. However, whilst the presence of women clergy is a welcome normality for most contemporary Anglicans, ordained women are far from enjoying parity with their male colleagues: stipendiary posts are almost twice as likely to be filled by men as by women (and whilst the reasons for this are complex, seasoned observers note the lack of mentoring and preparation for women to enter senior posts, and a tendency for appointments still to be made based on experience rather than aptitude).[3] Furthermore, women remain unable to become bishops: despite a recent General Synod vote to trigger the preparation of relevant legislation, progress over the past two years has been agonizingly slow as the Church wrestles not only with the question of the appropriate treatment of those who cannot accept women's priesting (not least the spectre of an autonomous province of 'traditionalist' Anglicans, whether officially sanctioned in an attempt to hold the Church together, or emerging spontaneously as churches decide to go their own way), but also wider Anglican Communion questions about the acceptable limits of diversity in doctrine and practice. As I write this, General Synod is about to receive the report of the drafting group for the legislation. The eventual outcome is uncertain. the Church in Wales faces similar uncertainty, with a proposal to open the episcopacy to women narrowly defeated due to an insufficient majority in the House of Clergy in a vote in April 2008. At the time of going to press, a solution to the stalemate had yet to emerge. However, whilst many of the influencing factors will be uniquely English or Welsh (respectively), and Anglican, the variety of international perspectives contained in this book give considerable food for thought about the shape of the forthcoming debate and the kinds of factors which may prove significant. May it similarly be so for Christians in all churches, at whichever point they find themselves on the journey to women's full participation in the work of the Kingdom.

Notes

1   With thanks to Kirsty Thorpe for making this observation.
2   Figures relate to ordinations in 2006 – the latest year for which figures are available at time of going to press. For full details, see: http://www.anglican.org/info/statistics/churchstats2005/statisticspg40.htm (accessed 15 November 2007).
3   Comments of Revd Rosemary Lain-Priestley, Secretary of the National Association of Diocesan Advisers for Women's Ministry, in a report on the BBC website: http://news.bbc.co.uk/1/hi/uk/7091976.stm (accessed 15 November 2007).

Index of Biblical References

Index of Subjects and Names

9–11, 13, 14, 16, 25, 27–8,
30–1, 36, 40–1, 44, 55, 57,
60, 83, 86n. 13, 103, 106,
117, 119–20, 123, 125–6,
128, 132, 134–5, 137–9,
148, 159, 162, 164ff., 178,
185, 189–90, 191, 196–7,
205, 210, 212, 216, 222,
225

cultures, denominational or
ecclesial 4–5, 8, 14, 45, 92,
96, 149, 208, 210, 225
Cyprian 22–3, 33–4

Deacons/diaconal ministry 1–2, 7,
22–6, 28, 46, 56–9, 123,
130–1, 133, 142n. 19, 145,
147, 148, 161–3, 174n. 22,
174n. 24, 180, 183, 187n. 4,
219, 220
deaconesses
in the early church 23–4, 26, 46,
56–7, 145–7
Mary as 'deaconess of salvation'
55
modern deaconess orders 46,
56–7, 60, 77, 116, 130–1,
142n. 19, 215, 217, 219–21
permanent diaconate and women
132, 145, 161, 162, 174n.
21–4
Deborah 196
declericalization 46–7
Dionysius 217
dissenting academies 91, 93, 104,
106–7
Djurle, (Revd) Elisabeth 117
Dunster, Robin 206

early church see especially chapter
1; also pages 7, 46, 55–7,
60, 77, 115, 145, 147–8,
194
ecumenism 1–2, 4, 6, 9–10, 15,
17, 22, 30, 40, 48–9, 58–60,
91, 95–6, 115, 119, 122n.
11, 126–8, 135, 144, 147–9,

158, 178–9, 184, 225 see
also unity
Ecumenical Decade of Churches in
Solidarity with Women 2,
127–8, 135, 174n. 33
Education see especially chapter 4;
also pages 1–3, 7–9, 11,
14–16, 56, 58–9, 89, 91, 93,
96, 102–4, 106, 108, 114,
116, 124–7, 131–2, 134–9,
159, 163, 169, 178–9,
181–2, 186, 188n. 19, 216
gendered theological education
see especially chapter 4; also
pages 135–9
higher education (excluding
training for ordination) 3,
11, 41, 44, 89, 93, 103–4,
106, 114, 130, 179, 181,
188n. 19
ministerial training and
formation see especially
chapters 4 and 7; also pages
8, 15–16, 44, 46, 91, 93,
104, 106–8, 127–9, 131,
134, 136, 161, 163, 165,
167–8, 170, 177–83, 185–6,
188n. 11, 207, 212, 213n. 8,
219–20, 224n. 1, 225
rising age of ordinands in United
States 167
theological education (general)
see especially chapter 4; also
pages 1, 8, 9, 56, 58, 91,
103, 116, 127, 131–2,
134–9
Edwards, (Revd) Ruth 13, 27–30,
32, 38n. 10
Eire (Republic of Ireland) 103,
204
Elijah 33
employment 5, 12, 24, 41, 44, 96,
114–16, 118, 124, 132, 134,
159, 168–9, 174n. 22, 177,
180–1, 185, 187n. 5, 204–5,
208–9, 211–2, 216, 222
Endokimov, Paul 29, 32